Hedge Fund
Due Diligence

Founded in 1807, John Wiley & Sons is the oldest independent publishing company in the United States. With offices in North America, Europe, Australia and Asia, Wiley is globally committed to developing and marketing print and electronic products and services for our customers' professional and personal knowledge and understanding.

The Wiley Finance series contains books written specifically for finance and investment professionals as well as sophisticated individual investors and their financial advisors. Book topics range from portfolio management to e-commerce, risk management, financial engineering, valuation and financial instrument analysis, as well as much more.

For a list of available titles, please visit our Web site at www.Wiley Finance.com.

Hedge Fund Due Diligence

Professional Tools to Investigate Hedge Fund Managers

RANDY SHAIN

John Wiley & Sons, Inc.

Published by John Wiley & Sons, Inc., Hoboken, New Jersey.
Published simultaneously in Canada.

Wiley Bicentennial Logo: Richard J. Pacifico

For general information on our other products and services or for technical support, please contact our Customer Care Department within the United States at (800) 762-2974, outside the United States at (317) 572-3993 or fax (317) 572-4002.

Wiley also publishes its books in a variety of electronic formats. Some content that appears in print may not be available in electronic formats. For more information about Wiley products, visit our Web site at www.wiley.com.

Library of Congress Cataloging-in-Publication Data:

Shain, Randy, 1965–
  Hedge fund due diligence : Professional tools to investigate hedge fund managers / by Randy Shain.
     p. cm. – (Wiley finance series)
  Includes bibliographical references and index.
  ISBN 978-0-470-13977-6 (cloth/website)
  1. Hedge funds.   I. Title.
  HG4530.S485 2008
  332.64'524–dc22

                                                    2007039388

Printed in the United States of America.

10 9 8 7 6 5 4 3 2 1

Contents

Acknowledgments

Embarking on this project was a new experience for me. (Hopefully, that won't be too obvious upon your reading the book.) I have edited thousands and thousands of 20+-page reports, accumulating a fair amount of knowledge of syntax, language, and tone in the process. Certainly, it's also true that I have spent nearly two decades specializing in background due diligence, so I thought, how hard could it be to write about it?

As it turns out, pretty damn hard. Writing an article here and there or expounding on the topic in a new business meeting (or, G-d forbid, to friends foolish enough to ask questions) is one thing. Writing 250 pages for an institutional audience turns out to be another. Still, I have taken to comparing the process to the feeling I get when I am watching a movie that fails to entertain me completely yet remains in my thoughts for a few weeks. The process itself might not be described as fun, but I am damn proud of the way this book has turned out and hope it helps do what John Wiley wanted it to do when the editors first approached me to write it.

One thing I relearned in penning this tome was the value I place on interacting with others who share my passion for this topic. The late management guru Peter Drucker had it right when he espoused the idea that employees are a company's value, not its cost. The staff at BackTrack, now part of First Advantage Investigative Services, is incredibly talented and hardworking. Beyond that, they proved time and again that when I needed help, all I had to do was ask. Of course, one could argue that since I am their boss they had no choice but to listen to me, and I am sure to some extent that cannot be factored away entirely. Yet, this cannot explain everything, or even most of the reason, for their competence, enthusiasm, and concern.

Specifically, no thanks are enough for Casey Drucker (née Kahl, a far more alliterative name, apologies, sort of, to her husband Steve). Casey's responsiveness and willingness to take on ever-increasing levels of responsibility paved the way for me to have enough time to write every day (albeit not all day, as that was well beyond my capabilities), without worrying about what would happen to the office. Casey runs our firm as if it were her own; there is no bigger compliment I can give, other than pointing out that there is no one else I'd want to run the show.

No less deserving of thanks are some long-time BackTrack researchers, two of whom, Sean Leadem and Alex Foster, contributed chapters here. My feelings about those two should be evident in the lead-ins I provided to their respective chapters (Chapters 7 and 10, respectively). To reiterate, both have demonstrated time and again why due diligence background research is not a commodity; the skills, instincts, and perseverance they demonstrate every day are a crucial difference between poor results and outstanding ones. Two other researchers, Joe Cadigan (who oddly posed as me during Casey's wedding, but that is a different book) and Chris Stevenson, are similarly skilled, and were only too willing to answer every question I asked during the writing of this book—and believe me there were a lot of them. I have said this before and repeat it here: I'd match up our group of researchers against any in the world.

Caroline Mak, who heads our Litigation department, was invaluable in helping me to answer intricate questions about our country's somewhat Byzantine court record-keeping system. She is absurdly professional and in some ways, irreplaceable.

Stephanie Kim is another BackTrack veteran who provided me with a terrific tutorial on identification sources (Chapter 5). The ability to distinguish between items that name a subject versus those that merely cite someone else with a similar moniker is a theme that is stressed repeatedly in this book; Stephanie and her group are adept at arming our staff with the information necessary to make these critical distinctions.

Although at one time I knew practically everything about the underlying areas of our research, as time has gone on and our firm has grown clearly, I have learned to rely on other people's expertise. Eileen Chan, who heads our Verifications unit, is one of the people on whom I now lean, and she was especially helpful during my discussion of this area (Chapter 9).

Leah Clarkson, a BackTrack editor and a published author, was always willing to use her practiced eye on a chapter. She has an amazing ability to be complimentary without making it feel as though she is being obsequious. Her points were and are always appreciated.

Barrett McInnis is an extraordinary interviewer and provided assistance in the vital chapter discussing the nonpublic records aspect of due diligence.

Our marketing department, headed by Aaron Smith, has done an admirable job battling the imitators, firms that claim they are offering due diligence but in reality succeed more at limiting their own costs and liabilities while leaving institutions holding the bag.

All those who work for BackTrack, now FADV, you know how I feel about our team. In case you don't, it says here in print that combined, we have managed to produce the most comprehensive hedge fund background reports of anyone, which is an achievement of which all of you should be proud.

I didn't receive help just from my colleagues. When vexed by legal lingo, I frequently turned to lawyer friends, who with one notable exception (Port Washington basketball players all know who I am referring to here) were universally helpful and accommodating. Thanks again to Ted Keyes, Mike Stolper, and Arnie Herz, who besides translating legalese also preached the idea of establishing your end goal before proceeding with any decision, a mantra I now follow religiously.

Along those lines, I received expert tutelage from a friend's mother, a person well-versed with the comings and goings of the IRS and who asked to be anonymous here. Her name is not here, but she'll recognize her contributions, which I greatly appreciate.

As you'll see in Chapter 6 on the courts, I spoke with two women who cofounded one of the most renowned litigation retrieval companies in the country. Karen Wolfe & Sheri Fister-Annable, owner-operators of Research & Retrieval (R&R), took the time to explain the Los Angeles court system, probably the most difficult of any in the United States to navigate. I have enjoyed working with them for nearly two decades and look forward to continuing to do so in the future.

Without Annette Bronkesh of Bronkesh Associates, there would have been no book. Annette has helped taken our company from an expert known mostly to institutional investors to one that receives media coverage on a monthly basis. Having previously tried and failed to garner publicity on our own, the difference in using a specialist like Annette and flailing about has proven to be astronomical.

Similarly, I must point out that not every boss would be so receptive to the idea of publicly discussing the secret sauce. Andy MacDonald merits great recognition for being such a forward thinker, and an all-around easy guy to work for.

To my friend Henry Abbott, what more can I say about someone than I already have many times? A preternaturally mature and wise person, Back-Track employee number 4, Henry consistently provides sage counsel on a multitude of topics, and was instrumental in convincing me that the opportunity to write this book was something that could not be passed up. Also, by selling his soul to ESPN, Henry freed up my time to even do the book, something for which in some ways I suppose I should be grateful.

Though we both know the way other feels, writing acknowledgements without mentioning my long-time business partner and friend, Chris Manthey, would be ludicrous. We worked together for six years before striking out on our own in late 1993, two New Jersey guys with new mortgages and the theory that specializing in due diligence would be valued by institutions that were used to either slip-shod work or useful searches but at extremely pricy rates. With complementary skills, we built a business from the two of us to one that now has more than 60 employees. Chris is brilliant; more importantly, although we have disagreed about how to handle things, we have never once had even the remotest discussion around ethical conduct, often forgoing seemingly lucrative offers made by clients asking us to do research in a way we deemed improper, ineffective, or both. Few partners can make this claim, I'd wager.

When we were looking for lenders and/or investors, my wife's late step-father, Jay Monroe, was a natural first stop. Instead of a check, however, we received extra motivation to succeed in the form of a letter that told me, among other things, that I was not an entrepreneur and "should accept my lot in life." Jay always told it as he saw it, and did so immediately and permanently. However, he was a good sport when he turned out to be wrong, and as people who know me know, I had no trouble reminding him of this miscalculation every chance I got.

Speaking of investors, two people who literally gave us the lifeblood we needed to get rolling were Chris's uncle, Bill Davis, and my brother, Jay Shain. I have related this tale many times but it never fails to amaze me that my brother, then not yet 30 years old and by no means wealthy, wrote us a check for $10,000 without seeing so much as a word describing our idea. Relying solely on a phone call, he asked merely, "You're doing what you did at the other place, right?" After I responding yes, he stated, "I'll write you a check right now. I only wish I could give you more."

To my parents, both now deceased, I think of you often. My father taught me many things, but two stand out as particularly relevant here. He impressed upon me from an early age the idea that you should always make a living doing something you like to do, because you spend an awful lot of time at work. I still love what I do, thanks both to my father and his brother, my Uncle Bernie, whose stories about his investigative job is what got me interested in this career as a 14-year-old. My father's other big mantra was that you do things the right way not because you are afraid of getting caught doing otherwise, but because you will always know what you have done, even if no one else does. Anytime anyone suggests cutting research costs to increase profits, or selling a report that is a mere compilation of indices to reduce labor fees, I think of what my father would say, and I understand implicitly that this is something we'll simply never do.

As for my mother, amongst the forest of lessons that are wildly inappropriate for this book stands one thing that is. Early on, my mother taught my brother Jay, sister Shelley (a better writer than me, by the way), and me to never accept mediocre results when excellence was within our capabilities. In Jersey terms, this translates to "don't be half-assed." My own kids, therefore, have their late grandmother to blame for the use of this term in our home on such a frequent basis.

My wife, Michelle, said many times during this process, "I am proud of you." I guess kind of like Renee Zellweger in the pivotal scene with Tom Cruise in *Jerry Maguire* ("You had me at hello"), I don't remember anything else she said, but nothing else mattered.

And to my kids, Jackson and Dillon, who have picked up my love of reading and might yet convince me to take a crack at a kids book next. I couldn't love any two beings more.

Introduction

Bayou. Wood River. Aurora. Amaranth. The Manhattan Fund. Integral Investment Management. For anyone who has invested in hedge funds or who follows the industry, these names are all associated with disasters. Although these hedge funds may have blown up, knowing this isn't particularly valuable. On the other hand, determining how to avoid the funds that are most likely to blow up is. This book provides a step-by-step methodology that gives readers an intimate knowledge of the most important variable: the hedge fund manager. A precise investigation of a hedge fund manager's career, combined with a clear understanding of what the information really means in practical terms are the building blocks of informed investment decisions. By deconstructing these and other hedge fund blow-ups of the past few years, the book will also chronicle the warning signs and how to spot them.

Professionally, for nearly 20 years, I have specialized in business background investigations and cofounded an investigative firm that specializes in hedge funds. I have had a hand in investigating more than 2,500 separate hedge funds and close to 4,500 hedge fund managers. Through all of that, consistent trends have emerged:

Not all hedge funds blow up. In fact, the vast majority don't.

Many hedge funds do indeed go out of business. Often, however, this is due to things reporters don't find sexy enough to discuss, like the fund's not amassing enough assets to allow its owners—the managers—to make money. This is no more indicative of fraud than a restaurant closing due to lack of customers.

Every nonmutual fund is not a hedge fund, even if the press describes it that way. (As I will explain, Kirk Wright, who has achieved a measure of infamy by losing a lot of money for professional football players, is no hedge fund manager.)

You don't have to invest in something secretive or unregulated to lose money. Ask people who had their money in Janus or other technology-centric mutual funds in late 2001.

Regulation is a noble concept but is by no means bulletproof when it comes to preventing fraud. One of the most tightly regulated financial industries is broker/dealers, the same folks who continue to spawn boiler rooms that prey on the unsuspecting to this day.

Good hedge fund of funds do a tremendous job weeding out the riskier hedge funds.

Individuals considering investing in hedge funds should not confuse their own business sophistication with hedge fund analysis expertise.

Most entities purporting to provide background reports on hedge fund managers provide little more than a false sense of security, based on mindless searches that result in incomplete, incorrect, or irrelevant information.

There is a way to predict and avoid most blow-ups.

That last point may be surprising. But it's really true. As you'll read, an examination of the backgrounds of the various portfolio managers in those cases listed above, and several others I'll discuss, yields data that at the very least would give informed investors pause. (The data itself, in the form of addenda, can be found at www.wiley.com/WileyCDA/WileyTitle/productCd 0470139773.descCd-DOWNLOAD.html.) In fact, many investors avoided those funds just for that reason. By analyzing these examples, and by explaining how you can develop this kind of research for yourself, this book will serve as a primer on how to make the most informed hedge fund investment decisions possible. And perhaps most important, with the tools presented in this book, you will have the knowledge you need to be able to deduce how a hedge fund manager's previous behavior is likely to predict future success.

Right now you may be thinking, "Is it possible for me to learn how to conduct background research all by myself?" The answer is that you'll certainly have all the information you'll need to do so. Whether you choose to roll up your shirtsleeves and do it yourself, staff a department devoted to this task, or outsource to an entity specializing in this research is your call. By pulling back the curtains on this Wizard of Oz, I hope to arm you with the ability to make this decision wisely and to ensure that either way you will have the tools you need to avoid reading about yourself in the next blow-up news frenzy.

How is any of this possible? A lot of it has to do with asking the right questions (of your staff, of the managers themselves, and of your vendors). Just as you know how to ferret out information from hedge fund managers, regarding their strategy, leverage, where they put the cash, how much of their own money is in the fund, and so forth, this book will, if I do my job correctly, serve as a guide for your manager due diligence questions.

It is hard to argue with the notion that the backgrounds and reputations of the portfolio managers, and others connected to the fund, are crucial to a fund's success. It is equally easy to prove the idea that a hedge fund of funds, a pension fund, an endowment, or any institution seeking to invest in hedge funds is not set up to learn, say, whether a hedge fund manager has been sued for fraud in a former position. No industry I have seen has recognized this more clearly, and has taken steps to rectify this imbalance between knowledge needed and ability to obtain that knowledge, than the fund of funds world. Although they may be criticized for excessive fees and a host of other purported ills, fund of funds routinely commit to some form of a background search as part of their due diligence process. Compared to venture capitalists, who despite getting crushed by their 1999 to early 2000 rush to fund the next greatest tech idea presented to them on a napkin in a room on Menlo Park's Sand Hill Road have seen no reason to change their diligence approach (I welcome the VC community to dispute this, and may well write a book about this travesty next), hedge fund of funds and other institutions investing in hedge funds know that due diligence does not mean do as little as you can, but instead refers to a standard of "due care" established more than 70 years ago in an effort to ensure that the stock market would function honestly and beyond reproach.

The problem, then, lies not in the desire to conduct effective background research, but in the ability to know it when you see it. Here, too, there is a wide disparity between the skills hedge fund investors typically have and the skills needed to know whether the information you are receiving is all that there is, whether it is important, and oddly, whether what you are reviewing even relates to the subject manager versus another person with that same name. Unfortunately, many investigative firms prey on this, knowing full well that they can pass off the same research they do on a potential 25-year-old secretarial-level employee as being all that is needed for a 43-year-old hedge fund manager. The industry is rife with firms who have entered the hedge fund field for the same reason that legions of investment bankers morphed themselves into hedge fund managers at the turn of this century (boy, that phrase sounds odd, huh?): low, to no, barriers to entry, combined with perceived riches to be made in a short period of time. Preying on the investment professionals' lack of sophistication regarding their work, these investigators often are able to provide just enough information to make their work seem useful (and scarily, to provide the worst kind of false sense of security), but not enough to actually do what due diligence is intended to do: that is, ensure that the investors have enough information to help them decide whether this investment will have a chance to succeed, and more importantly, whether the manager in question will not end up on the front page of a *Wall Street Journal* exposé into hedge fund fraud. So for those tired of that vague feeling of discomfort they get when they pick up the latest "report" they get from investigativegeneralistjustgotintothebusinessand-don'tsearcheverythingbecauseit'stooexpensiveandhard.com, read on, and be armed with the right questions to ask, and the answers to expect in advance. And, toss that other report in the garbage, where it will do you less harm.

CHAPTER 1

Hedge Fund Growth—What It Means to the Institution

Open any business publication or daily paper with even moderately in-depth business coverage and you'll see a story about a hedge fund. Most of these stories will describe how hedge funds are unregulated, implying that somehow this means hedge funds are The Wild West of investing, best left to only those willing to brave extraordinary frontiers and the risks associated with them. Other articles concentrate on the latest scandal to touch down on a "hedge fund," not distinguishing between a hedge fund and essentially a crooked enterprise masked as a hedge fund to take advantage of the zeitgeist of today. Finally, stories feature breathless descriptions of the fantastic growth in hedge funds, both in terms of the money they manage collectively as well as the number of funds in total. This book will touch on these issues, but this opening chapter will focus on the last point, specifically as it relates to the effect the tremendous increase in hedge fund formations has had on institutional investors.

The 2006 PerTrac Analytical Platform neatly summarized what daily and trade press have simply termed an "explosion" in hedge funds over the past several years. According to PerTrac's* study of various hedge fund databases[1]:

- Nearly 13,675 single manager hedge funds were identified, up from 8,100 single managers acknowledged in the 2005 study.

---

*An invaluable source for this and other hedge fund data is Matthias Knab's Opalesque.Com, a site that agglomerates news and other information relating to the alternative investments world. The PerTrac study was reported, for example, at http://www.opalesque.com/main.php?act=archive&and=show&nr=1240&anchor=topic33608#topic33608. The site is not free but few things worth this much are.

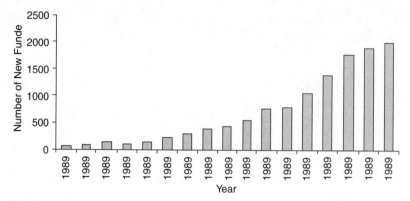

FIGURE 1.1   Number of New Single Manager Hedge Funds by Year
Used by permission of Opalesque.com.

- Single manager funds totaled more than $1.41 trillion under management.
- Approximately 250 funds have surpassed the $1 billion hurdle. By contrast, more than a third of single manager funds manage less than $25 million.
- Approximately 4,150 of the single manager funds appear to be clones of another fund.
- Figure 1.1 shows a steadily increasing arc of new single manager hedge funds over the past decade and a half; note that this figure does not even take into account those funds that didn't report to any database.

The *Wall Street Journal* added to this analysis by reporting, on January 3, 2007, that hedge funds managed approximately $500 billion five years ago. The *Journal* placed the figure at the time of the article at close to $1.44 trillion.[2]

What does all this growth mean to an institution? Certainly, one upside is capacity, or the ability for institutions to increase their alternative asset allocation percentage if they should wish to do so. Turning this coin over reveals, however, the inherent dangers of any industry that sees its membership increase so rapidly: dilution of talent, and consequently, increase in potential losses stemming from the selection of the wrong fund. Not too long ago most hedge funds had a similar starting point. A classic biography highlighted the manager's graduation from Harvard, followed by a Wharton MBA, a stint at a bulge-bracket investment house and then something of an apprenticeship at a place like Julian Robertson's Tiger Management. When the manager ultimately broke out on his own, an investor could be assured, knowing the manager had the necessary background to succeed.

Now, this is no longer the case. As hedge funds became more and more popular, and as other opportunities in the financial world became less attractive, if not, at one point, downright less available, the type of person seeking to become a hedge fund manager changed dramatically. From investment bankers to stock analysts, from physicians to pharmacists, from amusement park operators to real estate developers, all of a sudden everyone you know is a hedge fund manager. A few years ago, I attended a basketball camp and at dinner, the 18-some-odd group included an eclectic mix of careers, united only by a love of hoops. Going around the table, the spotlight turned to the only person there who then worked for an investment bank and the only person who by that time had managed to be somewhat universally irritating in his manner. Asked to elaborate on his career, he said he was leaving to start a hedge fund. I am quite certain he had little desire to be a hedge fund manager. His focus was prestige and money, not some innate love of esoteric trading strategies.

It is not the fact that people from so many walks of life are becoming hedge fund managers that is necessarily troubling. Rather, it is the reason they are doing so. Illustrated in the example above (though admittedly lost somewhat in the translation) is the fact that many people are approaching the hedge fund industry as if it were a fast, easy way to make a ton of money, all with a very low barrier to entry. The low barrier to entry part may very well be true (this is probably the best argument for increased regulation, though a libertarian would argue it is the worst); the easy money part is not. People's motivation for becoming a hedge fund matters precisely because running one is not easy. One needs a combination of trading experience, ability to deal with risk, conviction, honesty, and overall business skills (any fund seeking institutional money is no longer a guy clackety-clacking away on his basement computer; no, running an actual business is required now, too). People in it for just the fast riches often will find out the hard way that this industry is not what they thought; the key for the institution, then, is not to be the one colearning this lesson.

The trick for any institution is ferreting out which funds present an acceptable risk. This has been made simultaneously easier and harder by the drastic expansion in hedge funds from which to choose. On the one hand, given the plethora of funds at their disposal institutions no longer have to fear getting shut out of all the funds in which they might like to invest. Conversely, this very abundance of choices means it is no longer so simple to judge the quality of the people running the funds, since these people may very well be unknown to the institution and those in its circle.

Pointedly illustrating this are recent statistics on the heavy concentration of hedge fund assets in a relatively small number of funds. According to a March 2007 piece in *Hedge Fund Daily*, gleaned from its sister publication, *Absolute Return*, a unit of *HedgeFund Intelligence*, 241 U.S. hedge fund firms have more than $1 billion in assets under management.[3] Perhaps most astoundingly, the 20 largest hedge fund firms controlled approximately $386 billion, in total, or almost one third of the global hedge fund assets reported to surveyors.

A February 2007 report in *Hedge Fund Daily* presented slightly different figures, although not contradicting the general concentration point.[4] "The 10 largest hedge funds according to size control 63% of industry assets, according to Milken Institute's *Capital Access Index 2006*, while the top 1% control 19% of all global fund assets. Based on data from HedgeFund.net, the study found that . . . hedge funds with more than $1 billion in assets under management account for only 3% of the total number of funds but 35% of the industry's trillion in assets, while HFs with under $100 million AUM represent about 70% of the number of funds but just 12% of the assets."

The full list was published in *Absolute Return's* March issue. Unless noted otherwise, all asset figures are as of January 1, 2007, and are in the billions. See Table 1.1.

Even if you eliminate the bottom third of hedge funds that reportedly have less than $25 million apiece, what remains is a tremendous number of hedge funds to weed through, if you don't want to, or can't, invest in the aforementioned big boys. Speaking of which, one theory proffered in a recent *HedgeWorld* story is that investors are better served by getting into funds early in the fund's "life cycle."[5] According to this theory, penned by Shoham Cohen, a hedge fund has four stages, similar to what you might expect: introduction, growth, maturity, and decline. As might also be expected,

TABLE 1.1   Top 10 U.S. Hedge Fund Firms—January 2007

JPMorgan Asset Management	$34.00
Goldman Sachs Asset Management	$32.53
Bridgewater Associates	$30.20
D. E. Shaw Group	$26.30
Farallon Capital Management	$26.20
Renaissance Technologies Corp.	$24.00
Och-Ziff Capital Management	$21.00
Cerberus Capital Management	$19.15
Barclays Global Investors	$18.90
ESL Investments	$18.00

he does not believe that it is astute to invest during stage four; rather, he proposes that hedge fund investors often "shy away from funds with track records of less than five years, or assets under management of less than $300 million, in favour of more established funds. These vintage funds are usually past their prime."

Mr. Cohen avers, "Emerging funds can provide better returns, better capital protection, a longer-term investment prospect, and up-to-date investment strategies," while "historically, high-profile funds—in most cases—will add less value."

Although getting in while a fund is young, before it is hot, sounds appealing, these types of funds demand even more stringent due diligence analysis, for by their very nature they do not have the financial track record upon which you can rely.

None of this is meant to suggest in any way that all, or even the majority, of hedge funds are frauds or will blow up at some point soon. However, as with global warming, it now seems that the question isn't whether or not hedge funds are risky, but what can be done about it.

What can be done to lessen the risk of investing in a hedge fund that blows up? Specific prescriptions appear first in Chapter 4 and then throughout this book; it is enough to summarize here that the primary way to avoid the type of headline no one wants to see is due diligence. Proper, thorough research into the hedge fund manager's track record will go a remarkably long way toward ensuring a blow-up–free portfolio; no method is foolproof, of course, but relying on an ad hoc, hodgepodge of industry contacts, guile, and intuition is not only no longer necessary, but it is also no longer effective. And this is possibly the greatest distinction for institutional investors to recognize: the old way of hedge fund investing is no longer possible; no more can you simply invest with managers you know or with whom some acquaintance of yours has direct experience. But this doesn't mean you can't replicate the old experiences; it just means you have to work a lot harder to do so. Still, this work is not without its reward, because at the end of the day you can always move to the next manager on your list if your due diligence review should reveal that the first option is untenable. All in all, this isn't so bad.

DEMAND FOR HEDGE FUNDS

The discussion above focused on the increased supply in hedge funds, suggesting that this was in response, primarily, to hedge funds becoming popular and to their perception as easy money. Another critical factor, of course, and one you are likely to be at least partially aware of, is the concurrent heightened demand for hedge funds in which to invest.

Everyone knows about institutions providing ever-increasing dollars to hedge funds. (*Reuters.com* reported in March 2007 that a survey of more than 40 funds with assets totaling $1 trillion revealed that only 4 percent have no hedge fund investments, down from 16 percent the year before.[6]) Less well known, perhaps, is one of the reasons why this is occurring. According to a January 3, 2007, *Financialnews-US.com* article, the two largest US pension funds, the $225bn California Public Employees Retirement System and the $153bn California State Teachers' Retirement System, combined their unfunded pension liabilities of $49bn, as the state of California sought to address its funding deficits.[7] Though going forward, California and the many other pension plans in this predicament will plausibly seek to change from defined benefit plans to defined contribution plans, this will not address the immediate problem of unfunded, or under-funded, pension plans. One ready solution, however, is investing in more alternatives, including hedge funds, in order to "goose" pension plan returns and hopefully abate or even eliminate the funding gaps that currently exist.

Around this time, *HFN Daily Report* quoted a press release issued by Russell Investment Group, which managed more than $195 billion in assets for advisory clients as of December 31, 2006.[8]

According to the release, Russell Investment Group "predicted a drastic change in pension investment portfolios as corporations respond to pension reform and try to maximize returns while matching liabilities. ... 'Changes in pension policy are being driven by a variety of pressures, and these pressures are going to push different plans in different directions,' said Bob Collie, director of strategic advice at Russell and contributing author of the *Russell Pension Report 2007*. 'There will be a breaking up of the herd as organizations pursue a wide range of both liability-matching and return-seeking strategies, driven by different responses to recent pension reform and by increasingly diverse corporate objectives.'"

The Russell report added, "Regardless of which strategy or combination of strategies companies ultimately choose, the ability of plans to employ both return-seeking and liability-matching strategies is now more feasible and necessary than ever before, a finding that challenges the traditional presumption that the two investment strategies are mutually exclusive."

Eurakehedge had a related story about institutional investors driving hedge fund growth, based on an extensive survey* conducted in 2006 "through more than 100 in-depth interviews with institutional investors,

---

*For hard copies of "Institutional Demand for Hedge Funds 2: A Global Perspective," contact The Bank of New York, Hong Kong: Rosemarie Kriesel, rkriesel@bankofny.com.

investment consultants, hedge funds, funds of hedge funds and industry experts worldwide."[9] This was a follow-up to a similar survey conducted in 2004, both carried out jointly by Bank of New York and Casey, Quirk & Associates.

Among the study's conclusions were that institutional investors are by and large quite satisfied with their hedge fund portfolios and that this satisfaction means hedge funds are here to stay. The study also concluded that as recently as five years ago, hedge fund investors were comprised mostly of individuals, with a smattering of institutions joining in the fray. Now, more than 40 percent of hedge fund money is institutional (frankly, this still seems low to me, and in fact *Institutional Investor News* and *HedgeFund.net* released a report in mid-March 2007 in which Hedgefund.net estimated total hedge fund asset levels at $1.89 trillion, with $953 billion, or just more than 50 percent, from fund of funds[10]); by 2010, the authors expected this number to increase by half (to 60 percent—again, a figure I personally believe understates the case), with total institutional money in hedge funds predicted to be $1 trillion (said with a pinky in the corner of your lip, Dr. Evil–style). As for the whys, the authors believe that institutions are looking for both low correlation with the rest of their assets as well as absolute returns.

Perhaps the most important point from my perspective, albeit one that did not receive top billing in the research paper, was this one, "Factors such as scandal and regulation could slow predicted growth, though we would expect the impact to be marginal." As the following chapters will show, the press treats "hedge fund" scandals the way bears do salmon, ripping them apart rapidly and somewhat indiscriminately. For the hedge fund community, institutions especially, this means that vigilance is the watchword of the day. You can't rely on methods that worked when there were approximately 5 percent of the hedge funds that there are today. Today's hedge fund growth and turnover demands a level of scrutiny that this book will hopefully demonstrate how to execute.

WHAT ABOUT REGULATION? IS REGULATION THE ANSWER?

I guess it depends on the question. Most important for any institution to recognize, however, is that regardless of how stringent regulation becomes, and how successful regulatory agencies are in prosecuting frauds once they occur, regulation is not intended or designed to predict which hedge fund might blow up next. For that, you'll always need due diligence, both operational and manager research. To understand a manager's tendencies and track record, you must delve into these items. No regulatory body can possibly replicate your research, not just because they don't have the time or expertise, but also because this is inherently not their focus. Recognize, too, that regulatory bodies admittedly become involved in frauds against investors almost always after a whistleblower points out an ongoing fraud. At this point, you, the investor, can at best hope to recover only a portion of your investment, and you certainly can't prevent the damage from the avalanche of bad press that is sure to follow. We'll explore the role of regulators further in Chapter 8, but for now keep in mind that regulators cannot and do not obviate your need to do due diligence on the managers in which you are seeking to invest.

RECAP

1. Hedge funds are not a passing fad.
2. Institutional interest in hedge funds is likewise a long-term commitment, and is in large part a response to underfunded pension funds.
3. Today, 9,000+ hedge funds versus 500 hedge funds means more choice but also far more chance of finding a bad apple.
4. Ad hoc methods like calling on industry contacts are no longer an efficient or effective means of conducting due diligence on people.
5. Systematic management/people due diligence combined with operational due diligence allows for a great reduction in blow-up risk.

CHAPTER 2

What Is Due Diligence? What Are the Various Types of Due Diligence?

Googling "due diligence definition" produces an army of results. Among the herd, the following seem particularly relevant:

- The investigation and evaluation of a management team's characteristics, investment philosophy, and terms and conditions prior to committing capital to the fund. www.ventureeconomics.com/vec/glossary.html
- The degree of prudence that might be properly expected from a reasonable person in the circumstances; applicable to foundation personnel who act in a fiduciary capacity. (See Fiduciary Duty.) www.yscf.org/glossary.html
- The analysis and appraisal of a business in preparation for a flotation or venture capital investment. Investors have a right to expect that these investigations are carried out thoroughly. www.financingcp.org/glossary/glossary.html
- The process of systematically evaluating information, to identify risks and issues relating to a proposed transaction (i.e., verify that information is what it is proposed to be). strategis.ic.gc.ca/epic/internet/insof-sdf.nsf/en/so03149e.html
- The process of checking the accuracy of information contained in a company public statement, such as a prospectus, before recommending that company to others. Is also the act of one company investigating another company before buying its shares. https://www.shareanalysis.com/asp/glossary.asp
- A reasonable investigation conducted by the parties involved in preparing a disclosure document to form a basis for believing that the statements contained therein are true and that no material facts are omitted. personal.fidelity.com/products/stocksbonds/content/ipoglossary.html

- A legal requirement that stock brokers, underwriters and spin-off sponsors must meet to ensure that the statements made by a spin-off company or public company are accurate and complete. The purpose is to ensure the public has full and accurate information about a public company or a private company about to become a public company. www.goingglobal.com/equity/finance-glossary.html
- In an offering of securities, certain parties who are responsible for the accuracy of the offering document, have an obligation to perform a "due diligence" examination of the issuer; issuer's counsel, underwriter of the security, brokerage firm handling the sale of the security. Due diligence refers to the degree of prudence that might properly be expected from a reasonable man, on the basis of the significant facts which relate to a specific case. www.maverickenergy.com/lexicon2.htm
- An internal analysis by a lender, such as a bank, of existing debts owed by a borrower in order to identify or re-evaluate the risk. An independent analysis of the current financial state and future prospects of a company in anticipation of a major investment of venture capital or a stock-exchange flotation. A Venture Capitalist firm's examination by its lawyers and auditors of the records, accounts and any legal documents of an existing business. www.promitheas.com/glossary.php
- The process whereby an investor investigates the attractiveness of an opportunity, assesses the quality of the management team, and assesses the key risks associated with an opportunity. Due diligence starts on initial inspection of an opportunity and ends when the investment is in the investee's bank. www.tvp.com.au/resources/glossary.htm
- Investigation conducted by Underwriters and their counsel and, in some cases also by bond counsel and Issuer's counsel to determine whether all material items in connection with the Issuer, the Issue and the security for the Issue have been accurately disclosed in the Official Statement (or if a Private Placement in the Placement Memorandum) and that no material disclosure has been omitted. www.indygov.org/eGov/City/BondBank/glossary.htm

Although none of the above relates specifically to hedge funds, certainly the idea of what due diligence comes through via the various definitions. Running through these definitions is the theme about searching management teams and assessing their quality; this book will focus its entire effort on teaching you techniques for performing this very task. The book will not attend to the various other types of due diligence that are also important to analyzing hedge funds, but that are outside the scope of our expertise. The most prominent example would be operational due diligence, which might include, among other items, analysis of a fund's infrastructure; back office procedures; style and strategy; peer comparisons; financial statements; and risk management procedures. These are all very valuable, but they are also items that are best covered in a separate text, by someone with expertise in this arena.

Why focus on management team analysis? As each chapter will highlight, our premise is that effective, comprehensive management due diligence yields information about a manager's background that is itself critical to accurately predicting the future behavior of that manager. No amount of due diligence can account for market conditions or dramatic market changes, of course, but almost all people will exhibit their fundamental characteristics time and time again, over decades, and especially under pressure. Determining what those characteristics are, therefore, will give you, the institution, the ability to recognize how the manager is likely to act in specific scenarios, and allow you to act before these actions turn disastrous.

It is not too early to note that a multitude of service providers have cropped up to meet the obviously growing need for background reports/due diligence on hedge fund managers. Unfortunately, the quality has come nowhere close to the quantity, leaving most investors confused as to what exactly they should expect from a background report, if they were to outsource this. The book will clarify this issue as well and arm you with the questions you need to ask to understand whether what you are getting is actually comprehensive, effective due diligence, or whether it should be thrown in the nearest garbage can. Nothing is more dangerous to the investor than the false sense of security derived from a search purporting to be due diligence, but in actuality being closer to "do as little as you can get away with."

Comprehensive hedge fund manager due diligence is not achieved by magic (refer to Chapter 13, What People Think Is Helpful But Isn't). Rather, "people" due diligence means not shirking the details. Handling due diligence on your own via your corporate security department, without understanding the information presented in this book, will lead to mistakes. Your internal people can't fire themselves. Although they will never truly be perceived to be entirely independent, the lack of expertise is a far greater problem.

As mentioned in the Introduction, the other main problem in hedge fund manager due diligence is that institutions know or suspect that they are not aware of everything that they should be doing. Background search vendors prey on such worries, capitalizing on this ignorance by doing cheap, ineffective reviews designed to look like a search. Remember, like that phone one buys on the street in New York City, it looks good, seems good, has everything you need, except, well, the part that makes it work. Here too, this book will help you avoid these characters, and instead glean information you can really trust.

RECAP

1. Management Team Due Diligence is a critical piece of the entire due diligence puzzle.
2. Reviewing managers is not only wise, but might also be considered a fiduciary duty.
3. A manager's past is an excellent predictor of his future actions (results are always another story).
4. Comprehensive due diligence means attending to details, not avoiding searches to save money and time.

What Kinds of Hedge Fund Failures Does the Press Discuss? Why Do Most Hedge Funds that Fail, Really Fail?

Press accounts may prompt you to believe that hedge funds are failing every day, primarily because their operators are crooks. I am not really blaming the press, since it's their job to report newsworthy items, and people often do find stories about scandal more entertaining than stories about virtue. That said, two points need to be recognized and explored so you have a better understanding of the *real* risks in investing in hedge funds, as opposed to those that come via extrapolation from salacious stories.

Point one: Most "hedge funds" that fail are not really hedge funds at all. Nor are they vehicles in which the typical institution would ever dream of investing. As I am writing this the following story was published by *baltimoresun.com*[1]:

> *An Ohio investment manager ... pleaded guilty ... to two counts of securities fraud....*
>
> *The agreement ... calls for David A. Dadante to serve a minimum of 10 years in prison ... and make restitution to about 100 investors.*
>
> *More than $28 million was lost in what started as a Ponzi scheme and grew into a market fraud....*
>
> *Investigators say Dadante looted his fund to finance gambling junkets to Las Vegas and a luxury home in a Cleveland suburb.*

This story is as relevant to institutional investors as what Steve Cohen of SAC eats for breakfast, and perhaps less so. David Dadante, described here as an investment manager (and by a previous story in the same publication as a fund manager), was also provocatively referred to by the SEC as an unregistered investment advisor. He was also cited as a purported hedge fund manager by Hedgeworld. For the first time in my memory, in fact, a story actually describes the alleged fraudster as a "purported" hedge fund manager; that is progress at least in that the writer has seemingly recognized that calling yourself a hedge fund manager does not make you a hedge fund manager. (I can bake a mean cobbler but that doesn't make me Julia Child.)

Another notable facet of the story of Mr. Dadante's fund is that it had at least 110 investors. Given this number, it is almost certain these investors are individuals; if they were institutions these institutions would be named. This is reinforced by the assets under management figure ($51 million), an amount almost certainly too low to attract institutional attention.

Finally, and perhaps most tellingly, Mr. Dadante is accused of running a "Ponzi" scheme, which refers to a scam perfected by Charles Ponzi in 1920. The reason this scam works is that early investors do indeed get paid, handsomely, in fact, although with monies given by subsequent investors. This house of cards is destined to fail eventually, and in a further bit of mixed-metaphor-dom, the people who lose are those who are last to the party. But the real issue is that the first Ponzi scheme predated hedge funds by more than 40 years—and more like 80 years before the recent surge in hedge fund popularity. Ponzi schemes have nothing to do with hedge funds per se; they succeed because early investors tout their gains to their friends, who then want in on whatever the vehicle of the day happens to be. As hedge fund fever cools off, watch the next generation of crooks move on to another story that will explain how they turn your money into riches (for them).

So why do people who commit frauds call themselves hedge fund managers? For the same reason that criminals and con men have been immersing themselves in the popular financial terms of every era: because it works. Investors want to hear a story that resonates, a story that tells them that the storyteller knows something that the investor doesn't, something the investor is willing to pay for. Calling yourself a financial analyst just won't ring as sexy as laying out your ideas under the guise of hedge funds which are now perceived to be hotter than Beyonce.

By the way, I am not a lone wolf here. Commissioner Walt Lukken of the CFTC, according to Opalesque asserted[2]:

> [I]ndividuals who commit fraud by marketing themselves as hedge fund managers and bucketing the profits for themselves ... are fraudsters and have little to do with the concerns surrounding the legitimate hedge fund industry. These fraudulent individuals use the term "hedge fund" as a hook to illegally solicit funds from the public. From a regulatory standpoint, this behavior is not a hedge fund problem, per se—it is essentially an issue of fraud.

Point two: Most hedge funds that fail do so not because the managers are criminals, but because of either business forces or incompetence or demeanor issues. The latter two are still critical and have recognizable signs, which comprehensive due diligence efforts can reveal. The former refers mostly to the economics of investing and marketing, that is, if the fund does not market itself well enough, and achieve above average results quickly, it can find itself managing too little money, and thus unable to support the infrastructure it has developed to run the business at hand. Let's look at each a bit more closely.

BUSINESS FORCES

This term cuts through a wide swath of territory but can be pretty much narrowed down to some combination of performance issues and fund-raising/marketing issues. Although these issues are not to be minimized, they affect, primarily, the hedge funds themselves far more than the institutional investor community. Why? Well, hedge funds that are unable to raise enough money to sustain their business operation——are those that often have little or no institutional support, by definition; if they had institutions behind them, typically they'd be able to raise money from other institutions. And although this Catch-22 is clearly a dilemma to the small, fledgling hedge fund, it is beneath the radar screen of almost all institutions, and therefore will not receive further discussion here. (Check out http://www.crestmontresearch.com/pdfs/HF%20Myths%20Facts.pdf for a lengthier explanation.)

Regarding performance issues, even funds that have managed to attract institutional attention can fail without doing anything nefarious. Witness Scion Fund, which according to Jenny Anderson of the *New York Times* heavily shorted a sub-prime lender, one whose stock did ultimately crater.[3] Sounds great, right? The problem was the timing, with Scion making its bet a bit too early, something that almost led to its demise. You can be sure, however, that if Scion had gone under, attention to its closure would far outweigh any subsequent stories that outlined how it had been correct in its initial prognostication.

Then there was UK-based Westferry Global Markets, which according to a February 2007 snippet in *Hedge Fund Daily*, closed not long after it started. *Financial News* reported that the firm pursued a managed-futures strategy, and "from day one was losing money for its clients."[4] According to *Hedge Fund Daily*, telling investors to be prepared for drawn-out losses, while keeping the strategy itself a major secret, is "no way to build a hedge fund business," even if investors are told to expect positive returns eventually.

Other similar stories abound. Take Keel Capital Management LLC, which according to a February 27, 2007, *MarketWatch.com* piece shut down its $175 million fund because of "a lack of attractive short-selling opportunities and a strategy that it described as too restrictive."[5] According to the story, Keel Offshore Ltd., which concentrated on companies undergoing disruptive change, had a return below its benchmark but noncorrelated to the benchmark, something that is typically a positive trait. However, when some investors began withdrawing their money, Keel had to choose between shifting its strategy or shutting down. The article added an ominous note, "Hedge funds thrive on market volatility, because that creates mis-priced assets for them to trade. But as more hedge funds have started and others have grown into giants, trading opportunities have become scarcer and volatility has declined."

Finally, what about the billion dollar babies? Mid-March 2007 brought several stories about a number of large hedge funds that saw 2006 as their last year. *Hedge Fund Daily*, via *Absolute Return*, reported that nine hedge funds with over $1 billion in assets each ceased to operate in 2006.[6] Only Amaranth is likely to be recognizable to people looking for a sexy story; the others that called it a day were "Archeus Capital Management's *Animi Master Fund* ($2.65 billion); Sagamore Hill Capital Management's *Sagamore Hill* ($2.6 billion); Saranac Capital Management's *Citigroup Multistrategy Arbitrage/Saranac Arbitrage Fund* ($2.2 billion); BKF Asset Management's *Levco Alternative Investment Fund* ($1.9 billion); Ritchie Capital Management's *Ritchie Energy Trading* ($1.2 billion); Saranac's *Citigroup Archer/Saranac Total Return Fund* ($1.1 billion); MacKay Shields' *MacKay Shield Long/Short* ($1 billion); Mangan & McColl Partners' *M&M Arbitrage* ($1 billion); and Harbert Management's *Harbert Convertibles* ($900 million)."

These funds clearly closed not because they couldn't raise money; in fact, an argument could be made that they closed because they raised more money than they could effectively put to use. And again, except for Amaranth, most of the others barely earned themselves a line of type from the popular business press. Unless hedge fund failures reflect behavioral patterns, which themselves could or even should have led institutions to avoid investing in a certain hedge fund manager, ignore the blather.

INCOMPETENCE/DEMEANOR ISSUES

Hedge funds that do poorly, because of managers who are poor traders, poor businessmen, or both, do warrant inspection from the institutions, if for nothing else than for the sake of education, post mortem, as to what went wrong and what could have helped foresee the failure. The funny thing is, you won't see many stories about these kinds of blow-ups. In fact, most of the press wouldn't even consider these hedge fund closures a blow-up at all. But if public records and interviews with colleagues suggest that a fund is headed by someone who is so abrasive as to be completely unable to maintain key personnel for any appreciable length of time, the fund is not likely to be successful, unless it is so small that it can be run by essentially one person. Of course, such a fund wouldn't be seeking institutional backing, and therein lies the conundrum. A fund that goes from a one-man show to a billion dollar entity now needs leadership, the kind of leadership that is provided by someone as adept at managing people as at managing money. Managing people, though, takes a different set of skills from trading capital; some people may not be able to do both. This itself is not necessarily a problem, since many businesses survive, nay thrive, by having executives with complementary skills. But this issue becomes the death knell for a small or medium fund that is going big if its leader fails to recognize that people skills are a crucial component to a growing entity.

In the final analysis, what all of the above indicates is that, perversely enough, the hedge fund scandals that are discussed most often and most breathlessly are largely irrelevant to institutions. By contrast, failures that could be instructive are ones that don't receive a lot of press, and the lessons that could be learned are washed away by a sea of inattention. For institutions, therefore, the key is to study funds that have succeeded and those that have failed. The institution must look for the patterns that dictated why certain funds failed, to ensure that the next time around the institution does not invest in similar funds.

SIDEBAR: MANAGED ACCOUNTS, A CURE-ALL?

Several studies have suggested that managed accounts can transform, if not transcend, hedge fund investment risk. A February 7, 2007, piece summed up 2006 research by Terrapinn, along with industry reports by entities like Deutsche Bank (2003), by stating that "the greatest obstacles for institutional investors in their allocation to hedge funds are a lack of transparency, risk control and lack of regulation."[7] In this story, Simon Hookway, CEO of London's MSS Capital, averred that hedge fund failures are caused less by investment risk (40 percent

(continued)

SIDEBAR: MANAGED ACCOUNTS, A CURE-ALL? (*continued*)

of failures) than by operational issues (the other 60 percent). Mr. Hookway added that operational failures are "never the result of just one event," usually combining things like misrepresentation and unauthorized trading, among others.

Also commenting in this piece was John Cunningham of Stamford-based WR Capital Management, who asserted, "The benefits of liquidity, transparency, fraud controls, and controls over cash movements outweigh the associated costs or challenges with the separately managed account."

This theme is echoed by the renowned Jack Schwager, best-selling author and an executive with a fund of funds known as Fortune Group. On March 16, 2007, according to AllAboutAlpha.com, has redeemed his underlying hedge funds and "directed his managers to establish accounts on a managed accounts platform."[8] "'A lack of transparency is the root cause for all blow-ups and frauds in the hedge fund industry,' he says. 'Every problem, I don't care what it is—whether it's a fraud, blowup or whatever, is caused by one thing: a lack of transparency.'"

I am certainly no expert on the managed accounts structure and thus cannot begin to comment on whether its upsides, as elucidated by Messrs. Schwager and Hookway along with Dr. Jaeger, are worth whatever the downsides come with the managed accounts platform. What I can say, however, is that when we have examined hedge fund blow-ups (recognizing that it is hard to know if the failures alluded to in these studies are the garden variety failures discussed earlier in this chapter or if they are limited to blow-ups), almost all, if not all, of the managers had something in their background to suggest that a blow-up, while not imminent, certainly had more than the average risk of happening. Given this, due diligence on the people, while not an exact science like chemistry or algebra, can be mastered and can reduce the risk of investing with people whose characteristic behavior suggests they may be more problematic than a similar fund also under consideration. Again, for investors who are unwilling or unable to use the managed accounts method, due diligence is the answer. And for those investors reading this and thinking that of course a due diligence provider is advocating due diligence, listen instead to Jean-Rene Giraud,

Stephane Daul, and Corentin Christory, researchers at France's EDHEC business school (according to *Hedge Fund Daily*). In a *Journal of Alternative Investments* paper, "Quantification of Hedge Fund Default Risk," the authors contended that "thorough due diligence is an absolute requirement prior to investing." The authors stated that some funds "over-diversify," theorizing that by including 40+ funds, they have minimized the portfolio's operational risk. The authors conclude, however, that an increased number of funds may actually leave less time to investigate each individual fund; moreover, the more funds, the greater the possibility that funds with lower standards of operations might get in, thus plausibly increasing the default rate of individual funds.

The authors added that operational due diligence is best served by an "informed" process, to include general hedge fund risk factors like fraud, as well as, drum-roll please, the "management company under scrutiny."

So there.

RECAP

1. The press loves a salacious story.
2. Most hedge fund frauds and blow-ups receiving press are not hedge funds at all.
3. Hedge funds fail for similar reasons to other businesses.
4. Studying real hedge fund blow-ups is instructive.
5. Warning signs almost always exist before the blow-up.

suspected that perhaps everyone should have slowed down and taken

CHAPTER 4

Can the Chances of Investing in Future Failures Be Lessened/Prevented? How?

In the heyday of the late 1990s investment world, a frequent piece of advice given to young entrepreneurs seeking venture capital investments was to imagine finding themselves on an elevator ride with a VC, with approximately 30 to 45 seconds to make their pitch. Being able to reduce their entire business presentation to this blurb was supposed to be a way of honing them in on what was truly their so-called value proposition. History has since proven that perhaps everyone should have slowed down and taken some more time to analyze whether these businesses actually would produce profits, rather than well-crafted and bizarrely brief narratives. But just the same I like the idea of the elevator ride for the main premise of this book. Please take out your stopwatch, imagine we are on an elevator, then read on.

Unlike leopards, humans can, in theory, change their spots. Most, however, don't. And the ones with the spottiest of backgrounds, based on our reviews, are no exceptions. The central tenet of this book is that by careful scrutiny of hedge fund managers' backgrounds, institutions can indeed avoid the vast majority of potential frauds and a good many blow-ups by learning to first find and then recognize the warning signs that foretell later doom. Institutions have a fiduciary duty to check into the funds in which they are investing; this is indisputable. But more than that, their due diligence efforts benefit them directly by uncovering issues that they can either deal with upfront by confronting a manager, keep in the back of their minds for later use in dealing with a manager, or use immediately to simply move on to the next manager on their list. This is a powerful incentive to do due diligence, well, diligently. As this book will also make clear, due diligence on people does not tolerate corner-cutting. Like the Magic Eye hidden pictures within a mass of dots that were so popular a few years ago, the patterns of behavior that so clearly demarcate future actions are visible only if you really are looking for them. But when you find them, these pictures are spectacularly vivid.

I think I could say all of this in under 40 seconds, with most of it even being intelligible. To actually prove what I'm saying is a different matter. One way to do so would be through oratory. Another is via careful arguments, crafted in paragraph after paragraph, page after page, chapter after chapter. (Believe me, you'll get plenty of that.) For now, however, let's use another method: anecdotal evidence, in the form of a brief case study.

INTERNATIONAL MANAGEMENT ASSOCIATES: FELLING THE TOUGHEST OF THE TOUGH

Steve Atwater was a hard hitting safety for the Denver Broncos (and then perhaps regrettably, one season for the Jets). But he is no doubt wondering what hit him after investing with Kirk Wright's International Management Associates (hereafter referred to simply as IMA) and watching $20 million of his and six other former football players he helped to recruit vanish like a playing card held by David Blaine.

For those who have not followed the story, *Bloomberg* reported that on February 9, 2007, the SEC announced that a U.S. District Court judge in Atlanta ordered Mr. Wright to "forfeit $19.8 million and pay a $120,000 fine" for submitting "falsified statements about the assets and returns of seven hedge funds managed by his firm, Marietta, Georgia-based International Management Associates LLC."[1] The SEC had filed suit in February 2006.

According to the article, "the hedge funds 'have been providing investors with quarterly statements that misrepresented both the amount of assets in the respective funds and the rates of return obtained by them.' ... 'In fact, by 2005, the assets of the funds had been largely dissipated, and this fact was not disclosed to the investors.'"

Mr. Wright was arrested in May 2006 on mail-fraud charges for which he is scheduled to be tried in May 2007.

The SEC litigation release alleged that approximately $115 million, and as much as $185 million, was raised by Mr. Wright and investment advisers controlled by him.[2]

A debate between Atwater and other players and the NFLPA is currently playing out now in the courts, with the players essentially claiming that the NFLPA implicitly endorsed Mr. Wright by having him on its roster of registered advisers. The union and the league have countered that the NFL's collective bargaining agreement makes the players responsible for their own financial decisions. This book will not take a position on this battle, which will be up to the courts to sort out. However, as a matter of demonstrating the effectiveness of due diligence, laying out Mr. Wright's background is instructive.

Kirk Sean Wright was born on July 14, 1970, if criminal records (below) are accurate. According to news stories, Mr. Wright graduated from SUNY-Binghamton in 1993, then received a master's degree at Harvard's Kennedy School of Government circa 1995. (Harvard confirmed that Mr. Wright indeed earned a Masters in Public Policy, having attended from September 1993 to June 1995. SUNY-Binghamton requires a release to confirm educational credentials, but the confirmation of the advanced degree, by default, corroborates that Mr. Wright obtained some undergraduate degree.) Mr. Wright immediately went to work for Kaiser Associates, again according to news stories, then struck out on his own approximately year later, running IMA from his Manassas, Virginia, home.

So what do we already know? A year spent at Kaiser, itself a firm with a stellar reputation, is not generally enough to qualify someone as a hedge fund expert, Harvard master's degree or no Harvard master's degree. But I am getting ahead of the story.

You see, also in 1996 (October 21, 1996, specifically) an arbitration proceeding (Addendum 4.1, viewable, with all other addenda cited in this book, at www.wiley.com/WileyCDA/WileyTitle/productCd-0470139773.descCd DOWNLOAD.html) was brought before the National Association of Securities Dealers (NASD) regarding a matter in which Olde Discount Corp. alleged that a certain Kirk Wright failed to pay for 1,500 shares of Media Vision Technology, Inc. stock, which this Kirk Wright then sold. Mr. Wright did not respond to the arbitration and on June 19, 1997, Olde Discount was awarded more than $3,000. Although no identifying information was presented on the NASD document, based on the nature of this action it is plausible, if not highly likely, that this matter involved the Kirk Wright of interest (in a real report, interviews with Olde Discount or its attorney would be conducted to clarify this).

1996 was an up-and-down year for Mr. Wright, who aside from forming his business and apparently getting hit with the aforementioned arbitration award, managed to bounce a check that resulted in a misdemeanor criminal action. On March 8, 1996, Mr. Wright (confirmed to be the subject via a social security number listed on the criminal record), according to Prince William County court records (Addendum 4.2), issued a check for approximately $75 to Lowes, "knowing at the time that there was insufficient funds in the account to pay such check." The charge was eventually dismissed on March 7, 1997, though it is unclear why.

The 1996 criminal records associated Mr. Wright with an entity known as Kitty Hawk LLC. In 1995, according to Secretary of State records, Mr. Wright was an officer/manager of Kitty Hawk, listed to an address in Manassas, Virginia, that elsewhere links to Mr. Wright's date of birth and social security number. Meanwhile, International Management Associates LLC was incorporated in Virginia on February 12, 1997, according to Virginia State Corporation Commission documents. Mr. Wright is not mentioned in this filing, but the company is listed at 8451 Weeping Willow Drive, Manassas, Virginia. Elsewhere, this address is linked to International Management Associates Taurus and IMA Sunset, with which Mr. Wright *is* associated (in still other filings). Finally, Georgia secretary of state records state that International Management Associates LLC, filed in that state in 1999, making numerous subsequent filings in 2003. (Recall the firm was based in Marietta, Georgia.)

The 1996 incident was not, our research revealed, Mr. Wright's maiden criminal voyage. On January 11, 1990, in Broome County, New York (recall that Mr. Wright purportedly attended SUNY-Binghamton, which is located in Broome County), Mr. Wright, then 19 years old, was charged with a criminal trespass violation and "petit larceny" (a misdemeanor). According to the available information (see Addendum 4.7) he pled guilty to trespass and received a $50 fine and a conditional discharge; the second count was reduced to trespass and apparently incorporated into count one. The case file was marked as sealed. A little more than two years later, on September 19, 1992, and also in Broome County, New York, Mr. Wright found himself in a spot of trouble again. This time, the charges were two counts of "assault—third degree (misdemeanor)" and a disorderly conduct violation. On March 31, 1993, all three counts were pled down to a disorderly conduct violation and Mr. Wright was similarly granted a conditional discharge. Once again, unfortunately, the file was sealed. (As a side note, the only reason New York courts were even searched is because our review associated Mr. Wright with an address in the Bronx, and had attended school in Binghamton. As will be hammered home in the next chapter and throughout this book, this is the reason why searching only where someone is now, in this case Georgia, is insufficient—to put it very mildly.)

Okay, now what do we know? Besides having absolutely no experience as a hedge fund manager prior to forming his hedge fund, and having practically no work experience at all, in fact, we can see that Mr. Wright had other legal and regulatory issues at the start of his career. We also see the existence of an entity, Kitty Hawk, that oddly is not referred to in news stories about Mr. Wright. What this entity did, and for how long, is therefore unclear.

Combined, these various yellow flags would probably have made a sophisticated institutional investor more than a little nervous. Whether they would have been enough to cause institutions to walk away is not a question that can be answered with certainty, though an educated guess suggests that the response is yes (remember, no institutions got seriously burned here, based on court records and news stories; bankruptcy records, attached at Addendum 4.3, show that the largest creditor was Playa Del Rey, California-based Roger O'Neal Family Trust, with more than $12.6 million invested, but this entity, and other similar trusts, would not qualify, to me, as an institution). Of course, what no one but IMA officials knows is whether institutions were even approached to invest; having gathered approximately $185 million, by some accounts, from individuals and others like the above-referenced family trust, IMA may not have seen the need to go after more sophisticated investors.

For the sake of discussion, let's say, however, that IMA had approached institutions for money. Besides the above, were there other warning bells that were ringing in Mr. Wright's background? Here are some things to know:

Mr. Wright, during 2001 and 2002, accumulated hundreds of thousands of dollars in various tax liens, ranging from a $1,033 County Tax Lien filed against him on December 6, 2002, to a $383,680 Federal Tax Lien he incurred on August 28, 2002 (subsequently satisfied on November 1, 2004). IMA, too, didn't want to miss the lien party, getting tagged by the Department of Labor on March 22, 2001 with a $2,088 lien. Also joining the fray was Watson Andy Armstrong, who was awarded a judgment for $10,944 against Mr. Wright in Cobb County, Georgia, on March 5, 2001; a later judgment for $11,132 was entered in favor of Armstrong on October 26, 2001, almost certainly involving the same incident. Satisfaction was recorded on May 19, 2005.

For people who invested prior to 2001, this lien/judgment history would obviously not then have existed. But for those like the karma-challenged Mr. Atwater, who got in after 2002, this information would have been helpful to know.

These liens and judgments were not to be the end of Mr. Wright's legal troubles. Three suits naming Mr. Wright were found in a search of Cuyahoga County Common Pleas Court (Ohio) records. Summaries of these suits, all of which involved Mr. Wright's investment in a restaurant (itself something that should have caused alarms to siren, if only for the distraction it posed) follow.

Suit Number 1: Filed March 4, 2004 as case number CV04524272, was *Darden Co. et al. v. Phil The Fire, Inc. et al.*, including Mr. Wright. Darden

Company was the general contractor for a build-out of a restaurant known as Phil The Fire; Mr. Wright was an investor in the restaurant, according to news sources, and an officer of defendant PTF Downtown, LLC, according to the complaint (attached at Addendum 4.4). Darden charged (that is, was owed) more than $977,000 for its work but had not been paid. Mr. Wright and his partner, Philip Davis, also were alleged to have used corporate assets to pay their personal obligations, prior to paying corporate debts (like the ones owed to the plaintiffs); Messrs. Wright and Davis additionally and purportedly had advised the contractor that the project was fully funded, knowing, allegedly, that this was not true.

This suit was dismissed without prejudice on November 14, 2005, likely due to some type of settlement (we would typically recommend contacting the plaintiff to clarify this, although settlement information is often considered confidential).

Suit Number 2: *Smarthouse Integration LLC v. Phil The Fire, Inc., et al.* (Addendum 4.5), again including Kirk Wright (CV04529051). Filed on March 4, 2004, this suit, like the one above, involved claims of nonpayment for services rendered, here including installation of WIFI and both security and telephone systems, among other things. Smarthouse sought the nearly $22,000 it was owed plus $25,000 in damages. This suit was dismissed on October 27, 2004.

Suit Number 3: *Alexander Daniels v. PTF Downtown LLC, et al.* (Addendum 4.6), including Kirk Wright (CV-04-535970). On June 20, 2005, Mr. Daniels was awarded a summary judgment against PTF and Mr. Davis for more than $30,000; the suit does not specify the work Mr. Daniels performed for the restaurant, but does state this as the reason for the suit.

Other items of concern discussed in news reports following IMA's crash have included Mr. Wright's promises of extraordinary returns; according to one account, he claimed to be guaranteeing that he'd achieve 27 percent returns by shorting stocks. Add to this a showy lifestyle highlighted by fancy cars, lavish parties at his mansion and an over-the-top second marriage, and it is not hard to see why people somewhat unfamiliar with investing would be taken in by such an ostentatious display of success.[3]

Finally, lending one more dash of credibility were the two doctors who served as Mr. Wright's business partners. While withholding all judgment of what they knew, and when they knew it, a bigger question would be why having two doctors as board members/advisors/partners/whatever would be useful in any endeavor outside of a medical procedure. Honestly, what do doctors (except for those who are also trained in finance) know about investments or people's character?

Smart institutions already recognize the value of due diligence. Ask managers of funds of funds that have been around awhile, and they'll all say that they routinely combine intensive operational due diligence with manager visits and background research. All of this is done to avoid both investment failures, which of course are bound to occur, despite the best of efforts and intentions, as well as high-profile blow-ups, which may very well be part of the general landscape but do not have to be part of your portfolio.

Identifying signs that warn of fraud and other, more subtle, yellow flags, are vital to a healthy investment process. Most investors agree that the best kind of decision is an informed one. As the volume of alternative investments increases, so does the commitment to research. In the past due diligence on people may have been relegated to the back of the line, but nowadays investors recognize how fundamental this research is, and they are increasingly making this a standard—and early—part of the investment process.

This last point is one that I think merits a bit more discussion. Proper due diligence takes time. Flashy advertisements screeching about the ability to find anything you need to know in a matter of days are akin to claims that a burger cooked by some fast food joint in 20 seconds is the same quality as the porterhouse aged for weeks by a fancy steakhouse. Leave enough time to do due diligence correctly, and you will be more than compensated. From a purely background research standpoint, some situations that require even more time than normal are as follows.

TIMING ISSUES

1. *Private Investment in Public Entity (PIPEs) investors.* These can be the worst. A lot of the people operating in this space are, how would I put it, "colorful." Beyond that, recipient public companies usually continue to report PIPE financings in all their subsequent SEC filings, which can number in the hundreds every quarter. Further, PIPEs are objectionable to many shareholders and governance types, so there's often associated litigation. In addition, this was until very recently a hot area, so there's a lot of media attention (in fact, a relatively recent sub-library in Lexis reports only on PIPEs).

2. *Medical/pharma/bioscience investors.* Dozens of trade journals cover this field, many of which simply copy in full or rewrite press releases. In fact, it's often a field that's driven by press releases. So you might find four or five PR newswires announcing something followed by two dozen

articles repeating the press releases. Finally, lots of pharma investors do a fair amount of PIPE investing (overlap with point one, above).

3. *If a subject's first name can conceivably be a last name.* Most online searches are done by proximity. Researching Thomas Dean, therefore, means you'll also end up getting everything on Thomas Dean, Dean Thomas, "John Dean and Thomas Franklin," and so forth. Although ways to modify searches to drop out a lot of the extraneous results do exist, these kinds of names are still always more difficult.

4. *Certain ethnic names.* We were once approached for work for someone with the surname "An." As you might surmise, this is basically impossible to search in many key databases. Many Middle Eastern names, likewise, are not only common but also components of still other, equally common names.

5. *Women.* Often, research here has to include a maiden name as well as a married name. Divorces can add more names, forcing you to effectively search on two or three people. For instance, reviewing our Casey Brooke Kahl Drucker would mean searching at least Kahl and Drucker as last names. As Brooke also could conceivably be a last name, we'd probably have to search that too.

6. *Public companies.* Note that even when your focus is not on the public company, if the subject is or was a senior executive at one, and they invariably are, their names will be all over the company's many SEC filings, and so forth.

7. *Generic-sounding companies.* Company names are often part of several other company names. Naming a fund the European Investor's Fund is not altogether uncommon, and frankly, just cruel.

However you choose to handle your people due diligence, the most important things to have in your arsenal is the knowledge of what to expect and when to expect it. Few people know everything about everything. Like most endeavors, a key to success is not only knowing what you don't know, but also admitting it, and being okay with this. I think of it like this: when I go to an auto mechanic, the most I can say is that my car is making a rattling noise. When told that this means the catalytic converter may be on the fritz, the mechanic may as well be talking in Polish. If I had the knowledge to understand this gobbledygook, I'd probably be able to fix the car, too.

Hopefully this book will serve, therefore, as a Polish-English dictionary. And though the above example might be an exaggeration, at least knowing whether what the person (here a mechanic, for you an investigator or in-house researcher) is saying will go a long way toward making you feel confident that the correct decision is being reached regarding the actions being proposed.

RECAP

1. People's behavioral tendencies tend to repeat, especially in times of stress.
2. Discovering past behavioral patterns greatly improves present decision making by predicting and dealing with future problems, before they happen.
3. Due diligence is the way to discover these patterns.
4. Learning how to recognize these patterns is critical.
5. Due diligence knows no shortcuts.
6. Due diligence takes time.
7. Doing due diligence is not just for fiduciary reasons.

CHAPTER 5

Investigative Background Reports—The Beginning: Identify Your Target

Before you can even begin to gather information on a hedge fund manager, you must learn as much about that person's *identifiers* as possible. By identifiers, I am referring to things like middle initial or middle name, spouse's name, current home address, current work address, former home and work addresses, date of birth, social security number, and former employers. Some of this data is widely and easily available; the former employers' part, for example, you can obtain from the Uniform Application for Investment Adviser Registrations (commonly referred to as Form ADVs) or by simply asking managers for a biography. But although you can certainly ask managers for the other information, many may consider this request to be onerous, to put it mildly. You therefore need a mechanism for uncovering these data points on your own. Before we talk about how you can find this information, let's briefly touch on why this information is so important.

WHY A MIDDLE NAME CAN MAKE OR BREAK YOU

Nothing astonishes me more than the fact that so many institutions settle for data that they cannot tie to the subject manager versus some other schlub with the same name. Realizing that this is most likely, hopefully, due to ignorance, rather than willful neglect, is one of the things that motivated me to write this book in the first place. The very essence of people due diligence is ensuring that what you are reviewing is relevant. And although you and your staff can argue *ad nauseam* about what makes various snippets of someone's history relevant or not, what is inarguable is that for any information about the manager to have value, it, um, has to be about that manager. Although I may sound like the ultimate master of the obvious here, many investigative shops, from the work I have seen, make little to no attempt to cull through what they provide to an institution, instead taking the easy way out by hiding behind legal and other caveats to explain why they just don't know whether the information they are providing relates to the subject or to a similarly-named person. If you take away anything from this book, let it be this: a "report" that does not explain which news stories, court records, corporate documents, and so forth relate to the subject, and which don't, is not only worthless, it is actually harmful, because it sticks you with all the liability and none of the means to reduce or remove it. Why? Think of it this way. Suppose you receive a stack of news stories, 500 in all, and are told that it is unclear whether those stories involve your subject. In one of those stories, it turns out, is a blurb about that person that would have alarmed you had you read it and related it to your manager. But even were you to have read through all 500 nonsummarized pages, how would you have decided on the significance of the one interesting tidbit without being able to discern whether it was relevant to the subject? The answer, unfortunately, is that you wouldn't, unless you approached the subject directly, something that can get pretty embarrassing pretty quickly if your information is so sketchy.

Do yourself the biggest favor. When it comes to people due diligence, never settle for less than knowing that what you are reading relates to your subject, and you must have carefully elucidated reasons for why this determination was made.

WHAT YOU SHOULD ASK THE MANAGER

A huge mantra of mine is always to first identify your goal, because everything you do should then be dictated by this goal. Here, our goal is to ensure that we collect enough information to help us comb through mountains of data and ensure that the molehills that remain are on point: that is, that they cite the subject, and not another person (I kind of wish there was a catchy word for a similarly named person, sort of like a doppelganger for a person who looks like another person. Suggestions are encouraged.)

Keeping this in mind, it's time now to briefly discuss the elephant in the identification room, otherwise known as the social security number (note that a further discussion of this is present in a myth-busting Chapter 13, "What You Think Is Helpful But Isn't"). The thing about social security numbers is that they do indeed help you find out other pieces of identifying information, including address histories, dates of birth, middle initials, and spouse's names. However, this must be measured against the fact that many managers are reluctant, to put it kindly, to provide their social security number. What's more, civil court cases, one of the most important items in a background report, do not except in rare instances include social security numbers, rendering them immune to the comparative powers afforded by the nine-digit *Wunderkind*, also known as the social.

Given the above, it is our contention that bothering the manager with a request for his social security number is not worth the reward. Instead, a home address will suffice and is not likely to inspire the same trepidation and even anger that asking for the social often does. As you will see shortly, the odd part of this is that the home address leads you to the social anyway, thus obviating the need for creating disharmony with a manager you presumably are courting, at least in some ways.

Finally, the civil court case conundrum cited above demonstrates that even with a social, your identification tasks are not nearly over. Those familiar with court documents know that many bankruptcy and criminal court proceedings do indeed list a social security number, allowing for an easy understanding of whether that matter involved the subject or not. Civil courts, alas, don't. This forces you to be more creative and work harder, which may be why so few due diligence "experts" even discuss this when talking about their search capabilities. For your purposes, though, the important part of this is that you are not without hope when it comes to separating out relevant from irrelevant court records; you just have your work cut out for you.

MODERN-DAY IDENTIFICATION DILEMMAS: THE LAW OF UNINTENDED CONSEQUENCES

Determining a manager's address history, date of birth, spouse's name, and other similar facts oddly has become more difficult over time, despite the increase in sources dedicated to this task. As will be explained in more detail in Chapter 9 (Credentials Verifications), most schools and employers will no longer verify a former student's date of birth or social security number. (Although it certainly makes sense that one would not expect one's school to provide this number to any person who called and asked for it, failing to just confirm it is hugely counterproductive, since these items are a way of ensuring that accurate information is presented about the student/employee. Still, this topic is rich enough for another book and so will be dropped here. For now. I promise.)

Adding to this, and subtracting from your ability to develop identification data, is the fact that dates of birth and social security numbers are now often truncated by identification sources. With a technique designed to prevent identity theft has come an unfortunate unintended consequence: people are slammed more, because private investigators and others don't or can't sift through data to determine what relates to the person of interest as opposed to the numerous others sharing that name.

Because of all this, identification efforts have turned into an art, as opposed to a science. More guesswork and intuition is necessary now, because the needed facts are simply not always available. Coupled with the fact that the few places that actually retain extremely accurate identification information, DMV records and voter registration records, are typically not available in any simple, comprehensive way, more, not less, identification mistakes are possible. For you, therefore, the challenge is to ensure that you are not the ones making those mistakes. The material below should help you in that effort.

THE HOW TO OF SUBJECT IDENTIFICATION; HOW TO WINNOW

Acknowledging that the following techniques do vary slightly from person to person, and that obviously the more information you have directly from the subject manager the easier your task will be, here are methods to employ depending on how much data you have at the onset of your review.

What to Do When You Start with Nothing but a Name

If for some reason you are reviewing a manager and have nothing other than his name and the entity for which he works, step one is to find any biographical data that may exist about this manager. If the manager provided you with a biography, that's great. If not, check regulatory records (more on this in Chapter 8), the Internet (Chapter 11) and news sources (Chapter 7) as any or all of these often will have biographical data.

The picture you are trying to paint here is geographical and contextual. Where, physically, has your manager worked? Based on his schooling and career, approximately how old is the subject? What is the subject's middle name? Answering these questions leaves you less helpless, and ready to use an identification product known as LocatePlus (https://www .locateplus.com/welcome.asp).*

----

*For this and the other sources described in this section, you will need to contact the entities directly regarding the access they provide to non-investigative institutions.

Your task is easier now, once you have established certain parameters, but it is by no means easy, for you still are engaging in what amounts to a hunt and peck method. In LocatePlus, you will run your search using the subject's first and last name (below is a step-by-step demonstration of this). Now, the hunt begins. Eyeing the results, you effectively are reducing the number of possible matches by taking the basic address history and age data your biographical efforts produced and comparing them to the details associated with the people on the list. Next, choose the person that best fits the criteria you established and then, crucially, try to find an address tied to the person in question that matches, say, the subject's current company or any previous employer's address.

Step-by-Step

1. Enter user name and password. Click Login.
2. Agree to terms/conditions. The LocatePlus screen, at the onset of your review and after you have entered your user name and password.
    Click on "Agree."
3. Under the person search category, click on "name and/or address."
    LocatePlus has several options to search under the "person search" feature. The two most commonly used options are "name and/or address" and "social security number." Given that we are presuming in this situation that you do not have a social security number to start, you obviously need to click on the "Name and/or Address" method.
4. Enter first and last names.

Before you click the "Search" button, select the letter B for the MVR Disclosure question; although you are not conducting a vehicle search here, this answer best fits the scenario in question.

Then, for the Disclosure Statement, we select the fourth option. (Here again you will need to discuss this directly with LocatePlus.)

Now the fun begins. (Fun might be something of a misnomer here but depending on your perspective, it can either be incredibly rewarding to be able to find the hedge fund manager's needle amidst a haystack of raw, confusing data, or intensely frustrating.) If your search yields more than a few records, you will call upon the information you have developed and which we referred to earlier, that is, a middle initial (if you have found this), or a state (starting with current work state). Note that when you are entering a middle initial, be sure to pick the "start with" option.

As an example, I entered Randy Shain. Somewhat surprisingly, there are quite a few people who share my name. Now it so happens that I know I do not have a middle name, but a researcher would more likely presume that one had simply not been found. How, then, to narrow this search down? Bizarrely, not by age, for even if you knew I am 42, most of the Randy Shain imposters out there have a similar number of tree rings. But entering a state would do the trick nicely. By clicking on "Change Criteria," located near the top right of the screen, you are returned to the page where you had entered the first and last names. Entering New York, a place you'd know I'd been by reviewing nothing more than our firm's website, even without seeing my biography, and hitting "Search" leaves you with three overlapping "hits." One of these contains no data besides an erroneous address, so this one would be ignored. The other two, as noted, are actually one record, with the separation merely delineating my "confirmed home address," according to this source. With the addresses provided, you are on your way to beginning your court research, and you have built a foundation upon which you can evaluate data citing people named Randy Shain to determine its application to me. You also will compare this information to that which you'll develop using other identification sources, outlined below (redundancy in this world is as important as it is to technology geeks), to develop a full address history.

Note: Searches for social security numbers when starting with only a name are not, of course, always this fruitful. Some such searches, in fact, may end up being too unwieldy and ultimately, unsuccessful, even with the other tools described in this section. In those instances, you'll need to have the subject provide either a home address (the least likely of the three to prompt any indignation), date of birth, or social security number.

What to Do When You Start with a Date of Birth or Home Address

In situations where you begin your search with a manager's home address, your search is of course much simpler and involves many of the same initial steps as described above. With the added data, however, you'll simply capture the record that matches the home address or date of birth provided to you. In the example with which we just finished, entering my name *and* home address into LocatePlus yields only one hit. Though this is not always, or even often the case, even with multiple hits the address in question will make the correct answer visible. This record will then yield both addresses and the person's social security number.

With a name and a date of birth, the search is certainly simpler than with just a name, but not quite as simple as the one just described, that is, using a name and a home address. This is so because LocatePlus does not have a date of birth criterion to enter; instead, you will need to search by name, then scan the results for the corresponding date of birth.

Problems arise when the manager's name is common. In this situation, you not only will be faced with a tedious journey through screen after screen hoping to happen upon the date of birth you were given, but there is always a chance that you may encounter two people with the same name and the same date of birth. In those situations, we'd move to a second source, known as IRB (see below). Unlike LocatePlus, IRB provides an option to search by name and either a partial or full date of birth. The trouble with IRB, and the reason you wouldn't always simply start with this source (a logical next question), is that it furnishes only truncated social security numbers. Given this, you'll need to cross reference your IRB results with those you find in LocatePlus.

What to Do When You Start With, or Develop, a Social Security Number

When you start your review already possessing the manager's social security number, step one is to use the LocatePlus option to search by social security number, instead of using the search by name feature. Click on this search method, enter the number, check the appropriate disclosure boxes, and wait ... for maybe two seconds. Now you have an address history, and, by clicking on the hyperlinked name, at times a complete or partial date of birth. At this juncture, you are ready for IRB (https://secure.accurint.com/app/irb/main).

As usual, you will first be prompted for your user name and password before you can log in. Other steps are also similar to those you used in LocatePlus:

1. Click on "Person Search" in the "People" category.
2. Select **Click to Continue Fraud Prevention or Detection** (the purpose of your inquiry).
3. We select **Click to Continue Licensed Private Investigative or Security Services** (you'll need a different option, of course).
4. Enter the social security number you previously developed into the prescribed field.
5. Press the "Search" button.
6. Select the report that matches the subject's name and DOB (if any) by clicking the report icon.

Aside from some misspellings, the span of time covered here is breathtaking. For me, for example, addresses back to 1988, missing only addresses where I lived during my college years.

Select "Comprehensive Report." Though this report contains a fair amount of information you will be searching for via other sources, and should in now way be thought of as "comprehensive" when it comes to court searches, lien records, and so forth, it does have certain data that otherwise can be hard to find, including, at times, addresses other sources did not find, full dates of birth, spouse's name, motor vehicle records, and voter registration data. All of this can be useful in helping you weed out news stories, corporate records and crucially, court cases, that do not relate to your subject. What's more, IRB has a creepily neat family tree feature that can be used to help you find an interview source. (This is discussed more fully in Chapter 12, but the basic premise is that sometimes a source is identified but no contact information is found. Calling a relative can untie the knot.)

Two sources are good; three are better. After you have finished with LocatePlus and IRB, you'll want to use Choicepoint *AutoTrackXP* (https:// atxp.choicepoint.com/at/login.asp?ReferringPage=/at/mainmenu.asp). Here again, redundancies are your friend, in that they ensure that your subsequent searches are both broad and narrow, and more importantly, accurate. On to the play-by-play.

1. User name and password, please.
2. Select Option 3 in the permissible purpose screen.
3. Click on "Direct-to-Report Individual."
4. Using the social security number and subject's name, fill out the following section.
5. Select "Basic Report." The other reports, at this point, are superfluous.
6. Ignore Step 3. These options are either focused on linking your data in a way that is beyond the needs of your review, or gather data that by now you already have.
7. We select number 8 to answer the permissible purpose inquiry. It is likely that you would select number 3, though your legal staff should review this. (For use in the normal course of business by a legitimate business or its agents, employees, or contractors, but only (A) to verify the accuracy of personal information submitted by the individual to the business or its agents, employees, or contractors; and (B) if such information as so submitted is not correct or is no longer correct, to obtain the correct information, but only for the purposes of preventing fraud by, pursuing legal remedies against, or recovering on a debt or security interest against, the individual.)
8. Step 5 of 5: Click on "Submit Report."
9. Oddly, instead of seeing the results, you must proceed to the Results Manager, located near the top left of the screen. Click on this link.
10. Once the report is "available," click the link marked "Available."

Though the report did produce one address not covered by either LocatePlus or IRB, it also attributed "possible" addresses to me that are or were occupied by, respectively, my wife, cousin, and late mother. When viewing this data, always bear in mind that while it should serve as a guide for your court searches, and will help you tremendously in your effort to distinguish relevant data from that which merely applies to similarly named individuals, not all of it will be 100 percent accurate. Given this, the possible addresses should be treated with extreme caution (we don't use these at all, unless they are verified by other sources).

OTHER HELPFUL SOURCES

Lexis-Nexis (http://www.lex.lexis-nexis.com)—Lexis-Nexis, as will be explained in chapters to follow, has a tremendous range of libraries within its overall system. The ones to concentrate on for this section, though, can be limited to those cited below:

D&B; GDUNS

In the situation where the manager's entity has an unusually common name (not unusual in today's era of funds apparently subscribing to the same directory of names, combining a color or mythological creature with a word involving water or rocks), this library can be an efficient means of uncovering the company's precise address, presuming you have not yet begun your direct visiting process. The reason? This library allows you to search by the name of the firm along with the name of an officer; in doing so, you will find the correct company and its current address, something that as you now know can be used as a powerful linking tool to other data you are gathering. Other morsels you'll occasionally feast on here include a subject's year of birth and at times, a middle initial or middle name. And while this source's biographical information is much more limited than that offered directly by Dun & Bradstreet, this is not something that will affect this part of your search.

INCORP; ALLBIZ

Combining a vast swath of Secretary of State records from most every state in the U.S. with DBA (doing business as) professional files and limited partnership filings, this library's primary value stems from its ability to uncover entities for which the subject has been an officer, director, manager, agent, or principal, but which the subject did not specifically cite on his biography (see Chapter 10 for more). Here, however, you are looking for other chestnuts, including addresses you can match to those you have developed via your identification review, as well as middle names or initials and family members (who often are cited in oddball limited partnerships that function to, say, act as a family trust).

COMPNY; COMPNY

This library produces information similar to the two above, albeit from various company and industry reports as well as Securities and Exchange Commission (SEC) records.

NEWS; ALLNWS

This library encompasses the entire extent of Nexis's news files, an enormous mass of news information. The application to subject identification lies in the news' ability to provide context, that is, to report on where a manager has worked, geographically, for which employers, and often, for what period of time. Any or all of these facts can lead to the successful identification of a manager, helping to home in on the person's age and address history, as well as providing a basis for comparison of information obtained via identification sources with those records maintained by previous employers.

FINDER; USVOTE

Containing combined voter registration records for 28 states (see Addendum 5.1 for the complete list), this library is useful primarily because voter registrations are among the most accurate records of peoples' dates of birth.

ASSETS; ALLOWN

Covering property records for an array of locales, this library's primary function, identification-wise, is to name a subject's spouse.

FINDER; EZFND and FINDER; ALLFND

Both these libraries are similar to LocatePlus and others described above in that they can help you locate the manager's address history and other identifiers. (Again, the major limitation with this source is that it provides only partial social security numbers, and also contains a less comprehensive address history. What's more, one has to search by name and state, rather than social, a more time-consuming method.) EZFND often has a spouse's name; ALLFND is EZFND, in effect, with voter records added to it.

NON-LEXIS SOURCES

National Futures Association (NFA); http://www.nfa.futures.org/basicnet/

National Association of Securities Dealers (NASD): http://pdpi4.nasdr.com/pdpi/broker_search_form.asp

Investment Adviser Registration Depository (IARD): www.iard.com/

Each of these regulatory bodies (see Chapter 8 for more) contains, to some degree, employment information, which can help you confirm a social security number simultaneously with your verification efforts. Also found here are full middle names and dates, cities and states for a manager's employers—all of which are handy identifiers. State securities agencies, moreover, often have records containing a manager's complete social security number. For privacy reasons, these files are not available to the general public; they can, however, be available to you.

Dun & Bradstreet (D&B) http://www.dnb.com/local_home/local_home_US/

As you may know, this firm collects data on entities throughout the U.S. and indeed the world. Although the value of much of this information is questionable, at best, since it comes mostly from a subject directly, the age, biographical records, and middle initial listings nonetheless can be productive identifiers.

Martindale Hubbell http://www.martindale.com/

If your subject was or is a lawyer (this is becoming more common as institutions check into the history of hedge funds' compliance officers, who often have a legal background), this site is invaluable. Aside from providing a lawyer's schooling, it also will list a middle initial and a full date of birth for that party.

Note that individual motor vehicle records, while providing a precise way of determining a date of birth, are unfortunately not agglomerated, nationwide, by any source.

WHAT TO DO WHEN YOU JUST CANNOT COMPLETELY CONFIRM A SOCIAL

Below are three situations in which despite all of the above efforts, your efforts to ascertain the manager's social security number and address history, beyond any doubt, prove unattainable. Depending on your level of assuredness, as you will see, different solutions are suggested.

(continued)

WHAT TO DO WHEN YOU JUST CANNOT COMPLETELY CONFIRM A SOCIAL (*Continued*)

A. 99 Percent Confidence Level

Scenario

- Manager has an uncommon name.
- One and only subject match in LocatePlus/IRB.
- Address history is consistent with the subject's employment/educational history
- *But*, still unable to verify social through school/employment records or an address match.

At this point you may be scratching your head (as I was, when this scenario was first posed to me), wondering, well, how in the world can this really happen? Assuming no significant data entry errors occurred (or more to the point, assuming that these may exist but not so much so that your search can't overcome them), there remains the possibility that you can be practically Ivory soap certain you have found your subject's particulars, and still be wrong. How? The example is when a father and a son have both a shared address history (common, of course) *and* a shared work history (far less common) *and* have had their records conflated (unfortunately, completely plausible). This would hopefully be revealed by your employment verification efforts, as you'd often find that one person was at a firm for 25 years, while your subject is only 37 years old, making it clear this individual is the subject's father, not the subject. Meanwhile, consider requesting the manager to provide a home address, with an answer that will be sure to eliminate your angst and lower your blood pressure immediately.

B. 90 Percent Confidence Level

Scenario

- Manager has a common name.
- You have located a possible social via LocatePlus/IRB.
- Address history is consistent with subject's employment/educational history.
- You are unable to verify/confirm the social through school/employment or an address match.

The difference between this scenario and the one above is the commonness of the subject's name. In this situation, we would not proceed at all without a home address from the manager; our view is that the margin of error here is simply too high otherwise.

C. 0 Percent Confidence Level

Scenario

- Extremely common name.
- Could not locate possible social in lp/irb.
- Work *cannot* be completed without home address.

As you can see, the drop off between Scenarios B and C is beyond steep. In effect, here you are stumped; if presented with a manager named John Smith, you may be able to develop enough information depending on the biographical data you have collected, but in many cases you will simply need a home address to have any hope that your search is accurate.

MERLIN. NOT SO MAGICAL ANYMORE

At one time Merlin (https://www.merlindata.com/SearchASPs/MainMenu.ASP) was *the* source for developing identifying data, especially when you started a review with little to no such information. No longer. Now, Merlin is useless for this part of your research, with one slight change leading to one enormously negative result. The change I am referring to is the fact that Merlin now requires both a name *and* a state to conduct its searches. This is lovely if you actually have a state, but it flies in the face of the very reason you ordinarily need this product, that is, that you do not have this information. Combined with the truncated social security number currently provided, Merlin has safeguarded its way out of a business. One final note: for now, Merlin is still useful in helping determine how many people with the

(continued)

MERLIN. NOT SO MAGICAL ANYMORE
(*Continued*)

same name live in one area, something that has value when you are seeking to deduce the probability that a lawsuit relates to a subject rather than someone similarly named. (For more on this, see Chapter 6.) Instinct says, however, that even this niche will be short-lived as other vendors like the aforementioned LocatePlus almost certainly will develop a similar system eventually, thus cutting the last thread of value that Merlin provides.

TIP 1: KEEP ACCURATE RECORDS

Nowhere else will it be more important than at this stage for your record-keeping to be spot-on perfect. One data entry error for a date of birth, social security number, or address will not only screw up your search for identifying data, but it could very lead to false positives later on in your research. Given that this is exactly what you are seeking to avoid, caution is the watchword here. Keep an accurate tab of the manager's previous/current employment(s), affiliation(s), membership(s) and education, as well as personal data (date of birth, social security number, and address history) in a format you can re-use over and over again, and you will find Nirvana (that might be an exaggeration, I admit).

TIP 2: ERRONEOUS ADDRESSES

All men are created equal, Thomas Jefferson famously wrote. Addresses, alas, are not. Some addresses are what we term "strays," as they appear on the one or more of the various identification sources discussed above, but instinctively make no sense as sites at which the subject manager likely lived or worked. Some examples of what may be a stray/suspicious address are as follows:

- PO Box
- Incomplete (usually incomplete addresses are a variation of another complete address)

- Same street as a known address but in a different city and state
- Address in one database but not on the other two databases (especially if that address is the only one in that state)

When confronted with such an address, it is best to go back to look at other sources, including the biography and even Mapquest, to ascertain whether the location in question is one you need to pursue or simply, and more likely, some kind of a data entry error you can then treat no further.

TIP 3: RELEASES

Releases are generally used either to comply with a school or employer's request prior to verification of a manager's credentials (expounded on in Chapter 9), or to obtain a manager's credit report (Chapter 15), but they have an ancillary benefit. Even the most benign release will include spaces for the manager to insert his home address, date of birth, and even social security number for those who don't object to listing this. Considering this, we strongly advocate procuring a release from each and every manager, and we have attached at Addendum 5.1 an example of a release we use regularly.

TIP 4: STUPID INVESTIGATOR TRICKS

Unfortunately for you, David Letterman's stupid human tricks segments have not included one perpetrated by many data dumps that masquerade as researchers. These "services" may indeed run one or more of the aforementioned identification searches. Distressingly, they then use this information to do little more than beef up a "report" by providing reams and streams of raw data, filling page after page, with no explanation of what the data means, and worse, no attempt to use the data for what it actually does: eliminating information from other records that does not pertain to your manager. Failing to do this does nothing more for you than if they handed you a piece of paper with the subject's name and date of birth on it, and said "here, go invest." So if you see this, do what you do with other junk—throw it away.

RECAP

1. No identifiers, no due diligence.
2. Home address = social = past address history.
3. The more identifiers you find, the more relevant your other results will prove.
4. Always ask how a researcher determined information related to subject.
5. Winnowing out nonrelevant material is an art as much as a science.
6. Identification takes time, but no time you spend will be better spent.
7. Redundancies can be your pals.

CHAPTER 6

The Courts

Institutional investors are most preoccupied with one thing—what happens if a fund in which we have invested turns out to be a fraud? This concern is expressed by nearly every client who contacts our firm seeking a background report on a hedge fund manager. The method that is best able to answer this question but is also the most difficult for investors to do on their own is a comprehensive court search. But often this is the search that gets overlooked. Why? Precisely because it is difficult. The difficulty lies in the lack of knowledge and expertise, the lack of time and the cost inefficiency inherent in a task that is not now and likely never will be fully automated.

This chapter will not likely be able to help you, the institutional investor, do a complete court search, from cradle to grave, on your own. But it will arm you with enough information to understand what you are getting and perhaps more importantly, what you are missing, in the mechanisms you are currently or are considering employing. It will certainly help you understand what is available online versus what needs to be searched, and retrieved, manually; how to find search and retrieval firms; how to know what court documents to retrieve; how to quickly peruse and understand court records; how to ascertain whether a court case relates to the subject or merely to another person with the same name; how to determine whether a suit is important; how far back you can, and should search; and lastly, how to interview litigants involved in suits with the hedge fund manager, in the event that documents do not provide the answers you need to some of these questions.

HOW TO ENSURE YOUR COURT SEARCHES ARE COMPLETE

U.S. court cases are filed in either federal or state/county courts. Federal courts are broken up by geographical district; larger states like California and Texas, as you might expect, have multiple districts (California, for example, has four: Central, Eastern, Northern and Southern), while smaller states like New Jersey have only one. Federal courts include civil, criminal, and bankruptcy matters. State-level courts, by contrast, only include civil and criminal suits, since bankruptcy petitions are filed only at the federal level. State courts go under many names, including Supreme (in New York, of course, which may simply delight in being unnecessarily confusing), Superior, Circuit, Combined, Common Pleas, District, and Prothonotary's Office (which itself is not a name of a court, per se, but rather is a recording office for the county. Pennsylvania, for example, has Prothonotary's offices but its state level courts are called "Court of Common Pleas.")

Like federal courts, state courts are broken up geographically, except that these courts are sectioned off by county names, not by broad geographic regions. According to the USGS website, there are 3,141 counties and county equivalents in the 50 States and the District of Columbia, categorized as follows:[1]

3,007 entities named "County"

16 Boroughs in Alaska

11 Census Areas in Alaska (for areas not organized into Boroughs by the State)

64 Parishes in Louisiana

42 Independent Cities (1 in Maryland, 1 in Missouri, 1 in Nevada, and the remainder in Virginia)

1 District—the Federal District or District of Columbia.

Quick quiz: without using Google, can you name every county in your state of birth? The good news is you don't have to. Recall from the previous chapter, which outlined how to determine where a hedge fund manager has lived and worked, that there are thankfully easier ways to translate cities into counties, and then from there into the appropriate state and federal courts that need to be searched. Although free sites for telling you the county in which a city is located certainly exist (http://www.getzips.com/zip.htm takes you from the Zip Code to the city, state and county, at the push of a button), a multipurpose tool known as BRB Publications will ultimately be far more functional. For $124 per year, you can access BRB's web-based service (http://www.brbpub.com/), using it both to quickly find county information as well as to pinpoint the correct state and federal courts to search, *and* to then identify a search and retrieval firm in those particular areas, should you choose to go this route for document retrieval (a further discussion of the buy versus build strategy takes place below). As an aside, BRB also produces books on many public records topics; at this point, the website renders much of the hard copy information unnecessary.

Once you have paid the annual fee, you will establish an account, complete with log-in name and password (note that multiple users within your firm can simultaneously log in using the one log-in name and password). To identify the counties where your subject manager has resided (and then to know what courts to search), do the following:

1. Click on PRRS.
2. Type in the State in question. Obviously you'll need to repeat this for each state connected to the subject manager.
3. Type in the city your previous research had developed for the manager, under "Place."
4. Hit Go. Do not pass Go. Just hit it.
5. Enter the Zip Code. (Your preliminary research will have revealed this. Another place you'll find Zip Codes, at least for the subject's current address, is on releases or questionnaires they may have furnished to you.)
6. Click on the city that corresponds to the Zip Code you developed.
7. Under "County Courts," select the court you want from the drop down menu.
8. Under retrievers, you will see a drop down menu with a list of firms who search courts and obtain documents. When you select a name, you will be shown contact information, what areas and courts this firm searches/retrieves from, the firm's expected timing for searches/retrievals, and their area of specialization. It is this last piece of information that is the most critical: look for a firm whose specialty is in document retrieval, as this will be the area where you'll need the most help.

Another handy feature of this site occurs when you click on "Federal Level." Once you have entered the state, the city and the Zip Code, clicking on "Federal Level" yields the federal court that needs to be searched for that particular city. By way of example, this search shows that Dallas is covered by Texas's Northern District. Clicking on the hyperlink for the federal court, whether it be civil, criminal or bankruptcy, tells you where the court is located, as well as, among other things, its phone number. The latter can be used for finding an archived number of a suit you expect to be filed in one of the country's 13 Federal Records Centers, based typically on the age of the action filed. These 13 repositories are where federal records for archived suits are stored. In some instances, you'll be lucky in that the Records Center is near or even in the city where the suit was originally filed; returning to our Dallas example, we find that the Records Center for Dallas is located a hop, skip and jump away, in Fort Worth. However, New York City federal suits that get archived are somewhat inexplicably stored in beautiful downtown Lee's Summit, Missouri.

Archival periods vary from state to state and even within a state. In our experience, federal suits that are more than 10 years are typically archived. For these suits, assume they are archived, and as noted above, you will have to call the court directly to learn the archive number, which is necessary to retrieve court documents. This also helps skip the step of having a court researcher go to the court directly, only to learn that the suit is archived; while court personnel can then get you the archive number, too, there will be a fee for their "search."

In suits filed within the last decade, aside from those rare occurrences when the docket sheet, found on PACER (an acronym for Public Access to Court Electronic Records, and to be discussed at length below), alerts you to the suit's archival, you will need to have the retrieval firm do the search first to ascertain whether documents exist at the local courthouse or in one of the aforementioned Federal Records Centers. Here, too, however, the opportunity to cut expenses exists. Many vendors will propose that they order the retrieval for you, once they have determined that a suit has been archived. A federal suit filed in Connecticut, say, will be stored in the Records Center based in Boston, Massachusetts. Rather than use the Connecticut vendor to process the search, use BRB to identify the corresponding Federal Records Center, then to identify a vendor from that area to do the retrieval, undoubtedly saving you money.

Using BRB, how do you identify the vendor? Very easily. Once you have established the areas to search, another drop down menu, this one under the heading "County Level Record Retrievers," is available. Simply click on the menu for "Select a Retriever" and off you go. Just recall from above that the key issue is to select a vendor whose specialty is in retrieving documents from the court or courts in which the records you need are located.

COURT SEARCHES: THE BEGINNING

Once you have established where the hedge fund manager has lived and worked, you are ready to begin your targeted court search. An important note here, however, is that online sources are by their nature extremely broad, meaning they cover multiple jurisdictions simultaneously. Although at first blush this probably seems to be hugely beneficial, and certainly advantages of having more data do exist, a difficult puzzle occurs as well: how does one determine whether the suits citing someone with the same name as the subject actually relate to that person, or whether they instead simply involve someone else? Few items are more critical to conducting proper due diligence than this; while the mechanics of how to distinguish relevant from nonrelevant information are discussed below, for now just bear this idea in mind during this section.

HOW FAR BACK YOU CAN LEGALLY SEARCH

You will see over and over in this chapter that courts have records dating back sometimes over 20 years. A common misperception is that court cases that date back more than seven years cannot be reported to you by an investigative firm or other entity doing research for you. This has stemmed from a misreading of Fair Credit Reporting Act (FCRA) statutes, which hold that certain items cannot be reported if dated over seven years, in a pre-employment scenario (and even there, this relates only to jobs where the person will earn less than $75,000 per year). The institution seeking to invest in a hedge fund does not fit into this definition and is not, therefore, subject to the FCRA limitations. Please refer to Chapter 14 for a more detailed explanation but for now, suffice it to say that obtaining court cases from any year, in anticipation of a hedge fund investment, is fine.

ONLINE SOURCES: FEDERAL COURTS

A typical court search should cover at least the last 10 years. Federal court searches, including many dating back much further than this, are often available online via PACER. (To establish a PACER account, go to http://pacer.psc.uscourts.gov/ and click on "Register for Pacer.") PACER, according to its website "is an electronic public access service that allows users to obtain case and docket information from Federal Appellate, District and Bankruptcy courts, and from the U.S. Party/Case Index."[2] Every federal court that is available online is linked with PACER. Moreover, individual federal court websites can be used to augment searches in instances where PACER dates are not up to date. Individual websites are up to date (according to various court clerks from different courts, they may be a day or two off, but this is insignificant) and are therefore an excellent resource.

The amount of time covered in the various federal districts varies from court to court (that is, civil, criminal, and bankruptcy), state to state and even within states. Many bankruptcy searches date back to the mid to late 1980s. PACER's New Jerseys Bankruptcy Court records, however, date back to January 2, 1980. More striking is that Indiana's Southern District Bankruptcy Court has records on PACER extending back all the way to November 1, 1974. But before we get too excited, this same district's civil records are maintained only from April 12, 2002, and no federal criminal search in this district is available at all.

See Addendum 6.1 for complete bankruptcy court coverage from PACER; similar records available via Lexis's INSOLV; ALLBKT library are attached at Addendum 6.2. PACER's other federal courts (civil and criminal) are discussed below; here again, Lexis has a comparable system, found in its DOCKET; USDKT library. It is important to remember that the end dates reflected here are fluid; that is, information is added on a nearly daily basis, and the end dates change accordingly.

BANKRUPTCIES, DEFINED

Black's Law Dictionary defines Chapter 7 bankruptcy as "a proceeding designed to liquidate the debtor's property, pay off his or her creditors, and discharge the debtor from his or her debts." It can be either voluntary (started by the debtor himself or herself) or involuntary (started by the debtor's creditors). Other sources describe this as a declaration of insolvency.

Chapter 11 Bankruptcy shields a business from creditors while a partial repayment schedule is negotiated. An individual with over $750,000 in assets has to file Chapter 11 even if it is a personal bankruptcy petition.

Chapter 13 Bankruptcy, sometimes referred to as "wage earner" bankruptcy, establishes a repayment schedule to satisfy part of what is due to creditors, while a bankruptcy court trustee manages the personal bankruptcy plan and distributes the agreed-upon payments every month.

At Addendum 6.3 is a list of the federal court districts for every state, along with the dates of coverage provided by PACER (I have excluded PACER's bankruptcy data, which is contained in Addendum 6.1). Of course, this information is constantly updated, so by the time you are reading this book the end dates will be out of date; you can expect that in most jurisdictions, PACER's information is as close to real time as any database can be. Note, too, that yet another huge advantage of computerization is that records are not "thrown away," so over time information becomes more and more comprehensive. (This is not to be confused with all data, as unfortunately some states, companies and regulatory bodies have decided to throw away information after a set period of time. And while some argument can be made that companies are under no legal obligation to retain all data in perpetuity, advances in storage technology make it particularly unseemly for, say, places like Broward County, Florida, and worse, much of Connecticut's state court system, to toss court records, yes throw them away, sometimes within less than two years of a suit's closure.)

HOW TO USE PACER

Learning to use PACER is not very difficult. Still, below is a walk-through of a search.

> Step 1. Once you have logged onto the PACER system, click on "United States Party/Case Index."
>
> Step 2. Click on "All Court Types."
>
> Step 3. Leave the default setting to "all courts."
>
> Step 4. Do not enter a file date; this will ensure that the search is as broad as possible.
>
> Step 5. Type your search name—last name, first name—using all capital letters (years ago we found a glitch in the system in which certain searches using lower case letters did not work; it is not clear whether this problem remains but better safe than sorry). To broaden the search, we use last name, first initial; for someone with a common name, we will limit the search by state but continue using only the first initial. The reason? Suits are at times filed on PACER using only a first initial, or a first initial and a middle name; other suits might spell the first name incorrectly. All three of these situations are addressed by the first initial entering system.
>
> Step 6. Hit "search."

Example: Entering "Shain, Randy" yielded one bankruptcy, no civil suits and no criminal actions (thankfully). Oddly, the bankruptcy action named a Randy Robert Shain and a Beth Michelle Shain (names purposely altered), and my wife's name is Michelle. Luckily, I don't have a middle name, and my wife's first name is not Beth. But if you didn't know that, you'd proceed to Step 7, below, which begins our guide through the actual case documents found on the PACER system.

Step 7. To view a document, click on the case number. Note that before you do this, I suggest you mentally or physically delete the duplicate suits that appear. By way of example, numbers 23 and 25 are the same suit, as indicated by the case number 1:2003mc00107. One is listed under Ray E. Shain, while the other more specifically names the litigant as Ray Elliot Shain. Either way, this is only one action, not two.

Step 8. For bankruptcies, click on "Party"—this will show an address and a partial social for easy clarification of the petitioner's identity. In the example above, the Randy Shain in question had social security number xxx-xx-9247, different from mine and marking him as another person who happens to have a name similar to mine.

Step 8a. For civil and criminal actions, click on "Docket Report," then "run report," which brings you to the actual docket.

Step 9. Anything hyperlinked (blue and underlined) can then be reviewed, for a fee; PACER will alert you to the fact that a charge is about to be incurred. Using case number 22, entitled *Board of Ed. v. Ray Shain*, clicking on the case number will bring you to the docket sheet. Scrolling down, you'll notice three columns: Date Filed, # and Docket Text. In the number column, the numbers are in blue highlights; click on number 1, as this will show the case's complaint (the Docket Text describes what will be found, so you do not have to guess). You'll then click on "Number 1," which corresponds to "main document." Hit "View Document" and voila, the 24-page complaint appears.

Caveat: The availability of complaints is somewhat random. In our experience, complaints are not necessarily available based on where or even how recently the suit was filed. Regardless, you'll know when they are available, and in situations where you are either certain the suit relates to your hedge fund manager or in those where you are unclear but the suit itself is important, retrieving documents this way is both remarkably inexpensive as well as incredibly time-saving. For those suits where PACER does not have the complaint, as always, manual retrieval (again, discussed at length below) is necessary.

As for the other classifications cited by PACER, they are mostly repeating the information provided elsewhere but are being segmented for your easy perusal. The following sets out what these denotations mean (also check out http://pacer.psc.uscourts.gov/documents/pacermanual.pdf for an easy, if lengthy, referral guide):

Alias. This is somewhat self-explanatory—an alias refers to other names to which the litigant has been tied. So an R. Shain might have AKAs (also known as) of Randy Shain, Randall Shain, Randolph Shain, or other similar permutations.

Associated Cases. These are suits that are related to the action you are reviewing.

Attorney. Needs no explanation. You might click on this first if you are trying to deduce whether a suit names a subject manager, which you could learn by comparing an attorney in a suit that you know relates to the subject with the attorney cited in the other action.

Case File Location. This is used by the courts to locate a file folder. Like the part of the forms marked "office use only," you can disregard this.

Case Summary. The case summary is a very useful mechanism for easily viewing, on one page, who sued whom, where, when and to what result. It does not tell you the underlying reason for the suit in any detail; for that, you'll still need to review the complaint.

Deadlines/Hearings. This refers to the pending hearings and deadlines for the suit. Hyperlinks for documents exist here too and can be useful if you are interested in this level of detail; for most suits, this will not be necessary.

Filers. Filers are those parties who have filed documents in the suit, typically meaning the plaintiffs and the defendants. Clicking on a name will bring you to what the person filed; the hyperlink will then take you to the actual document. This allows you to home in on what your subject has filed—whether it be a complaint, an answer to a complaint, or some other motion (which if not in the first two items mentioned, is likely to be outside of the scope of your interest).

History/Documents. Here you will find a list of the publicly recorded events for this suit. In essence, this is a reformatted docket sheet, albeit one with hyperlinks to those documents available for review. Although this is better than reading a hard copy docket and then returning to the court for a document you may want, using the Filer mechanism above is probably an easier way of homing in on your subject and avoiding the items (various motions, the always thrilling notices of appearance and the ubiquitous time extension filings) you needn't review.

Party. This is a relisting of who is suing whom, along with the attorneys representing the litigants and whether any litigant has been added or terminated from the case; this could be an easy way for you to see whether your manager is still involved in the suit.

Related Transactions. These detail transactions that are related. Make sense? Examples are helpful: you might find the complaint, then the answer to that complaint; or a motion to extend the time for an answer, and another motion seeking to dismiss the motion to extend. All in all, this is not hugely relevant to you.

Status. I have no idea what this means, even after reviewing the manual and discussing this with a PACER representative. One would think this relates to whether the case is open or closed. And, in fact, this is what the manual suggests. Having reviewed many cases, however, I have concluded that you should just pay no further attention to this button, and be happy you'll waste no more time on this.

OTHER TIPS

1. *How to answer typical questions.* If the PACER manual cited above is too cumbersome, PACER had segmented a "frequently asked questions" section, located at http://pacer.psc.uscourts.gov/faq.html.

2. *How to immediately determine the basic premise of a civil or criminal suit.* Look at the column marked "NOS," located between the columns marked "Filed" (the date the action was filed) and "Closed" (the date the action was closed, if it was). NOS, or Nature of Suit, uses a numerical code to indicate a suit's essential cause. Examples of actions that might concern an institutional investor would be 850, which stands for "Securities/Commodities/Exchanges"; 470, "Racketeer Influenced and Corrupt Organizations" (RICO); 370, "Other Fraud"; 220, "Foreclosure"; and 160, "Stockholders Suits."
   For a complete list of the NOS codes, refer to http://pacer.psc .uscourts.gov/documents/natsuit.pdf.

3. *How to view one suit after you have reviewed another one.* Hit "Back" until you return to the screen with the list of cases on it.

4. *How to ensure you capture the most hits.* Make sure you do not add a space at the end of your search string. A search of "Shain, Randy" will work better than one that seems to be almost the same, "Shain, Randy_"

ONLINE SOURCES: STATE COURTS

An excellent compilation of state court indices can be found on Lexis's state docket file (hereafter referred to simply as "State Docket"). The following outlines how to open an account here, how to do a search, and how to know what you'll need to do with the results.

State Docket

1. Go to www.lexis.com
2. First, you need an account. Call 800-227-4908. Under "contact us," the site also has a hyperlink entitled "contact a sales representative form."
3. Enter your new ID and password.
4. The "Search" tab at the top of the screen should be the default setting. If it isn't, hit this tab.
5. Click on the "Public Records" tab.
6. Click on the link known as "Combined Civil and Criminal Findings"; this is on the right hand part of the screen, near the top. (The libraries to search include DOCKET; CRIMNL and DOCKET; STDKT, described by Lexis as a "Combined File of Civil Filings from 20 States & Criminal Filings from 11 States.")
7. Click on "New Search."
8. Enter your *search terms. (The math behind search terms is explained in more detail in Chapter 7.) Be certain to account for all possible names (AKAs) the subject may use or have used; first name Donald, for example, should be searched under Donald, Don and Donnie.

    Trying Randy w/2 Shain, which means any suits citing people named Randy within two words of Shain (this broadens the search and encompasses a middle name or middle initial) yields, thankfully for me, nothing. For you, of course, this does no good. Let's search Christopher or Chris w/2 Stevenson. Enter this, then

9. Hit "Search."
10. 263 "Hits" emerge, with 10 listed per page (you'll see this number in the top middle of your screen). Unfortunately, now you have to look through them, individually. This is unless, of course, you have some identifier that immediately rules the suit out, such as a conflicting middle initial. In this case, we'll assume we have found that our subject manager has middle name Matthew. Given this assumption, numbers 1, 2, 3, 4, and 6 can be eliminated from consideration immediately, as the person cited by the index for each of these actions has a different middle initial or name from Matthew (M). Other cases we'd avoid reviewing would

be those marked small claims (see #9) or parking (#107), or those that were filed when the subject would have been a minor. To learn whether the remaining actions are relevant, and important, reviewing at least the index is, regrettably, necessary.

What you see from clicking on each entry is an index of sorts, with the case name, the name of the court, the date the action was filed and sometimes the type of action, the money being sought, and the outcome of the suit. But here, "sometimes" is not all the time, and so we return to the idea that retrieving actual court documents, including the complaint and the docket sheet, is critical to your understanding of the importance of the suit and how it might affect the manager going forward. (Take, for example, entry number 18. On the index, it is listed merely as "Contracts—Collections." What is missing here is the amount in dispute, which forces you to obtain the actual records.)

Still, to start, focus on eliminating as many actions as possible by ascertaining that they relate to someone other than your subject. Outside of the obvious measures described above, that is, seeing if a middle name or initial is different from the one you have tied to your subject manager, the first and most productive step to take now is to associate other actions with those involving these other parties, thus eliminating these actions as well. For example, recall that entry number 4 shows a Christopher "J" Stevenson, clearly not the subject; clicking on the hyperlink shows a specific Oregon address for this person. Any other entry with a person with this address is, ipso facto, also not your subject. Once you know this, you'll need to hit "Back" to return to the list of actions. Then start clicking through pages and actions, always keeping this address in mind.

Another easy suit to avoid is an action that does not even name a Chris Stevenson. In this search, #33, is "Battle, Christopher v. Stevenson, Edward." By the quirks of search strings, this action is brought up, but obviously it has nothing to do with your manager. Similarly, if the litigant is listed as a "Minor," no further action is required by you.

One other mechanism at your disposal is comparing spouses. Your early research (again refer to Chapter 5 for details) will have revealed, hopefully, the subject's spouse, and even given you some idea of how long they have been together, and whether the subject had previously been married to someone else. Keeping these names and dates at the top of your head when reviewing the indices will often lead to your being able to reduce substantially the amount of actions that will require more attention.

Remember, too, that this source has a fairly concentrated search range, geographically. This will result in numerous hits on individuals in certain areas, including, mostly, California, New York, Connecticut, and even

Colorado and Oregon. If your subject has not been placed to an address in one of these states, you should be skeptical of the relevance of these actions.

This brings us to individuals with common names. In these instances, the search should be narrowed by tying the subject manager to his entities, the states where he has been located and, for those with extremely common names, by adding a middle name or middle initial. The narrowest terms would be as follows: ((aaron w/2 smith) and (backtrack) or (first advantage) or (new york or ny) or (Pennsylvania or pa))) or ((aaron p or aaron Patrick) w/1 smith). Doing so reduces the number of hits from 2312 (with a search of aaron w/2 smith) to a far more manageable 111. And, yes, there is a tradeoff, in that it is remotely possible you'd miss something this way. In our experience, however, the types of actions that would most concern you would be found by this search method.

Returning to Chris Stevenson, using middle name Matthew or middle initial "M" limits the results you'd view to four. Two of these were filed in 1979 and 1980, respectively; assuming we discovered our subject was born in 1971, these would immediately be dismissed. The other two matters were filed in Colorado in 1993, and are listed as criminal case filings. Clicking on one reveals it is a "Traffic—Motor Vehicle" action, seemingly something you can ignore. But the other is more serious, being a Traffic matter but more specifically, also a driving under the influence action. Now even if your subject manager has not lived or worked in Colorado, it is always possible, particularly given that in this instance he would have been 22 years old at the time of the incident in question, that this matter did indeed involve the subject. Before panicking, however, you'll see that the index lists a home address for the defendant. Returning to lessons learned in Chapter 5 on preliminary research, your next move is to try and develop this person's age, full middle name, partial social security number or some other identifier, using this name and address. Only if this didn't work would you obtain court documents, which likely would yield further information you could use to identify the defendant.

Tip 1. Make sure you are searching for suits citing the individual manager as well as the entities with which he is associated. We'd also recommend adding entities the subject formerly owned or for which he served as president or CEO (uncommon titles in the hedge fund world, but as you know, not every manager has come strictly from this world).

Tip 2. To capture the cases you want to retrieve, you can either do a cut and paste job, copying the data from the indices of interest and pasting them into, say, a Word document you create, or you can use Lexis's "Fast Print" option. The latter method, of course, will result in a batch of paper, while at least the former yields a computer searchable file, which to my mind is always preferable.

Tip 3. You can always hit "Back" repeatedly to return to previous searches you have run.

One last tip. Westlaw (www.westlaw.com) has a similar service, with docket coverage found at http://west.thomson.com/westlawcourtexpress/map/default.asp?tf=90&tc=16. Westlaw, according to a Thomson West representative, has been investing significant resources into developing this search, and has purchased an entity known as CourtExpress. According to this representative, Westlaw's CourtExpress Docket program has over 70 million dockets loaded onto the system, which is "the largest repository of Dockets in the world. We are also loading 2000 Court Documents, such as Briefs, Legal Memos etc, each week onto our platform, and giving us the greatest collection and coverage, anywhere, of these materials as well."

Per the representative, among its offerings Westlaw provides coverage in 26 states, 10 of which are full statewide systems. Also covered are all 13 U.S. Court of Appeals (back to 1997), and all but one of the 94 U.S. District Courts. Finally, Westlaw offers a database that allows for full Word Searching capability across its entire grouping of federal and state courts.

An outline of the coverage offered by Westlaw, in a side-by-side comparison to that furnished by Lexis's State Docket search, is attached at Addendum 6.4. (Where the word "Limited" is used, it indicates that either not all counties within that state are covered, these searches don't date back at least 10 years, and/or the searches cover civil or criminal records but not both.) Just remember, these sources are not meant to serve as the be-all-end-all of court research and document retrieval; using them this way, as I know some people do or are tempted to do, will lead only to a false sense of security. Reviewing the Courtlink material, for instance, reveals the following holes in its state court system:

- Counties where only civil records are covered, not criminal.
- Counties where a third party vendor is used (all counties where "via assisted search" is listed).
- Counties with incomplete records.

Courtlink, meanwhile, is exceptional, compared with the absolute dreck available on the Internet. Trolling the Web yields a panoply of sites claiming to help you "check arrest records," "Get all the facts right now!" or "Find anyone's record nationwide." When examined a bit closer, you find that these sites either merely link you directly to a courthouse (worthless), or, if they do allow an actual search, do not indicate where you should search, how you should know whether the suit names your person, what documents to retrieve (if any, as this doesn't seem to even rate a mention on many sites), or how to retrieve documents. One site I reviewed, for example, found a court case on Bayou (a much-publicized hedge fund blow-up discussed at length below), but without documents knowing that the suit existed was pretty much useless. What's more, a huge suit and resultant seven-figure judgment against Bayou was not found in this search; knowing this I relegated this site to the trash heap.

Another search engine one comes across when trolling the Internet for court searches is http://www.pretrieve.com/. This engine's "court" search section brings you, however, to the court's direct link, something that is of virtually no value. The search and retrieval aspect of the court review will not be handled by court personnel (oh, if only). I suppose for those rare occasions when you are seeking information about how far a court's records go, or some similar question, the links are useful in that a phone number can be found. But this information is available via the phone book or another easy Internet search, without the convoluting, tempting instant "court" search feature that is neither instant nor a court search.

These sites are not worth your time.

MANUAL SOURCES: STATE COURTS

As you may have surmised, the online world is not yet ubiquitous in its coverage of state court records. In fact, no online source, or even collection of online sources, will allow you to search every state-level court, civil and criminal, in the country. Manual court searches, therefore, are an absolute necessity to effective due diligence. Temporarily tabling the conversation about retrieving documents (a huge limit to the online sources, but one that is examined at length later in the chapter), let's instead focus now on the limits of online sources only as those limits relate to searching for court cases.

Many hedge fund managers, as you know, are concentrated in metropolitan areas. Still more managers reside and/or work in the Northeast, particularly in Connecticut. Given this, a study of Connecticut's online vs. manual court record system is in order.

On the surface, Connecticut state courts are covered exceptionally well by the aforementioned State Docket system. Civil cases are documented from January 1994, while criminal matters are searchable back to January 1, 1986. The big "however" is that the records are updated only monthly, thus necessitating a manual search. You may wonder why I say this. While it is true that the likelihood of a suit being filed in the one-month period that the database does not cover is remote, it is also equally true that the rare instance that this occurs will result in extraordinary embarrassment to the investor who didn't discover this suit, especially as it would have occurred quite recently—by definition.

DOCUMENT DESTRUCTION

Even more problematic, unfortunately, is something that no search can fix. Connecticut's state courts, according to Addendum 6.5, routinely make case materials unavailable (sometimes even discarding them). Connecticut state courts have established a practice whereby they hide or destroy documents in cases that have been closed for one of the following four reasons:

1. Dismissed more than 20 *days* (italics mine) ago. I had to read this twice since I presumed they meant 20 *years* ago. But no, it is 20 days. According to Debbie Stoutenburg of CT Search Link, (860) 613-2621, ctsearchlinkllc@sbcglobal.net, all cases, whether they were dismissed, withdrawn, or are dormant, can be destroyed in all Connecticut state courts according to the statutes. Some courts handling a large number of suits do hold on to documents longer than other courts; for example, Fairfield County, where many hedge fund managers reside, disposes of withdrawn cases approximately six months to one year after the withdrawal date.
2. A "nolle" was entered more than 13 months ago.
3. The case resulted in an acquittal or a finding of "not guilty," again using the more than 20-days-ago timeframe. (Clearly this refers to criminal matters.)
4. The file is "sealed by statute or court order."

Now for a personal rant. Treating the above in reverse chronological order, reason number 4 is the most justifiable. Any suit that is sealed by statute or court order is, presumably, sealed for a reason determined by a judge to be important enough to outweigh the public's right to review records pertaining to that document. This is quite dissimilar, though, to a suit being unavailable because the State decides it doesn't want people to see the documents.

Reason number 3 is also one that has a certain amount of logic to its credit. I am supposing that the court here is taking the "innocent until proven guilty" ethos of our country to an extreme, but I can see why they might do so. Of course, an acquittal does not mean a person was not guilty, and an institution seeking to invest in a hedge fund headed by a manager who was "acquitted" of fraud would surely still be interested, and I would strenuously contend, entitled to know, that this charge had been levied.

Reason number 2 is similar to reason number 3. A nolle refers to the prosecution deciding not to prosecute any longer. According to Nolo.com, a nolle "is an admission on the part of the prosecution that some aspect of its case against the defendant has fallen apart. Most of the time, prosecutors need a judge's permission to "nol-pros" a case."[3]

Reason number 1 is where I have a real problem. A case that is dismissed, as will be hammered home throughout this chapter, is not an indication that the suit was merit-less. Most cases, in fact, are not tried; instead, they are settled before trial. Clearly, it is beyond illogical to presume that all settlements are going against the plaintiff. If we accept, then, that sometimes plaintiffs are winning, why on earth would it be acceptable for records of these suits to be unavailable? This is made worse by the fact that so many hedge fund managers live and/or work in Connecticut. In our experience, as many as 75 percent of the reports we do on hedge fund managers who have had a Connecticut address result in a suit being found, though it is stressed that many of these suits likely involve other people with the same name as the manager, rather than the hedge fund manager in question. That itself, of course, is not something that can be proven, because without documents it is impossible to always tell whether a suit is relevant or not. Regardless, in approximately 70 percent of the cases where we find these hits no documents are available to help us navigate whether this suit names the subject. Even presuming that only a tiny amount of these cases did involve the subject, it still stands to reason that in some of those situations the manager has done something that would influence an investor's decision to invest.

Admittedly, I believe that even in principle, destroying or hiding documents is a bad idea. It comes down to a general theory: in a business situation who has the right to know what? I maintain that the person who has to the most to lose trumps all; here, the institution seeking to invest, to my mind, has far more to lose than the manager seeking those funds. What's more, hiding or destroying documents is a way for the state to say that it knows more than you do; that is, it has "judged" this suit to be irrelevant to your needs. But how can it possibly know this? Isn't it more likely that you know what is a concern to you, and what isn't, and can act accordingly?

If any part of this rant has you as fired up as I am, perhaps a letter-writing campaign, a blog or some other mechanism should be put in place to reverse

TABLE 6.1   Lexis State Docket New York Coverage

Bronx Co.	11/1985	Nassau Co.	2/1978	Queens Co.	12/1985
Dutchess Co.	8/1985	New York Co.	11/1985	Richmond Co.	11/1985
Erie Co.	11/1988	Orange Co.	8/1985	Rockland Co.	9/1985
Kings Co.	11/1985	Putnam Co.	8/1985	Suffolk Co.	3/1983
Westchester Co.	1/1981				

this trend. Holding back documents is bad enough; once documents get destroyed, they can never be replaced.

Other metropolitan areas frequently searched in hedge fund manager cases include New York, Texas (Dallas mostly), and California. Each has significant coverage via state docket; each also has significant holes that need to be filled by manual searches, as outlined in the Court Coverage Chart (attached at Addendum 6.6).

New York

The New York counties covered by state docket are depicted in Table 6.1.

As you can see, these 13 counties are primarily composed of those in or around New York City. Although most hedge fund managers do live or work in these counties, others have certainly been in other areas of New York, which itself has 62 counties in total. So for anyone who has lived in any city in any of New York's 49 counties not covered by state docket, a manual search of civil courts is necessary. (Here again, it is important to note that although State Docket covers less than 25 percent of New York's counties, it does cover those with the highest population bases and those where most hedge fund managers have had an address.) Large New York cities that are examples of those not covered by the online state docket database include Rochester, which is in Ulster County; Albany, the state capital and part of the eponymously named Albany County; and Monticello, in Sullivan County, the southeast part of New York and approximately 90 miles from New York City. Two vendors we've found to be expert at researching and obtaining documents in these areas include:

Access Information Services (northern district: Monroe County, Ulster County, Albany County, etc.)

Contact: Jackie Lee

Tel: +1 (800) 388-1598

Walsh Process & Legal Services (Sullivan County, etc.)

Contact: Heather Walsh

Tel: +1 (845) 896 3566

More importantly, the state docket search in New York is limited to civil courts only; criminal courts anywhere in New York need to be searched manually. I will repeat this: state level criminal courts in New York are *not* available via a database.

One method of handling New York state-level criminal court searches is via G.A. Public Record Services, Inc. (You may wish to contact Erica Hillman at 1 (800) 760-2468, ext: 319 for information.) G.A. provides a web-based search and requires a contractual agreement to get started. They also search the New York criminal courts on a statewide basis, though you must be able to provide the hedge fund manager's full date of birth to ensure that results will be accurate. Another limitation G.A. has is that they do not retrieve documents; for this, you must hire another service, like one of those mentioned above or another vendor depending on the area in which the criminal record was filed.

Dallas, Texas

State docket coverage in Texas is fairly limited, as can be seen from Table 6.2.

San Antonio is the most well known city in Bexar County. Denton County, along with Collin and Tarrant Counties, are part of the Dallas-Fort Worth region. As can be seen from Table 6.2, Tarrant and Collin Counties are not covered by state docket at all. And while 21 years of Dallas civil court records is impressive, you are again faced with the aforementioned monthly lag problem as well as the database's total absence of criminal

TABLE 6.2 Texas State Docket Coverage

Civil Courts		
Bexar	From 1982	11/01/2006 (updated monthly)
Dallas	From 1985	11/22/2006 (updated monthly)
Denton	From 1/90	10/31/2006 (updated monthly
Criminal Courts		
Bexar	From 1950	12/01/2006 (updated monthly)
Denton	From 1/90	9/29/2006 (updated monthly)

court records in this county. Moreover, many managers who work in Dallas live in Tarrant, Denton, or Collin.

California

State Docket's California's records vary wildly from county to county. While some counties in California are somewhat covered, you will need to order *manual* county searches for *all of California* based on the limits set forth in Table 6.3 below.

As can be observed, this list is extensive, but by no means comprehensive. Northern counties like Marin and especially San Francisco are covered rather poorly. And though some of the major southern counties, including Los Angeles* and Orange, are relatively up to date, the files are still updated no more than monthly, an unacceptably long period.

Other areas where hedge fund managers have had some history, according to our experience, include Massachusetts, Virginia, and perhaps surprisingly, Florida. Massachusetts and Florida state courts are not covered by State Docket at all. Virginia's criminal courts are not part of the State Docket system; its civil court records are, though they are slightly dated (typically within a month or two of current, again necessitating a manual search). Virginia, like a number of states (again, refer to the Court Coverage Chart for other states' web systems), also has several web-based search engines outside of Lexis's state docket mechanism. These, unfortunately, are of limited application. One, located at http://208.210.219.132/courtinfo/vacircuit/select.jsp?court, is a civil/criminal docket search engine, which according to the site, "is the case management system for circuit courts in Virginia. This is a project with a limited number of courts. Cases may be searched using name, case number, or hearing date. Searches must be done by individual courts. Statewide searches are not possible."

Another type of search, this one for the district court level (the lower level, for misdemeanors, civil suits seeking under $15,000, or small claims cases, typically), is at http://208.210.219.132/courtinfo/vadistrict/select.jsp?court and is "the case management system for General District

---

*An interview with a Los Angeles County court guru, who explains the intricacies of perhaps the nation's most difficult system to navigate. Also note that California Superior Court criminal records include felonies; misdemeanors and traffic violations are filed separately in various municipal courts within each county (which are not targeted in our reports, given their perceived lack of relevance, especially when weighed against the cost involved).

TABLE 6.3   Lexis State Docket California Coverage

Civil Courts

Contra Costa	From 1980	8/31/1998 (no longer updated)
Fresno	From 2/1/76	09/29/2006 (updated monthly)
Kern	From 1/1/75	07/31/2006 (temporarily suspended)
Los Angeles	From 1/1/83	12/20/2006 8 am (updated monthly)
Marin	From 1986	6/30/2006 (updated quarterly)
Orange	From 1989	11/30/2006 (not listed)
Riverside	From 1/1/73	09/30/2006 (updated monthly)
Sacramento	From 1975	12/1/2006 (updated monthly)
San Bernardino	Superior Court	from 1/1/1972–3/29/2002 (7/02/2006; see Lexis) (updated monthly)
San Diego	From 01/01/76	12/15/2006 8 am (updated monthly)
San Francisco	From 1987	9/30/2001 (suspended)
San Luis Obispo	From 2/3/75	4/1/1998 (no longer updated)
San Mateo	From 1/3/89	10/13/2006 (updated monthly)
Santa Barbara	From 1964	11/03/2006 (not listed)
Santa Clara	From 1/94	6/27/2003 (suspended)
Ventura	From 7/1/69	10/31/2006 (updated monthly)

Criminal Courts

Alameda	From 2/1/68	03/10/1998 (suspended)
Butte	From 1/1/88	9/30/1999 (suspended)
Contra Costa	From 1/1/90	09/12/2006 (updated monthly)
Fresno	From 1/1/70	6/30/2006 (updated monthly)
Los Angeles	Municipal Court	from 1/1/1993–12/4/2006 (updated monthly)
	Superior Court—From 1/1/79	12/4/2006 (updated monthly)
Marin	From 1/1/77	6/30/2006 (updated monthly)
Orange	From 1989	11/30/2006 (not listed)
Sacramento	From 1/1/89	10/02/2006 (updated monthly)
San Bernardino	From 12/1/96	6/30/2006 (updated monthly)
San Diego	From 1/1/76	12/9/2006 (updated monthly)
San Luis Obispo	From 1/1/86	7/12/2002 (no longer updated)
San Mateo	From 1/1/89	10/13/2006 (updated monthly)
Santa Barbara	From 1/1/65	10/05/2006 (not listed)
Santa Clara	From 1/1/91	12/22/2006 (updated monthly)
Santa Cruz	From 2/20/90	5/7/2004 (updated monthly)
Ventura	From 9/5/52	3/30/2006 (updated monthly)

Courts in Virginia. Cases may be searched using name, case number, or hearing date. Searches must be done by individual courts. Statewide searches are not possible."

Better than nothing, but not a substitute, in most instances and regrettably, for going to the dusty shelves at the local courthouse.

STATUS OF A SUIT

Clearly the Lexis State Docket system is an excellent start to your court research, but it is by no means a panacea for all your needs. Aside from its geographical and real-time limitations, which as shown above can be significant, its chief flaw is its inaccuracy regarding a suit's status, that is, whether that suit is open or closed. According to the aforementioned addendums, particularly Addendum 6.6, many courts in the State Docket are not updated close enough to "real time" to reflect when a suit has been closed. This then leads to suits being classified as "active" that are actually no longer open. This, in turn, means that actual docket sheets need to be obtained to allow for a more complete understanding of a suit's outcome.

In other instances, it is not the updating that is the concern. Many state docket indices just don't list the status of the suit at all, regardless of whether that particular court is up to date or not. Yet another problem, this one endemic to the court system itself rather being ascribed to Lexis's state docket, is the fact that parties sometimes settle out of court and don't go promptly tell the court about this settlement. In this situation, the suit will still be considered ongoing in the State Docket system.

Still another way that suits get closed is when they result in a judgment. Finding judgments (and liens, which are awarded to, typically, governmental agencies, as opposed to judgments, which are awarded to individuals or entities, ordinarily) is not difficult, as you'll see below. The real trick lies in being able to match the judgment you locate to a suit you have found elsewhere; no "source" does that for you, other than you.

LIENS/JUDGMENTS

Both Choicepoint and Lexis offer judgment and lien search capabilities. Choicepoint's search, as shown below, is run via a social security number; Lexis's (insolv; allbkt), conversely, is run by name.

Choicepoint's judgment search chronicles:

1. Go to popular searches→ court searches→ nationwide searches→ bankruptcies, liens and judgments→SSN/FEIN
2. Enter social security number in the SSN/FEIN Search field.
3. Hit "search" button
4. Wait.

Name:		**Example: Walpole Albert or ABC Construction**
State/Territory:		**Example: Florida**
Address:		**Example: 1234 Hickory Lane**
Zip:		**Example: 12345**
SSN/FEIN:		Example: 123-45-6789
Case Number:		**Example: 1234567**

5
1

Search $

Because Choicepoint's system uses a social security number, you will not need a complicated mechanism to determine whether the judgments you find relate to the subject or not. One difficulty lies, instead, in the fact that some matters that are not judgments, but instead are just notices of a suit's inception (termed a "civil case filing") are erroneously stored in this database. Also, some items will be repeated, either because a judgment was first filed then subsequently satisfied (paid) or because two or more creditors are listed separately but for the same action. More strenuous is the fact that you must manually connect the judgments that are judgments to suits you have located, if indeed the underlying suit was found, to make sure you are not in effect attributing more actions to the subject than really occurred. Still, a judgment search can be a quick way of getting a snapshot of someone's character; hedge fund managers who are debtors in a half dozen five-figure judgments are, to say it mildly, worthy of judgment: yours.

CASE STUDIES

Theories about court searches, results, and values are all well and good. Dispensing with theories is even better. It's time for a few case studies.

Bayou

When hedge fund industry people think of Bayou, I'd bet most think of the information that was discussed by the press and others after the blow-up of this ironically named fund. It is not hard to see why, as the stories behind this spectacular implosion are certainly titillating. From Sam Israel sort of hiding out in his Westchester mansion, to the visual of him lying down in his office for great periods of time, in an effort to alleviate purportedly crippling back pain, from his colleague, Dan Marino's 2005 confession/suicide letter delineating how the two had perpetrated a fraud for seven years and ultimately going through somewhere between $350 million to $450 million, to the firm's "independent auditor" turning out to be anything but independent, the stories started in mid-2005 and went on and on, culminating in one mention of Mr. Israel sending a more than $3 million check, that later bounced of course, with a picture of cartoon character SpongeBob SquarePants imprinted on it (luckily for Mr. Israel he didn't bounce a check to Mr. Krabs). But the real story lies in what was known by those people who checked into Bayou, *before* the fund imploded. And few stories are more instructive as to the value of actually obtaining court records rather than relying on an online index to tell you what a lawsuit is really about. Listen to what Paul Westervelt, former Bayou employee, had to say in court documents filed in March 2003, several years before the Bayou situation was to explode onto the national scene in what I think will be looked back upon as a seminal moment in hedge fund fraud history.

On March 26, 2003, Paul T. Westervelt, Jr. (along with his son, Paul Westervelt III, a minor player in this saga) sued the Bayou entities (Bayou Management, LLC; Bayou Securities, LLC; and Bayou Funds), along with company founder Samuel Israel III and the above-referenced Daniel Marino—also a principal of Bayou—for breach of contract and "an unlawful violation of the Louisiana 'Whistleblower Statute,'" in regard to his March 17, 2003, termination as principal at Bayou, according to court documents (attached as Addendum 6.7) filed in the U.S. District Court, Eastern District of Louisiana. (Immediate note to readers: I have struggled to remember another whistleblower court case involving a hedge fund manager but have come up empty. This in and of itself should give great pause to anyone thinking of investing in a manager with a similar issue.)

According to the complaint, Mr. Westervelt was a 33-year veteran of the investment world, and in the summer of 2002 was working in Louisiana at a firm known as Johnson Rice and Company of New Orleans. He was recruited to join Bayou, a Stamford, Connecticut–based hedge fund/investment firm by Sam Israel, a long-time acquaintance who himself was a Louisiana native. (As you'll discover, afterwards much was made of Mr. Israel's purported pedigree, and how this helped him raise money. We will examine the folly of this thinking later, in a fuller case study of the Bayou blow-up.)

After several months, Mr. Westervelt agreed to join Bayou, becoming a principal and shareholder in the business on September 30, 2002 (receiving at the onset a 25 percent stake in Bayou Management LLC).

The honeymoon lasted for less time than a Hollywood marriage. Mr. Westervelt alleged that shortly after his hiring, Messrs. Israel and Marino "severely impaired" his ability to conduct business by denying him access to "critical business documents and financial information relating to Bayou."[4] What was it exactly that Mr. Westervelt was asking to see? Was it Mr. Israel's ATM code, or Mr. Marino's wall-safe combination? Hardly. Examples of items he sought but was not given, as cited in the complaint, included—get this—"income statements, balance sheets, [and] monthly account statements." What documents he was able to lay his hands on provided even less comfort. A Spear, Leeds and Kellogg capital trading account, according to the December 2002 account statement, showed a balance of more than $7.8 million on December 1, 2002, but only $379,000 30 days later. According to Mr. Westervelt, he was given no explanation for the rapid, near total fund withdrawal by either Mr. Israel or Mr. Marino, despite repeatedly asking for one.

Mr. Westervelt also alleged that he witnessed possible SEC and NASD violations at Bayou. "[Mr.] Westervelt, upon entering into the business arrangement with Bayou and its principals, Israel and Marino, discovered what he perceived to be possible violations of SEC regulations governing the operation of hedge funds, as well as other perceived possible violations of SEC and NASD rules and regulations. In addition, [Mr.] Westervelt became concerned that Bayou, Israel and Marino might intend to use the North Carolina brokerage office for a purpose that he believed was improper and unethical and would be detrimental to Bayou's investors," again according to court documents.

Expressing his concerns to Mr. Israel in a March 9, 2003, letter led not to a rectification of the problem, but to Mr. Westervelt being fired eight days later, less than six months after he first joined Bayou. This, in turn, spawned his lawsuit.

Mr. Westervelt, it turns out, had a right to be concerned. His insight into the inner workings of this hedge fund was eerily prescient, and foretold a significant problem with which any possible institutional investor viewing these court records would have to contend.

A PI PRACTICE THAT WILL KILL YOU

We have been told several times of investigative firms that search for, or retrieve, only suits that are pending. In practice, this is saying to the institutional investor that cases that have been dismissed are not worthwhile to review. Of course, you need only review the above-described Westervelt action to know how ridiculous this theory is. Moreover, as elucidated above, most cases do get dismissed, and this is by no means reflective of the relative merits of these actions. If someone tells you that this is how he searches, politely decline to buy.

Why tell this story? Yes, clearly the press found it newsworthy, though Paul Westervelt surely would rather have found out Bayou's problems from the outside rather than from his inside post. The real illustrative nature of this story, however, is demonstrating just how crucial it is to retrieve court documents, and not simply rely on a court index to explain a court case. Figure 6.1 shows what we got from an early July 2003 PACER search on Sam Israel and Bayou.

Really helpful, huh? I'm not criticizing PACER, which remains an especially useful tool for uncovering federal court cases. And in this instance, because this particular court happened to be one where actual documents are available online, and because we found this suit shortly after it had been filed, we were able to retrieve the aforementioned complaint via PACER itself. That said, only a handful of courts (depending on the state and even the district within that state) make complaints available online and then typically only when the suit is current, that is filed within the last year or so. Regardless of whether you retrieve the document in the rare instance in which it is available via an online source or obtain it the more common, old-fashioned way, manually, the key is to get the actual complaint. If you click on the case number, 2:2003cv00860, both the docket sheet and the complaint are available (again, this is relatively rare). More importantly, you have already seen that reviewing the index provided by the online source indicates, at best, that a case exists. The docket, attached at Addendum 6.7, is not much better, describing the cause of the action as "diversity-breach of contract." You can plainly see that without obtaining the complaint, you'd be left at best wondering what happened here, and at worst thinking it was a banal contract issue not worthy of your inspection. We often say there is

2 Total Party matches for selection ISRAEL, SAM after 02/01/2003 for ALL COURTS
Search Complete

Tue Jul 8 10:02:12 CDT 2003

Selections 1 through 2 (Page 1)

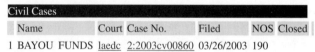

Bankruptcy Cases				
Name	Court	Case No.	Filed	Chapter
1 ISRAEL, SAMP.	njbke	03-01769	05/12/2003	AP

ISRAEL AND SAVIA

Civil Cases					
Name	Court	Case No.	Filed	NOS	Closed
2 ISRAEL, SAM III	laedc	2:2003cv00860	03/26/2003	190	

WESTERVELT vs. BAYOU MANAGEMENT LLC

1 Total Party match for selection BAYOU FUND after 02/01/2003 for ALL COURTS
Search Complete

Tue Jul 8 10:02:49 CDT 2003

Selections 1 through 1 (Page 1)

Civil Cases					
Name	Court	Case No.	Filed	NOS	Closed
1 BAYOU FUNDS	laedc	2:2003cv00860	03/26/2003	190	

WESTERVELT vs. BAYOU MANAGEMENT LLC

2 Total Party matches for selection BAYOU M after 02/01/2003 for ALL COURTS
Search Complete

Tue Jul 8 10:03:01 CDT 2003

Selections 1 through 2 (Page 1)

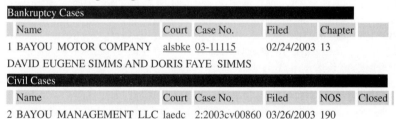

Bankruptcy Cases				
Name	Court	Case No.	Filed	Chapter
1 BAYOU MOTOR COMPANY	alsbke	03-11115	02/24/2003	13

DAVID EUGENE SIMMS AND DORIS FAYE SIMMS

Civil Cases					
Name	Court	Case No.	Filed	NOS	Closed
2 BAYOU MANAGEMENT LLC	laedc	2:2003cv00860	03/26/2003	190	

WESTERVELT vs. BAYOU MANAGEMENT LLC

0 Total Party matches for selection BAYOU P after 02/01/2003 for ALL COURTS
Search Complete

Tue Jul 8 10:03:27 CDT 2003

No Matches Found

FIGURE 6.1   PACER Search Results

1 Total Party match for selection BAYOU SEC after 02/01/2003 for ALL COURTS
Search Complete

Tue Jul 8 10:08:50 CDT 2003

Selections 1 through 1 (Page 1)

Civil Cases					
Name	Court	Case No.	Filed	NOS	Closed
1 BAYOU SECURITIES LLC	laedc	2:2003cv00860	03/26/2003	190	

WESTERVELT vs. BAYOU MANAGEMENT LLC

FIGURE 6.1   (*Continued*)

no way of knowing what you have missed unless you look. The corollary is that though some indices do provide enough data to allow you to avoid obtaining further documents (as, say, in a suit clearly marked "personal injury" or similarly, "other tort-negligence," both examples of actions not likely to be a cause for alarm in this type of review), many indices, like the PACER example here, are less descriptive, and thus require you to read the complaint to understand whether the action is noteworthy or not. Since there is no substitute for doing this, do not allow anyone to provide you with an index and assert that their court search is complete.

As a case study, the Bayou situation is fascinating, offering a little bit of almost every type of yellow flag (discussed further below and in Chapter 16). We have discussed at some length the whistleblower suit filed in late 2003 by Paul Westervelt, a former Bayou principal, all within a space of less than six months. Recall that Mr. Westervelt's allegations boiled down to the fact that though he was brought on as a principal and was expected to help the firm by leveraging his hard-earned reputation, the company refused to show him basic internal financial documents, refused to explain why an account suddenly and inexplicably had most of its money withdrawn, and refused even to properly and formally document his ownership interest in the firm. This combined with what he saw as possible breaches of regulatory rules led to Mr. Westervelt's documenting his concerns in a letter to Sam Israel, a letter that resulted in Mr. Westervelt being fired and that subsequently prompted his suit.

But this suit, which ultimately was dismissed on November 4, 2003, was not the only signal that something was decidedly unkosher at Bayou (a bit of a mixed metaphor I hope you forgive). Our research, conducted before the press caught wind of the problem that eventually doomed the firm, revealed a multitude of warning signs in Mr. Israel's history, delineated as follows.

1. *Regulatory disciplinary actions.* The National Association of Securities Dealers (NASD) reported on April 10, 2003 (Case #C11030011) that Mr. Israel allegedly violated NASD Membership and Registration Rule

1031, and NASD conduct rules 2110 and 3010. According to NASD documents, "Respondent Israel, acting through member firm [Bayou Securities LLC], permitted two individuals to execute transactions concerning over-the-counter securities without first obtaining registration as equity traders in accordance with NASD's Series 55 requirements. Respondent Israel supervised the individuals required to be registered as equity traders in accordance with NASD's Series 55 requirements. Respondent Israel did not properly register as an equity trader in accordance with NASD's requirements. In addition, respondent Israel, acting through member firm, also failed to update written supervisory procedures reasonably designed to achieve compliance with said regulations and rules of NASD with respect thereto."[5] Mr. Israel was censured and fined $8,500, according to the NASD. See Addendum 6.8 for copies of this NASD record.

Now before you say that $8,500 is chump change to a hedge fund manager, consider this more a sign of the fecklessness of our regulatory apparatus than an indication that this issue was insignificant. See also Chapter 8 for a further discussion of the various regulatory bodies that cover the hedge fund industry.

Shortly after this action, on September 10, 2003, the NASD filed a consent order alleging that Bayou Securities "failed to keep the records required by Section 36B-31-14A of the regulations under the Connecticut Uniform Securities Act." Bayou Securities was fined $7,500 and was ordered to provide the NASD with copies of customer complaints on a quarterly basis for two years.

The above matters were not the only run-ins Mr. Israel and/or Bayou were to have with regulatory authorities. NASD records show that a customer complaint was initiated against Mr. Israel on September 19, 2002, but was not reported to the NASD until July 9, 2004. The unnamed customer charged Mr. Israel with the following offenses: misrepresentation, churning/excessive trading, failure to disclose, fraud, unauthorized transactions and unauthorized use or borrowing of customer funds. According to the records, the customer sought $520,609. in damages. This matter was settled on April 5, 2004; here again, settlement data was not provided, and usually is impossible to gather.

Three disciplinary actions filed within a one-year time span is a considerable amount, when compared to the amount of similar problems faced by the average hedge fund we have reviewed (we have looked at over 2,500 hedge funds). And when added to the issues discussed next, a real pattern of frightening behavior emerges.

2. *Lack of education.* According to his biography, Mr. Israel "attended" Tulane University. Tulane's office of the registrar advised that Mr. Israel began at the school in the fall of 1978 before being placed under academic suspension on October 16, 1979. Mr. Israel returned to the school in 1980

but discontinued his studies in December 1981, leaving the school without receiving a degree, again according to the registrar. In fairness, Mr. Israel's biography makes no claims of a degree, stating correctly that he "attended" the school. Nonetheless, the absence of an Ivy League or similar education, much less the absence of even any undergraduate degree, is considered a yellow flag in our book. And although one would not necessarily want to judge one's friends based on their education (though obviously many people do), judging a hedge fund manager on his education as one criterion is not only okay, it can be quite relevant.

3. *A series of short tenures at various firms; omissions and untruths regarding other employment periods.* Mr. Israel's biography listed several brief stints at entities like FJ Graber, Gruntal & Company hedge fund affiliate ARA Associates (which advised that Mr. Israel was an account executive, not a senior trader, from May 1990 to January 1991) and HMR Investors, LP. HMR, it turns out, had a James Marquez as its general partner, according to a February 1994 *Futures* story. Mr. Marquez likewise headed Bayou Securities. Not cited on the biography but listed on an alternate biography given to the NASD was Mr. Israel's time at something known as JGM Management (April 1991 to April 1992). Corporate records showed Mr. Marquez as chairman of this entity.

From June 1992 to December 1992, the NASD biography continued, Mr. Israel was at the Purchase, New York, facility of Concorde Asset Management, a company that, like the above JGM Management, does not appear on his biography.

Next, according to the NASD, Mr. Israel was employed by Omega Advisors. The NASD gave his dates as January 1, 1993, to June 1, 1995; Mr. Israel's biography stated he served as the fund's "head trader" from 1992 to the 1996 formation of Bayou. The former dates were closer to correct, but in either case the biography he was presenting was clearly not accurate, either in the length of time he worked for Omega or the role he had there, according to a former colleague with whom we spoke during a review of Bayou.

One ex-colleague actually corroborated Mr. Israel's title, and made no disparaging remarks about him at all. In fact, this person was quite complimentary of Mr. Israel. That said, this individual recalled that Mr. Israel was with the firm for approximately two years, which would be more like what the NASD biography showed but markedly different from the biography Mr. Israel was using to attract institutional money.

Another Omega person, however, remembered Mr. Israel's role differently. This person took pains to explain that Omega was not set up as a typical trading firm and that neither Mr. Israel nor others at the trading desk were giving directions or functioning as head traders. And though this individual believed Mr. Israel was honest (we all make mistakes, obviously), he did assert:

"I recommend your client study his record carefully," this individual cautioned, "if [Mr. Israel has] done consistently well and there's an audited record. [If Mr. Israel] portrays a position of being consistently right in his trading, I would ask for an audit of the record.... Your client has to understand they're not dealing with a fundamentalist, they're dealing with a guy that's a trader and if he presents an attractive record that gets them interested they should check with a respectable accounting firm too, because I can't speak to that."

Finally, and not to be cast aside too quickly, this party offered that Mr. Israel was given a small amount of money to trade in addition to his execution responsibilities; when Mr. Israel failed to make money, this function was eliminated.

What lessons are imparted here? To begin, it seems clear that Mr. Israel's biography exaggerated both his position and the length of time he held that position. This presents two problems:

1. *Character.* Mr. Israel's lack of honesty is itself a concern. And for those people tempted to say that everyone puffs a biography/resume and that this is not a cause of concern, we'd respond by pointing out that a number of hedge fund frauds or blow-ups, upon inspection, featured managers telling little white lies like this one. One possible explanation for why this later becomes so telling flips the above everyone does it theory on its ear: if people are willing to lie about something seemingly so innocuous, what do you think they'll do when presented with a very difficult situation, like a fund that is losing money? I think it is safe to say that telling the truth at that point is not likely, particularly considering that oftentimes a fund that loses money faces redemptions, then staff departures, and at times, closure. And in this case, the facts bore out this theory.

2. *Lack of experience.* Lost in the muddle of the half-truths, misstatements, and omissions was the fact that Mr. Israel, in effect, had not really proven himself as a trader prior to branching out on his own. The real question is not whether you necessarily believed that he had done something wrong, but rather, as my partner was fond of saying in situations like this, what had he done right?

Many of the pre–blow-up news stories focused on Mr. Israel's family connections and his philanthropy in his home town of New Orleans. (The May 16, 2002 *HedgeWorld Daily News* reported, for instance, that Mr. Israel grew up in Louisiana and "has generously endowed New Orleans' Tulane University," his alma mater, sort of, you'll recall.)[6] These twin topics helped to confer upon Mr. Israel a sense of respect from the investment community that his record almost certainly did not merit. One post–blow-up story summed up the problem nicely. On September 6, 2005, *Infovest21 News* reported that the now notorious Samuel Israel III is a member of the Israel family of ACLI Israel, a New Orleans coffee and sugar merchant they formed in the early 1800s.[7] His grandfather, Samuel Israel I, was known as Ace Israel, owing to his trading talent. The firm became ACLI International, an international commodities and futures trading business, which the Israels sold in 1981 to Donaldson, Lufkin & Jenrette for $42 million, making the Israel family the largest shareholder of DLJ at that time.

Dating back to the 1950s, the Israel family formed ACI Capital, a still active private equity and alternative investment firm. Thomas C. Israel, chairman of A.C. Israel Enterprises, one time CFO of ACLI International and formerly a manager of the ACI Capital America Fund, was described as a cousin of Samuel Israel III. Another story indicated that Mr. Israel's brother, Larry, worked at Prudential-Bache Securities.

Here's the real kicker. According to the *Infovest* piece, "Several veteran commodities traders, who had experience trading with ACLI and the Israels, said that they were 'very reputable people.' Samuel Israel III as a trader, didn't have direct experience in commodities and futures, and didn't work for ACLI. 'This seems to be a case of someone riding on the family reputation,' one of the commodities traders said."[8]

Easy to say, in hindsight. But based on what has been described already, along with some matters to be discussed below, it was almost as transparent before any problems had been made public.

4. *A driving under the influence (DUI) charge against Mr. Israel.* In July 1999, the Property Clerk of the New York Police Department filed suit against Mr. Israel and Hann Auto Trust, in the State Supreme Court, New York County (see Addendum 6.9 for documents). The complaint alleged that Mr. Israel, confirmed to be the subject via an address and social security number listed on the documents and matching those of the subject—was arrested on May 11, 1999, by police while operating a car leased by Hann Auto Trust, allegedly while "under the influence of alcohol." Furthermore, he was charged with "criminal possession of a controlled substance in the Seventh Degree." At the time of the arrest, the Jeep Mr. Israel was driving was seized by the police. The civil complaint sought to allow the police department to maintain permanent custody of the Jeep, based on Mr. Israel's violations of the aforementioned criminal statutes.

A discontinuance was issued in the civil forfeiture case on June 19, 2000.

What immediately jumps out here is not the resolution of who is entitled to the car. To me what is perhaps most illuminating is that Mr. Israel was almost 43 years old when this incident occurred. Though drunk driving can never really be excused, a person who commits this type of offense at 22 years old might be thought to have learned a lesson, and 10 to 15 years later, provided that he has not committed a similar offense again, it is certainly conceivable that an investor might then overlook this incident. But for a man in his forties to drive while intoxicated, and have drugs in the vehicle, is far more serious, both in terms of the remarkably bad judgment it demonstrates as well as the idea that it might indicate a bigger, more pervasive problem with substance abuse.

Side note: Regarding the criminal case mentioned in 403084-99, our court researcher found no records on file through OCA or the Supreme Court in Kings County, NY on Samuel Israel. When contacted, the clerk at the Supreme Court informed our researcher that the documentation we have was a police instrument reflecting that the individual did have property taken and that he was arrested. Additional information regarding this is available "only from the Police Department," who in our experience release data only to the defendant himself.

5. *Other lawsuits.* Another lawsuit, this one filed May 31, 2002, by D'Amore Consulting Company Inc. in California's Marin County Superior Court against Mr. Israel and the various Bayou entities (see documents attached at Addendum 6.10), also foretold possible problems. Though much of the file was "destroyed" according to court officials, the court docket described this as a breach of contract suit. Perusing the docket reveals that on September 9, 2002, D'Amore Consulting was awarded a default judgment of $2,660,784.50 (that's not a misprint—it is indeed more than $2.6 million). A default judgment was entered here, as it often is, because "no appearance by or for the defendants" was made, according to the docket. The case was reopened on January 17, 2003; the judgment was then vacated and set aside on January 24, 2003. Finally, the case was dismissed with prejudice on January 31, 2003, again according to the docket. (According to law.com, a dismissal is "1) the act of voluntarily terminating a criminal prosecution or a lawsuit or one of its causes of action by one of the parties. 2) a judge's ruling that a lawsuit or criminal charge is terminated. 3) an appeals court's act of dismissing an appeal, letting the lower court decision stand. 4) the act of a plaintiff dismissing a lawsuit upon settling the case. Such a dismissal may be dismissal with prejudice [as occurred here], meaning it can never be filed again, or dismissal without prejudice, leaving open the possibility of bringing the suit again if the defendant does not follow through on the terms of the settlement.")

Black's Law Dictionary 5th Edition presents a similar explanation: "**With Prejudice:** An adjudication on the merits and final disposition barring the right to bring or maintain an action on the same claim or cause. . . .

Without Prejudice: Dismissal without prejudice to the right of the complainant to sue again the same cause of action. The effect of the words 'without prejudice' is to prevent the decree of dismissal from operating as a bar to a subsequent suit."

It is stressed again that a dismissal does not indicate that a suit had no worth, and is frequently tied to a settlement executed between the parties. In this instance the docket obliquely refers to an arbitration, records of which are not normally public.

Based on the above, the final outcome of this matter is unfortunately unclear. (Typically, any hope of clarifying this would rely on contacting the litigants, in this case D'Amore Consulting Company. More often than not, however, settlements and arbitration results are made with the understanding that making them public is forbidden.) Regardless, the size of this action combined with the initial lack of appearance would certainly lead to it being classified as a yellow alert signal.

Yet another suit (Addendum 6.11) was filed against Mr. Israel, this time by a landlord alleging that he failed to pay $12,000 in rent. Sutton East Associates 86 sued Mr. Israel in State Supreme Court, New York County on May 11, 1992. Lest you think this was a nasty New York landlord trying to boot a tenant unfairly, the complaint alleges that Mr. Israel had failed to pay rent from September 1991 through April 1992; as the lease ran from April 1991 to April 1992, Mr. Israel was accused, in effect, of failing to pay two-thirds of what he owed. By July 15, 1992, court documents indicate, Mr. Israel had yet to respond (sound familiar?), prompting the landlord to seek a default judgment. (A form for a statement of default judgment was attached to the complaint, but it was filled in, stamped with court seals, or entered.)

One forest not to be missed in the surfeit of trees discussed above is that a narrow, targeted search for court actions likely would have missed all of the above suits. Remember, Mr. Israel lived in Westchester County, New York, and Bayou was based in Stamford, Connecticut. Recall from above that the whistleblower action was filed in Louisiana; the DUI and the failure to pay cases were filed in New York County, New York; and the $2.6 million breach of contract suit was filed in Marin County, California. So while a broad-based search has its own problems (namely the difficulty that ensues regarding which suits cite the subject as opposed to those that involve merely a similarly named individual) the benefits of this approach far outweigh its costs.

6. *Independent auditor in name only. Literally.* Bayou's CFO and long-time Sam Israel colleague was Dan Marino. Just before the fund blew up publicly we were asked to clarify the current or former connection that Mr. Marino had to Bayou's auditor, an entity known as Richmond-Fairfield Associates. Business reporting sources for 2005 listed Mr. Marino as the manager of Richmond-Fairfield Associates, located at 111 John Street, Room 1720, New York, New York. But as these records are notoriously spotty,

this was not considered "proof" of any conflict, and was at any rate not clear about the present relationship between Mr. Marino and this firm.

New York Department of State records, meanwhile, indicated that Richmond-Fairfield Associates, Certified Public Accountants, PLLC, was incorporated on October 10, 2000. Mr. Marino was not listed in New York Department of State records as an officer of Richmond-Fairfield; this was unsurprising, however, as these records typically do not cite officers. New York Department of State records also list Mr. Marino as the contact person and CPA at an inactive entity, JGM Management Company, Inc. whose address, 17 Whitaker Place, Staten Island, New York, is linked to Richmond-Fairfield. The aforementioned James G. Marquez also was listed in the records as an officer and director of JGM; recall that Mr. Israel's biography indicated he worked at JGM from April 1991 to April 1992.

So far, so ... nothing. But here is when things got interesting (a euphemism here meaning "oh boy").

We were advised by someone familiar with the firm that Richmond-Fairfield's address is 575 Madison Avenue, Suite 1006, New York, New York. Calling the firm at night (a favorite ploy in situations like this, and to be discussed further in another chapter), we reached Richmond-Fairfield's night-time voicemail, which said: "You've reached the office of Richmond-Fairfield Associates, Mr. Richmond is either on the phone or away from his desk ... leave a message." Using a suitable pretext we called the office and spoke to the company's receptionist, who confirmed the above address and said that "Matt Richmond" is the contact person for Richmond-Fairfield. (Note that we found numerous entities tied to this address and suite number, suggesting that it is a mechanism for firms to maintain a prestigious address without the expense of doing so on their own.) The receptionist also said that she has no Dan Marino listed "on her screen." When asked if it was possible that he'd left the firm, she said he might have or just might not be listed. Note also that our search of address identification sources for a Matt or Matthew Richmond in New York found no connection between the Matt/Matthew Richmonds found and Richmond-Fairfield's reported business addresses.

Note also that we attempted to contact Richmond-Fairfield's office at 111 John Street, New York, New York, via its phone number (212) 766-4233; this number is not in service. Note, too, that Staten Island is in Richmond County, and that Mr. Israel has been placed to addresses in Fairfield County, something that could account for the name of this entity.

New York CPA records show that Daniel E. Marino (License No. 063559) has been registered since July 9, 1990, and is registered through August 31, 2008. The records also show that Richmond-Fairfield Associates CPA Services, PLLC (Company ID No. 41980) filed on October 10, 2000, and its status is current at the aforementioned 17 Whittaker Place, Staten Island, New York, address. Mr. Marino is listed in the records as the member/manager of Richmond-Fairfield. Note that no listings were found for a Matt Richmond or a James G. Marquez in New York CPA records.

The AICPA advised that the only Matt Richmond they had in their records was an individual based in California. California CPA records show that a Matthew Frank Richmond was issued his license on August 1, 1991 (License No. 59658); though this was set to expire on November 30, 2005, the records listed his registration as inactive. The records also show that Matthew Frank Richmond's address is 8271 Woodshill Trail, Los Angeles, California. Our research shows that Matthew Frank Richmond has resided in California, Michigan, and Indiana, and was not connected to any addresses in New York.

Based on the above, it was not possible to assert with 100 percent conviction that Mr. Marino was in fact the "independent auditor" used by Bayou. Having conceded this, it was, however, eminently clear that something decidedly bizarre was going on, especially considering that the Matt Richmond referenced by Richmond-Fairfield's receptionist did not seem to in fact exist. Of course, ultimately it was proven that Mr. Marino and Richmond-Fairfield were in effect the same thing, and that Bayou's audits were therefore, essentially, worse than worthless.

Bayou Postscripts

Long after the first of several investor lawsuits, the following stories appeared.

"WHITE PLAINS, Dec. 15 [2006] (AP)—James Marquez, a founder of the Bayou Group, conceded in federal court "that he had conspired to defraud investors of more than $10 million."

James C. Marquez is facing up to five years in prison, according to the story. Like, Sam Israel and Daniel Marino, who also pleaded guilty to conspiracy and fraud, Mr. Marquez was awaiting sentencing.

Mr. Marquez admitted the three men claimed that Bayou was earning "big profits" when it had in fact been losing money for several years.

Bayou filed for bankruptcy in May 2006 and is now suing some former investors "who may have received "fictitious profits" from the Bayou fraud."[9]

December 17, 2006—According to the *New York Post*, Bayou lost 12 percent in 1996; 1997 was also poor, with profits stemming solely from Bayou's broker-dealer's commissions being directed back into the hedge fund, according to prosecutors trying James Marquez. By 1998's conclusion, desperate to avoid explaining the failures of the previous two years to clients, Mr. Marquez conceded to launching the fake number scheme.

"The cause [of the Bayou collapse] lies with Jim Marquez at the beginning and Sam Israel in the end," according to a 2005 "suicide note" penned by the now infamous Dan Marino.[10]

All told, the Bayou case is one for the ages, and were it not for people getting hurt by this situation, the story would be almost comical. At least if reviewed in hindsight, it allows for investors going forward to avoid the Bayou morass (forgive the tortured word play).

Another hedge fund blow-up, this one involving John Whittier's Wood River Associates, mirrored the Bayou scandal in several odd ways, but differed in many other respects. Like Bayou, John Whittier's Wood River started out seemingly doing well. (The "seemingly," in the case of Bayou, later turning out to be the operative word.) According to his biography, Mr. Whittier left Donaldson Lefkin Jenrette (DLJ) in September 1997 to form Wood River Capital Management, LLC. The biography also states that from September 1997 through 2003, Mr. Whittier's primary activity was "managing a family office, which he continues to manage," as well as "several investment portfolios consisting of public and private equity securities." Wood River Partners, LP was formed in February 2003, with Wood River Associates, LLC serving as the general partner, also according to the biography. New York Department of State records show that Wood River Associates and Wood River Capital Management were both formed on November 18, 1997. The records likewise show that Wood River, LP, which is listed with the same address, 711 Fifth Avenue, New York, New York, as Wood River Associates, was formed on November 19, 1997. California Secretary of State records indicate that Wood River Partners was formed on April 30, 2002, and list Mr. Whittier as the registered agent. Note that a registered agent frequently takes no active role in a company's management, and is more often merely acting as an investor or in some perfunctory, legal manner (though Mr. Whittier's role was clearly more significant).

The year 2002, however, was not kind to Wood River or Mr. Whittier. His biography indicates that the fund lost money for the period from 2001 through 2002, but beat its benchmark. What the biography doesn't say is exactly how far down the fund was, something that should have triggered alarm bells. Beating a benchmark is nice, I suppose; beating a benchmark by losing 40 percent, rather than losing 60 percent, is still not altogether impressive. What's more, not being specific about a failure is something of a classic poor character indicator: business people who are overly specific about their accomplishments but unusually vague about their low periods will often repeat this pattern, typically to the regret of those relying upon them. Mr. Whittier, case in point, stated in his biography: 'The public equity portfolio of the family office managed by Mr. Whittier out performed its benchmark (the NASDAQ) index since 1999. In 1999 the portfolio more than doubled in value [note here—success spells specifics]. In 2000, with the NASDAQ declining nearly 40 percent in value, the portfolio returned an absolute gain of nearly 2 percent. [Again, a gain, especially compared to others' enormous losses, leads to specific numbers being presented. But read on.] From 2001 through 2002, like many funds focused on communications and technology areas, the value of the portfolio of the family office declined (although it outperformed its benchmark)." And there you have it. When faced with describing a two-year period of losses, suddenly Mr. Whittier's memory of actual numbers is Alzheimerish. Institutions seeing this vagueness need to recognize that it is obviously intentional, that given the desire to obfuscate, the numbers are not positive, and perhaps most importantly, that a person who engages in this type of smoky language will likely do the same thing again, particularly if confronted with the same situation again.

As will be pointed out throughout this book, hedge funds, perhaps more than almost any business, have a built-in disincentive to be forthright. Once hedge funds, especially smaller or nascent ones, have to admit that they are losing money, investors frequently flee, as do analysts and traders, in many cases leading to a downward spiral from which the hedge fund cannot escape. Given this, it should come as little surprise that a fund in this situation would consider at least obfuscating its results, or even, as in the case of Bayou, simply making them up. (This obviously ignores the fact that many hedge funds, in fact the majority of them, will be and are honest. Nevertheless, it is impossible to discuss hedge funds without acknowledging this fundamental conflict.)

Numbers manipulation was not to be the only link between these back-to-back, notorious hedge fund scandals, however. Recall that Mr. Israel was sued at one point for failing to pay rent over a fairly long period of time. Amazingly, Wood River topped this by likewise getting sued for failing to pay rent, a suit I cannot remember seeing filed against any other hedge funds, before or since. In August 2002, OTR, an Ohio general partnership, as Nominee of the State Teachers Retirement Board of Ohio, sued Wood River Capital Management, LLC, *et al.* for allegedly defaulting on its lease at 44 Montgomery Street, San Francisco, California (an address linked to the subject company via identification sources). Mr. Whittier was not personally named in court documents. OTR charged that Wood River, whose first least payment was due September 1, 2000, missed rent payments of $31,464.17 on June 1, 2002, July 1, 2002, and August 1, 2002. On July 12, 2002, OTR served Wood River with a "Three-Day Notice to Pay Rent or Quit" the lease, according to court documents. Wood River made a partial payment of $32,318.12 to OTR on July 17, 2002; however, that payment did "not waive any of OTR's rights or remedies" under the Three-Day Notice, according to the complaint. OTR sought the total amount of rent due of $67,885.47, immediate restitution of the property, and declaration of forfeiture of the lease, among other things.

According to court documents, this matter was dismissed without prejudice on September 3, 2002. Recall that the term "dismissed without prejudice" indicates that the case has been closed (often due to a settlement) but can be brought again.

In a far more significant suit, one that resembled the action that occurred as Wood River was drying up (forgive me), the company (Wood River Capital Management, LLC, Wood River Capital Management, LP, specifically) and Mr. Whittier individually were sued by Credit Suisse First Boston Corporation in State Supreme Court, New York County for failing to pay $1,620,214.02 (yes, over $1.6 million) in Gemstar and AOL securities losses. On April 23, 2002, Credit Suisse First Boston (CSFB), which acted a prime brokerage clearance firm for Wood River, alleged that Wood River and Mr. Whittier failed to instruct one of Wood River's prime brokers—in this case Morgan Stanley—to take receipt of the Gemstar and AOL securities and pay CSFB, as per the agreement between CSFB and Wood River. The complaint states that Morgan Stanley "refused to settle" the Gemstar and AOL securities since Wood River "had not provided them with any instructions regarding" the transactions, this despite Mr. Whittier having previously advised CSFB to book the six transactions to Morgan Stanley.

CSFB repeatedly instructed Mr. Whittier to have Morgan Stanley take receipt of these securities and pay CSFB for them. CSFB, according to the complaint, informed Mr. Whittier on April 9, 2002, that "if delivery of the securities was not accepted by April 11, 2002, CSFB would liquidate those securities and hold Wood River liable for the resulting losses," then estimated at approximately $1.5 million. According to the complaint, on April 17, 2002, Mr. Whittier purportedly told CSFB during a telephone conversation that he was the "only person who had the authority to request securities transactions on behalf of Wood River" and also informed CSFB that it "would not be receiving payment that day or anytime in the near future." (For the layman, this statement is unbelievably harsh. For Mr. Whittier to essentially give the bird to CSFB in this scenario is roughly akin to a Jeopardy! contestant spitting in Alex Trebek's face.)

Court documents state that this lawsuit was dismissed with prejudice on May 17, 2002.

Another similarity between the Bayou and Wood River debacles was the benefit of a broad-based court search. Wood River (the management company, Wood River Capital Management, LLC, specifically) had offices in San Francisco, California, and Sun Valley, Idaho, where Mr. Whittier lived. Though the rental suit was filed in California, the critical CSFB action, you'll recall, was filed in New York, and thus would not have been found had the search been limited to only those areas where the subject was at the moment of the search. And without this suit, Wood River's history looks decidedly less problematic; a pattern of behavior, of course, can only be detected if one is searching for all the pieces of the puzzle, in all the places where those pieces can be found.

In addition to the lawsuits mentioned above, our search revealed four state tax liens filed against Mr. Whittier and one filed against Wood River. Two liens naming Mr. Whittier were filed in Idaho: one in December 2004 for more than $86,000 and another in July 2002 for approximately $80,000. Two more were entered against him in California: one in April 2002 for almost $46,000 and another in December 2003 for approximately $54,000. No satisfaction (payment) was found for any of these liens save for the July 2002 lien, which was released (that is paid) in February 2004, according to payment records (which are sometimes incomplete, leading us to suggest that managers with liens on their records provide evidence of satisfaction, should it exist).

The lien naming Wood River, also filed in California, was issued in October 2004 for under $2,400. Here again, no satisfaction was shown.

For the uninitiated, having four personal tax liens, all over $40,000 and only one paid, within a span of less than three years, is not a good omen. An entrepreneur who has owned and operated multiple businesses and is being considered for a venture capital investment might, and I stress might, be able to overcome such a record, with the presumption that he was merely "sloppy" rather than a poor businessman or a crook. A hedge fund manager, conversely, who is not paying his taxes properly is telling the investment world that he is capable of managing their money, yet utterly incapable of managing his own, a decidedly incongruous creed. This takes on even more significance when one considers how many opportunities to correct a tax underpayment (see sidebar, below) one has prior to having a tax lien filed against you.

AVOIDING A TAX LIEN

Many people, reading that a person has had tax liens entered against them, would think that this might have been the result of an overzealous government, or a simple filing error, or perhaps sloppiness at worst. And as a staunch libertarian, I am certainly no fan of taxes. This said, I set out to discover the process by which a tax lien is filed, theorizing that taxpayers almost certainly are afforded multiple opportunities to pay prior to an actual lien being assessed against them.

Going straight to the source, I first went to a friend who works for the Internal Revenue Service (IRS). I was directed to the collections area, where I received both literature as well as some answers to questions I had posed. What it boils down to is that taxpayers are given many chances to correct the underpayment or nonpayment prior to the lien stage. First, they are simply sent a bill, indicating they owe the government money. If no response is received, a letter is sent (certified, with a return receipt signature required) by the government demanding payment. Only if the taxpayer "neglect(s) or refuse(s) to fully pay the debt within 10 days . . ." does the IRS even consider filing the notice of Federal Tax Lien (FTL). This lien, by the way, is notifying creditors that the government now has a claim against the taxpayer's property. A levy, conversely, is the process by which that property is actually taken to satisfy the taxpayer's debts.

Meanwhile, as documented in a standard "final notice" letter sent by the IRS to a delinquent taxpayer (see Addendum 6.12), an appeals process is also possible; here the taxpayer can appeal the debt (if they think it is incorrect, say) within 30 days and thus temporarily kibosh on the lien procedure. A further option is to pay in installments; here the taxpayer must pay what they can immediately, then establish a plan with the IRS in which they agree to pay a certain amount every month until the debt is satisfied.

All in all, sounds pretty reasonable, especially by scary IRS standards. And in reviewing state tax liens, the procedures seem almost identical. The California State Board of Equalization discusses this at http://72.14.209.104/search?q=cache:1XRqNv3fE4kJ:www.boe.ca.gov/pdf/pub54.pdf+california+state+tax+lien+procedures&hl=en&ct=clnk&cd=2&gl=us; again, the taxpayer is sent a bill, and can discuss this prior with a representative to paying. Here, too, if it is determined that the bill must be paid, an installment plan is available.

The net net? Pretending that a tax lien was filed against you without your knowledge and without you having a chance to fix your tax situation prior to the lien stage is ludicrous.

So all in all, this was a bad time for Mr. Whittier and Wood River. Now we return to what he said about 2002, and it becomes apparent, or at least plausible, that the reason these suits and some of these liens occurred was due to the losses the fund was suffering. Nevertheless, the suits and liens by themselves, exacerbated by how Mr. Whittier handled them, show either poor business execution, poor judgment, or both. The failure to pay rent action may seem relatively unimportant, unless of course you are a commercial landlord. But for a company that is in business to manage money, the abject inability to manage your own is surely something most possible investors, had they known about it, would frown on.

As for the CSFB action, it is hard even to know where to begin. The suit itself again speaks to Wood River's inability, or unwillingness, to pay what it owed. Strangely, Mr. Whittier's reaction made a terrible situation look even worse, something that is not easy to accomplish. As a rookie investigator, I recall with great vividness researching numerous real estate developers in advance of multimillion dollar loans. The New York real estate market, those familiar with it might recall, hit some "turbulence" in the late 1980s–early 1990s, causing any number of foreclosure actions to be initiated against developers who suddenly found themselves unable to pay back their debt. In the case of two developers in particular, a search of court records revealed numerous suits filed against them, both separately and some jointly. However, one developer's actions following this downturn stood in stark contrast to his sometime partner, according to interviews we conducted with many of the lenders involved. Whereas Partner Number One dragged his heels at every turn, forcing the lenders to spend countless hours and dollars pursuing ultimately worthless lawsuits, Partner Number Two immediately stepped to the dais, took responsibility and announced that he could pay a certain amount on the dollar. The latter's reputation, unsurprisingly, not only survived this crisis, but flourished, particularly compared to that of his former colleague. Though no one was privy to the conversations between CSFB and Mr. Whittier other than the parties themselves, if we are to believe CSFB's account Mr. Whittier's statement closely resembled that of Partner Number One in the example outlined above. And in the final analysis, this statement probably has a far longer lasting negative feeling attached to it than the underlying event ever could.

WOOD RIVER POSTSCRIPT

From a March 2, 2006, *PR Newswire*:

> *Edison Fund Limited, successor to BNP Paribas, has sued Wood River Hedge Funds' auditors, outside counsel and financial professionals.*
>
>   *This suit follows the October 2005 SEC action against John Whittier, Wood River Capital Management, et al., which alleged, among other things, that Wood River accumulated 60% of the stock*

of End Wave Corporation, "secretly, and in violation of the repre-
sentations it had made to investors." EndWave's stock price demise
led to Wood River's, which led to the investors' fall, ultimately
prompting the SEC lawsuit.[11]

The wire placed investors' losses at over $200 million.

As I am writing this, *Reuters* reported on February 1, 2007 that Mr.
Whittier "was charged with defrauding investors of $88 million in 2004 in
a case that exemplified the risky nature of hedge funds."[12]

"[Mr.] Whittier, 40, faces a four-count federal indictment for violating
his firm's investment mandates and failing to file required stock holding
disclosures with the U.S. Securities and Exchange Commission, according
to the U.S. Attorney's Office for the Southern District of New York," the
article added.

The collapse of Mr. Whittier's estimated $265 million fund, "became a
poster child for the dangers of investing in lightly regulated hedge funds."

What have we learned here?

1. If someone says he is losing money, ask him to specify how much, as
   opposed to telling you he is doing better than his money-losing peers.
2. Search courts broadly (a familiar theme to be echoed throughout this
   chapter).
3. Obtain and review court documents.
4. If a person has been sued by a landlord, has multiple, mid to high
   five-digit tax liens and tells an investment bank, its prime brokerage
   clearance firm, to go scratch, rather than paying their bills, run.
5. See number 4. Rinse. Repeat.

For those still not convinced of the value of court searches, we need to
chat about Ed Ehee (rhymes with sleazy). Waking up on November 9, 2006,
sitting down to *Opalesque.com* (to be discussed further in a later chapter),
I was greeted by yet another sordid tale of a "hedge fund" gone bad. According to a November 8, 2006, SEC litigation release, "the Securities and
Exchange Commission today filed fraud charges against the head of several
San Francisco–based hedge funds, accusing him of misappropriating millions
of dollars from investors nationwide, including senior citizens. According to
the Commission, Edward Ehee, 43, of Oakland, defrauded investors in the
Compass West Fund, Viper Founders Fund, and Viper Investments, divert-
ing much of the money towards mortgage and car payments, vacations, and
personal bank accounts. Among other things, the Commission's complaint

alleges that although the Viper Founders Fund essentially ceased operations by late 2002, Ehee was continuing to raise money as recently as May 2006, using bogus account statements and phony financial reports showing millions of dollars in non-existent fund assets to lure new investments."

Describing this as a "classic Ponzi scheme," the release noted that to "conceal his fraud and induce further investments, Ehee provided investors with account statements showing that their money was safe and continuing to generate positive returns. . . . Ehee even fabricated an audit opinion letter from an accounting firm that had never actually audited the fund."

According to the complaint, the SEC sought, along with penalties, an accounting and disgorgement, permanent injunctions prohibiting Mr. Ehee and his firms from future violations of various securities laws.[13]

Disclosure. I am not sure I have any pet peeves more irritating than this; that is, the SEC telling someone not to do something again that they are not allowed to do in the first place, or, well, then they will get told not to do it again, again.

Aside from ranting about the fecklessness of our regulatory bodies, who more often than not show up long after all the money is gone and thus are as useful to investors with losses as the gift certificate I received to a store that had gone out of business, several issues are instructive here. The first is more obvious: news organizations love to talk about negative things, and are frequently tempted to describe any such occurrence using the zeitgeist of the period. In this instance, that means labeling Mr. Ehee a hedge fund manager, then going on to more correctly characterize his alleged methods as a Ponzi scheme. While it is true that a hedge fund scam can certainly be conducted via the Ponzi method of paying old investors with new investors' money, then having old investors talk highly of the fund, leading to even more new investors clamoring to get in, it is equally true that Ponzi schemes have predated hedge funds by several decades. (The original Ponzi was Charles Ponzi, who in 1920 promised investors 50 percent profits in 90 days. After landing many millions of dollars, he landed in jail, only to move from Massachusetts to Florida, take a new name, and perpetrate a second fraud. But that's a story for a different book.) Moreover, because you call yourself a hedge fund manager doesn't make you one; I'd argue that the majority of so-called hedge funds to have blown up recently, especially smaller ones, were hedge funds the way I am Stephen King.

The story does not make it clear whether Mr. Ehee (who according to a Jenny Anderson *New York Times* piece was formerly a Kidder Peabody sales associate who in 1993 established Global Capital Partners, which became the Viper Founders Fund in 2000) was a trustworthy person who somehow went haywire, or whether anything in his background might have indicated his ethics were askew. Drum roll please. . . .

Troubling ethics? Behind door number one, we have a winner. A court search of Mr. Ehee, limited specifically to the Oakland/San Francisco, California areas, was quite revealing:

1. *Suit Number One.* On July 27, 2000, in State Superior Court, San Francisco County, Senyon Kim sued Mr. Ehee, Viper and Global Equity Partners on a number of charges, among them conversion (which sounds tame but is a serious allegation; according to The 'Lectric Law Library conversion is "the unlawful turning or applying the personal goods of another to the use of the taker, or of some other person than the owner ..."), breach of covenant of good faith and fair dealing, and the big mama, fraud.[14] According to Mr. Kim, he had invested money with Mr. Ehee and Ehee's entities beginning in 1994. In March 2000, Mr. Ehee, the aptly named Viper and Global signed a promissory note indicating they owed Mr. Kim $300,000. Instead of repaying this money, however, the defendants allegedly "converted" it for their own use. In English, they stole it. Asked to return the money, Mr. Ehee purportedly refused. Mr. Kim also alleged that he relied on Mr. Ehee, with the latter knowing Mr. Kim was unsophisticated regarding investing and in fact, spoke little English. All told Mr. Kim sought the return of his money plus $1 million in punitive damages. On October 10, 2001, Mr. Kim filed to dismiss this suit with prejudice.

2. *Suit Number Two.* On April 5, 2001, an individual named Jack Mason sued Mr. Ehee (confirmed to be the Ed Ehee of interest because the complaint indicated the defendant could be served with process at Viper Capital) for a little under $9,000. Mr. Mason's complaint indicates that he became employed by something called Serengeti Software on April 5, 2000. In October 2000, he spoke with Mr. Ehee (whose connection to Serengeti is not made clear by the court records) about Serengeti's being slow to pay Mr. Mason's expenses. Mr. Ehee allegedly personally guaranteed Mr. Mason's expenses from "that point forward." Mr. Mason then accumulated $8,976.69 worth of expenses, which, you guessed it, Mr. Ehee allegedly refused to pay, prompting the suit. The case was dismissed with prejudice, according to Mr. Mason's motion, on July 10, 2002.

3. *Suit Number Three.* On March 26, 2004, Simon Cho brought a suit against Mr. Ehee, this one in State Superior Court, Alameda County, California but for the familiar counts of fraud and breach of contract. According to Mr. Cho's complaint, in January 2003 Mr. Ehee asked Mr. Cho to borrow $500,000. On February 1, 2003, to his lasting dismay, Mr. Cho agreed. According to the promissory note, Mr. Ehee was required to pay Mr. Cho $555,000 on January 31, 2004. He failed to pay this, or any money, in spite of repeated demands from Mr. Cho. Mr. Cho also alleged that Mr. Ehee had deposited the money into an account in Bermuda, without telling

Mr. Cho of this. On May 10, 2004, this suit, too, was dismissed without prejudice.

These three court actions were found in a five-second search of California courts. Documents themselves were then retrieved from the courts in question, and help paint a picture of Mr. Ehee as someone who clearly has breached people's trust in the past. At the time this is being written, Mr. Ehee's fate is unknown. But what is certain is that a review of the courts, combined with a retrieval of court documents, would have helped anyone considering investing with M. Ehee make an, ahem, more informed decision.

METHODS OF CONDUCTING COURT SEARCHES

Now that you know the value of an exhaustive court search, the next logical step in the process, is to ascertain how to go about actually searching courts, when records are not available online. A classic buy versus build dilemma confronts you here (though I will argue that the build strategy is beyond foolish, both in terms of cost, and more importantly, success). Four basic methods of searching courts and retrieving documents exist:

1. *Do everything on your own.* This means having staff available in 3000+ counties, although this is mitigated by the fact that most hedge fund managers have lived and worked primarily in larger metropolitan areas; many counties are close enough to one another that one person could handle multiple counties within a state; and, as noted above, a fair number of counties are covered online. However, and this is a huge "however," the last point is accurate principally for searching courts, and will therefore not be much, if any, help when it comes to retrieving documents. And although the first two points made will indeed limit the number of counties one needs to staff up for, the total number of counties not even covered for searches is enormous (for civil courts, approximately 250 counties are covered by state docket, and many of these are not updated in a way that makes them acceptable; this leaves 90 percent of the country's state-level civil courts not covered).

   One caveat here. I was at an industry conference where I heard an investigative company claim that they fly their staff around the country to retrieve documents, as an alternative to having full-time staff in various locales. I am guessing they were just blustering, for if this were actually true, it is an incredibly dumb idea.

   Overall, the intractable problems with this approach are expertise and cost. As you'll learn in the following section, court systems vary, sometimes wildly, from state to state and sometimes even within states. Though this book will certainly provide enough details to get you started, no book can replace the experience amassed by professional court searchers. The only way I can see even considering this is by going ahead and hiring people who are working as court researchers now, and bringing them in house.

But that brings us to cost. A staffer with enough experience and intelligence to handle the tasks at hand will cost you, by the time you are done with salary, insurance, and FICA, approximately $40,000—$60,000+ per annum, not even taking into consideration raises, bonuses, vacations, and so forth. Next you have to factor in the time and energy your people will need to spend training the new person (though this could be obviated, somewhat, by hiring only experienced personnel). Finally, you'll need to multiply this figure by the number of places you'll need to cover, some of which may only be searched a few times a year. Simply put, even if you could teach yourself everything you need to know about the court system (with this book as one guide), there is no way you'll ever achieve the economies of scale to warrant this expenditure.

2. So if you shouldn't build a court search and retrieval team from scratch, what can you do? Hire a former FBI or other governmental agency investigator, in each location necessary, to search and retrieve for you. This approach does have some merit, in that it at least gets you on the way to the recognition that hiring someone, or really multiple someones, to handle this aspect of your review, is the correct move. Several problems with this approach, however, make it untenable:

   a. How do you find these ex-FBI agents? If you know an ex-FBI agent, they will have access to a little brown book that is a directory of former agents. Of course, this is a bit of a Catch-22. Still, this directory can be had, with some effort.

   b. In my experience, the ex-government person is often more expensive than a professional court researcher, owing, I'd surmise, to the economy of scale issue alluded to earlier.

   c. Timing problems. Most of the time the ex-government person is on a pension, supplementing this via court searches and other investigations for other former colleagues. But as they are a one-man show, you will be subject to the constraints put on them by whatever job they happen to be handling when you need them to retrieve a court record for you.

   d. The real killer. Ex-government investigators still envision themselves as, well, investigators. Why is this bad? Because this is not what you need. Court searches can be complicated. They are often laborious.

And they are almost always tedious. But the expertise necessary to handle these searches is not the expertise typically developed by the ex-governmental investigator. Perhaps more problematic is the fact that the former Fed wants to peruse records and draw conclusions; what you need, by contrast, is someone to merely obtain the records and quickly forward them to you. For the integration of data from multiple sources, as has been and will continue to be stressed throughout this book, is ultimately what allows you to see the patterns of behavior that in turn, help you predict which hedge fund manager may represent an outsized risk to your portfolio.

This mismatch of expertise is what results in the Fed not obtaining a record, in a court case he considers to be unimportant, when it turns out that the data in those documents was critical. And while you can establish all kinds of procedures designed to prevent this, the process will never be as easy or efficient as merely using technique number 3 (below).

3. Hire a professional research and retrieval firm. Okay, getting closer. From the above, you'll see I am strongly in favor of your buying, rather than building, your court search capabilities. Moreover, it is clear that I believe strongly in the idea of using the specialist, that is, going with a firm that does nothing but court searches and retrievals for, well, court searches and retrievals. So are there any problems with this approach? A few, some of which are easily overcome, and others that aren't.

   a. Similar to the aforementioned solution, how do you identify research and retrieval firms? In this case, the answer is actually pretty easy. Recall that BRB Publications (http://www.brbpub.com/) has a website and a book containing a list of vendors providing research and retrieval services in their respective states and counties. There is a small cost ($124 as of this writing), but the list is quite extensive and is well worth it.

   b. How do you know who is good and who isn't? As with most things, unfortunately, you'll learn via trial and error, which in this instance as in most will be an expensive process. (As Ben Franklin said, "Experience is a dear teacher, but fools will learn at no other.")

   c. Speaking of costs, the price you'll be charged will likely be high, as you will not be a high volume user.

   d. Integration of data. It all comes back to this. And it is difficult, if not impossible, to get past the fact that it is significantly harder for an institution focusing on all the things it has to do to see the importance of various pieces of data than it is for a person or team that specializes in doing just that.

4. Hire an investigator that uses professional research firms. If you didn't know this was coming, you just weren't paying attention. Regardless, this method will ensure that you get the information you need, at the best price, and analyzed in a way that makes sense.

LOS ANGELES COUNTY COURT SEARCHES: AN INSIDE LOOK

In this section, you'll get a first-hand look at the Los Angeles (LA) County court system, probably one of the nation's most difficult to navigate. LA County Superior Court really consists of five courts, owing to LA's interminable sprawl (in case it's not obvious enough, I don't care much for LA, frankly). And as noted in the previous section (on ways to do court searches—buy vs. build strategies), I am by no means advocating that you conduct court searches on your own. Having said that, I am reminded of an experience I had in college. As a Rutgers University freshman, I took calculus, presuming that since I'd had it in high school, it would be a breeze. Studying for my first test, I wisely opted to concentrate on what I already knew, completely ignoring topics I didn't understand. Voilà, a 44 (out of 100). Calling my brother, then a sophomore Electrical Engineering major also at Rutgers, I discussed my grade. His response? "What's the matter with you? You're too smart to fail. You're going to come over to my dorm twice a week, and I will teach you. I'll show you more than you'll ever need for your tests, and that way you'll always get an A." As I was in no position to argue, I did it his way, miraculously ending up with a B+ for the semester. (I ran out of exams.)

So what's the point? Simple: You may be thinking, as this section ensues, that you'll never need to know this level of detail. But knowing it will ensure that you'll always be able to obtain whatever court searches and documents you need, whether someone else handles it for you, or you do it yourself.

Rather than explain LA's Byzantine court system myself, I have opted to let an expert do it for you. What follows is the result of a series of e-mail interviews I conducted with Karen Wolfe & Sheri Fister-Annable, owner-operators of Research & Retrieval, better known as R&R, the foremost court researcher in the LA area and a service I have used for nearly 20 years. (Note that the answers provided have been quoted directly; I did reorder certain questions after reviewing them and realizing it would make more sense to do so.)

Me: Sheri/Karen, exactly how long have you been handling LA court searches and document retrievals? (Sorry if this is like asking your age.)

Sheri/Karen: We have been in this business since February of 1990. Prior to opening Research and Retrieval Karen worked at another company doing this same type of work for 2 years and Sheri worked at the same company for a little over 1 year.

Me: Please explain the various courts that comprise the LA County system.

Sheri/Karen: The court is comprised of 12 districts that include 48 different court locations. You are able to access both civil and criminal information that covers the entire county through the main system's computer. However, to pull any case files or documents you still need to go to each individual courthouse.

Me: How does LA compare in terms of difficulty to other areas? Why?

Sheri/Karen: The thing that can give you the most difficulty is the actual geographical size of the area that LA County covers. The LA courts serve close to 10 million people and cover a 4,000 square mile county. To add to the problem the courts are usually located in densely populated areas known for their traffic and lack of parking.

Me: Is this a problem mostly because of the time it takes to then retrieve documents at each locale? Can the average person quickly discern the location they'll need to hit to retrieve their documents?

Sheri/Karen: The problem with Los Angeles Courts is that there are so many and they are so far apart—you can index civil at any branch court—but you may for example be indexing in Torrance and your case is in San Fernando but that court is over 45 minutes away to go over there and get the file.

There is no public computer system to index criminal—you can pay a $5.00 per name fee at all courts but they aren't as accurate as the downtown branch court in Los Angeles. And again once you locate the case # you have to know the codes in order to determine which branch court the case is located at.

We have 12 districts and 48 court locations ... it isn't as easy as it looks as the courts are so widespread.

Me: How much of the information is available online?

Sheri/Karen: You can go to the court's website at lasupercourt.org and obtain the following:

If you have the case number for a civil case most docket sheets are available to print. Documents for some cases are also becoming available online. Before accessing any of [the] court's information, you must first set up an account with the court using a credit card.

Me: But most complaints are still available only manually, correct?

Sheri/Karen: Yes, most doc[ument]s still have to be pulled manually.

You can conduct a countywide civil, small claims, family law or probate search by name for $4.75 per name. Any documents that may be available can be purchased for a flat rate of $7.50 per download up to 10 pages. Anything over 10 pages is $.07 per page with a $40.00 limit.

Keep in mind that these types of searches and document requests may return incomplete information as the courts all started putting their information onto the system at different times. Some of the courts provide information back as far as 1995 while some [are only] as recent as 2005.

You can conduct a countywide criminal search for $4.75 per name [for] up to 99 names, then the search fee is $4.50 per name. No criminal documents are available online.

Me: The key phrase here seems to be "that may be available." Can you estimate the percentage of complaints that are available online now?

Sheri/Karen: I would say less than 30 percent.

Me: How does one know which of the courts to search?

Sheri/Karen: There are 13 main superior court locations with many other court locations spread out throughout the county. Each court has specific case numbers that identify that particular court. For example, #BC252481 would indicate the case file is located at the Central courthouse in downtown Los Angeles where[as] #PC007853 would indicate the case file is located in the North Valley courthouse in San Fernando and so on.

Me: Is there a chart for people to use to decode this information?

Sheri/Karen: Yes, for the Upper Superior level, but not for the Muni[cipal] level, [where] we usually have to either ask a court clerk or that information is listed on the index downtown as well.

Me: Are civil and criminal records stored in one location? If not please explain.

Sheri/Karen: No, the civil and criminal records are stored at separate locations.

You can access countywide civil information at any of the court's public computer terminals.

There is no public computer system for the criminal index. You can do a hand search on microfiche that may or may not cover the entire county. To be 100 percent sure you need to submit the search to the clerks and pay the $4.75 per name fee. If you submit more than 5 names you will have to wait 24 hours, more than 10 names may take up to one week.

Me: Again, most documents are still retrievable only manually, at the correct location, right?

Sheri/Karen: Yes.

Me: Walk us through an actual search and retrieval—that is take us to, then through the buildings, where one goes, etc.

Sheri/Karen: You can access civil information through the public computer terminals in room 111 at the Stanley Mosk Courthouse @ 111 N. Hill Street, Los Angeles, CA.

If you want to view any case files or order copies you must go to room 112 and fill out a request form with the case information on it. You hand the request form to the clerk and if the file is available, they hand you the case file. You fold back the pages of any documents you need copies of and hand the file back to the clerk. Copies are $.50 per page and can be paid for by cash, check or credit card. Any copy orders under 30 pages are usually filled that same day. Larger copy orders may take anywhere from 1 to 2 days or up to a week depending on the page count.

To access criminal information you must go to the Clara Short-ridge Foltz Criminal Justice Center @ 210 W. Temple Street, Los Angeles, CA.

You can either index the name yourself, using the microfiche system, or place the request with the clerks as explained above.

If you want to view any case files or order copies you again request the file from the clerk. After viewing the file and paper clipping any documents you want copies of, you fill out a request form with the case information and document title, date filed etc. and hand the file and list of documents needed back to the clerk. She will hand you back a copy of the request form to take to the 5th floor to pay for your copies. After you have paid for your copies you will need to bring the receipt back to the clerk on the 2nd floor so they can start processing your copy request.

Me: When would a file be unavailable? Archived? Lost? How often does this occur? Are cases archived according to a fixed schedule or via some other means?

Sheri/Karen: Each court does have a list, by case number, on what the cut off is for cases housed there and cases sent to archives. Some of the branch courts archive their cases sooner because of space issues so the cases they send downtown may be more recent because they simply don't have the space to hold them.

Me: How does one make copies? What is the cost? Is change needed? How do you send the documents to the client? Straight from the court? etc.

Sheri/Karen: All copy jobs are ordered through the court clerks. Copies are $.05 per page unless certification is needed. The court charges $6.00 per certification and can certify by document or entire case file. The documents can be returned either by FedEx, fax or scanned and emailed to any location requested.

Me: Any chance these records will get digitized?

Sheri/Karen: The courts are always changing and updating their systems. Maybe sometime in the future there will be a fool-proof system in place with every case and every document available online. As for now, there is no such system in place.

Me: What else am I missing? What else do people doing court searches in LA need to know?

Sheri/Karen: Cases are many times not available or at the locations they should be. Because of the volume of cases being heard downtown another courthouse called CCW or Central Civil West has been opened. This court hears special proceeding cases and the files are always in a department and must be ordered directly from the department clerks. This process usually takes several days. Also, if a case file is with the judge, the research attorney, checked out to a staff member or out for an upcoming hearing the file will not be available. These files can stay unavailable for as much as 30 days or more. Also, older cases are housed either in the basement of that particular courthouse or shipped to the main "archive" facility downtown. Very old cases are on microfilm reels and housed in the archives at the downtown courthouse.

Me: How do people reach you? (full names/phone/email)

Sheri/Karen: Research & Retrieval Contact: Sheri Fister-Annable or Karen Wolfe Tel: (310) 798-8100 Email: order@researchand retrieval.com

HOW TO READ A LAWSUIT

So far this chapter has explained about the importance of broad-based court searches, what courts are searchable online versus those that must be searched manually, how to retrieve court records, and how to go about conducting such a search. What it has not done, so far, is explain how to actually read a court case, once it is obtained. You might think reading a court case would be as simple as, well, reading. That would be true, if lawsuits were written by people not seemingly trying to be confusing (I'd apologize to my friends who are lawyers here, but they know they are guilty of drafting brutally dense and arcane documents, and are thus not owed anything but a rebuke, or worse).

Rather than talking in hypotheticals, I thought it would be more instructive to take you through the process of perusing an actual court case or two. Let's think back to the Edward Ehee/Viper debacle mentioned earlier in this chapter. Recall the suit filed by Senyon Kim against Mr. Ehee, Viper, and Global. Step 1 is to understand what documents you actually need; as mentioned earlier, I'd always obtain, whenever possible, the docket sheet, complaint, and final disposition. There is an argument to be made for retrieving other records, as well; answers to a complaint, in some instances, can have some useful information, for example. But on balance, it is not, I believe, cost effective to embark on what I would consider to be a fishing expedition by looking for and obtaining every last document stored in the case file.

The docket sheet can be described as a chronological index of a suit's history, and this is the place where I'd begin when reviewing a suit. This said, be cognizant that at this point all you are attempting to learn is who sued whom, when that suit was filed, and, hopefully, the amount being sought and what was the final outcome to the action. What the docket will not do is provide any information as to the actual genesis of the disagreement at hand; for this, you'll need the complaint.

The complaint details the guts of the suit. It will reiterate some information contained in the docket sheet, including the litigants' names, the case number, the date the action was filed, and where the suit was filed. It will then go on to list all of the charges being brought, whereas the docket often will list only one cause of action (this was certainly true in the *Kim v. Ehee* suit, as will be explicated below). Most critically, the complaint is the document that explains what the suit is really about. For the layman, the downside to complaints is the legalese, which tends to be repetitive, sometimes confusing, and almost always verbose, all of which can obscure the suit's central themes that may be or are of concern to you, the investor.

The final disposition is what it sounds like: a document that says when a suit has been closed (dismissed), settled, or both. It may sound obvious, but I'd be remiss if I didn't point out that a suit that is open/pending will not have a final disposition record attached to the file. Furthermore, the docket sheets in pending actions may not be clear as to exactly where the suit stands, because of delayed recording of events that have transpired or simply because a suit is languishing and has not seen any action for some time. In any event, when a suit has been closed, there typically will be some record of this, though this document may not necessarily be termed "final disposition" or final anything, for that matter. Note that when there isn't a readily available final disposition record, referring back to the docket sheet will be the way to discover what happened to that case.

THE DOCKET

Returning to the *Kim v. Ehee* case, the docket sheet, attached at Addendum 6.13, is a good starting point. The docket, here a "Register of Actions," is in reverse chronological order, so you'll need to proceed to page three of the three-page record to see the beginning of the suit. In any case, the court is identified clearly at the top of each page, as is the case number (helpful in keeping various records together, and discrete from other records) and the case name. Reading upwards from the bottom of page three, you see first that the complaint was filed for "breach of contract" on July 27, 2000. (As alluded to earlier, the complaint, to be discussed next, actually lists 11 causes of action, only one of which is breach of contract.) A summons was issued on this same date. Similar to a summons presented for a traffic violation, a summons is the piece of paper that is sent to the defendant and that commences the lawsuit. The summons requires the defendant to respond within a certain number of days, most commonly by either filing an appearance, an answer or a motion to dismiss the complaint that is attached to the summons (although a complaint is not always attached to a summons).

Although docket sheets present somewhat arcane information, and are certainly not the most interesting reading, someone needs to go through them. If you don't have a lawyer on staff, or are tired of waiting for that lawyer to read and decipher materials for you, or are not hiring someone else to analyze the records for you (or even if you are, returning to the "it never hurts to have knowledge theory" espoused above), the following should help you interpret a typical docket sheet. As you get more experienced reviewing these records, you'll learn to skip over many of the items cited, allowing yourself to concentrate on finding the few pieces of data you need to know (when the case was filed, and what was its outcome). One final note: different court clerks enter things differently, as there is, of course, no one key that everyone uses (heaven forbid that the legal system should operate in a way that makes it easy for the layman). So abbreviations and other shorthand used here might not be precisely replicated by a court clerk in, say, Texas or New York. Anyway, as my seven-year-old is fond of saying, moving on.

Other items, again in reverse chronological order, can be explained as follows (you'll note that certain items on the docket sheet have been skipped; these were deemed to be too repetitive even for this discussion):

"Plan I status conference date: Hearing set for Dec-29-2000 ..." This refers to a case management plan, more often called a case management order (CMO) or scheduling order. This is a pretrial meeting in which the attorneys advise the judge about what is occurring in the case, how long they expect the trial to last, whether a settlement is being negotiated, and so forth.

This is one of the notations I'd gloss over in the future (others to be scanned then ignored going forward are marked with an asterisk (*), following).

Summons filed. This is a summons filed by the plaintiff, who also has to file a proof of service (below) after serving the summons on the defendant. The defendant responds by answer, motion to dismiss or appearance of some kind; the next item, in fact, details the defense's answer in this suit.

Order to show cause re dismissal/sanctions (mailing) from 12/29/00.... An order to show cause is a type of motion, typically used when someone is in a rush or wants to limit the responding parties' time to respond and get a court hearing or ruling on an expedited basis. Here, the order to show cause re dismissal/sanctions likely means the defendant responded to the summons and complaint by seeking a dismissal of the action and sanctions on the plaintiff (for filing a spurious suit, presumably). How do you know this order was filed by the defendant, and not the plaintiff? The docket does not make this clear, but context does. If the plaintiff seeks a dismissal of the action, something he can do at any time, the docket makes this evident and terms it something straightforward. (In fact, here this actually happened, albeit much later, on October 9, 2001, with the citation reading "Request for dismissal, with prejudice compl[ain]t only.") It is only the defendant who would need to file an order to show cause motion regarding a case's dismissal.

"OSC [order to show cause] dismissal/sanctions hearing set for Feb-13-2001 ..." This is exactly what it seems, finally. The court docket is merely reflecting that a hearing date has been set to review the defendants' motion to dismiss the action and have sanctions placed on the plaintiff.

Proof of service. Proof of service, as anyone who obsessively watched 1960s/70s police dramas like *The Rookies* and *Mod Squad* knows, is an affirmation that the defense was served papers indicating a suit is being filed.

Req[uest] to enter default—entered as to: Edward S. Ehee; Viper Investment Group; Global Equity Partners. This is very odd, as a default or a request to enter a default is made when the defense fails to respond to a suit.

Here, this belies the fact that the defense has made a motion to a defense, which certainly counts as a response. To understand this, one would have to contact the attorney directly.

Status and setting conference statement by Senyon Kim. Before you have a conference with the judge, you need to submit a summary of the case, so the judge knows what there is to conference about.

Declaration confirming service. This is exactly what it sounds like: the court is indicating that the defense was properly alerted to the suit.

Supplemental to status & settlement conference statement. Moving on.

Response to OSC re dismissal & sanctions. This is filed by the plaintiff, who is answering the defense's motion to close the case. Unless the plaintiff agrees to dismiss the suit, which typically would occur only if they suddenly realized their suit had no merit, or thought the suit itself would be too expensive to litigate, or most likely, reached a settlement with the defense, the plaintiff is obligated to respond to the plaintiff's motion to dismiss by asserting that the case should continue.

Declaration of Edward S. Ehee in supp[ort] of m[o]t[io]n to set aside default. This is fairly straightforward. Mr. Ehee is telling the court that a default should not be entered because he had indeed answered the complaint.

Declaration of Hartford Brown in supp[ort] of mtn to set aside default. Mr. Brown, confirmed to be an attorney, likely represented Mr. Ehee. Anyone with evidence/facts to submit must do so via a declaration, otherwise that evidence is not entered into the court proceedings. A declaration is a synonym for an affidavit.

Mtn to s/a (set aside) default—grtd (granted). 10 days lve (leave) to ans[wer] or otherwise respond. Req[uest] for sanctions denied. You win some, you lose some. Mr. Ehee was victorious in his efforts to have the default entry removed (a default, if it is not already clear, is an automatic loss for the defense). He lost, however, in his attempt to have the plaintiff penalized for filing the suit in the first place.

Note, too, that this was filed on April 10, 2001. On April 17, 2001, Mr. Ehee indeed filed an answer to the complaint, ensuring he fulfilled the court's order to answer within a ten day period.

Ntc (notice) of mtn for continuance of trial date, Calendar Motion: Continuance of trial date hearing set for Sep(tember) 28-2001.... A continuance is what you might suspect it is: that is, a delay. Here, one side is seeking to move the trial date, and a hearing date is thus set to determine whether that will occur.

Deft (defendant) Edward S. Ehee, Viper Investment Group & Global Equity Partners' ex parte appl[ication] for an OST (order shortening time) for defts' mtn. "Ex parte" shows that only one party has been in contact with the court. Except for things like Child Protection Orders or search warrants, where notifying both sides would adversely affect the goal of the action, ex parte applications are somewhat frowned upon.

Declaration of Edward S. Ehee in supp[ort] of mtn for summary judgment. Summary judgment is a decision made based on statements and evidence (recall the declarations cited above) presented for the record, obviating the need for a trial. A summary judgment occurs when the facts of the case are not in dispute, and one party is entitled to judgment as a matter of law. This last point is critical, for the court at this point is not making any findings of fact, but is instead just making a finding of law. This can only transpire if both parties agree on what constitute the undisputed material facts in the suit. The court could also rule for summary judgment if some facts are disputed but are themselves determined by the court to be immaterial. If, on the other hand, there are facts that are disputed and material, according to the judge, then summary judgment will not be issued.

Mtn to cont[inue] trl (trial) date—off calendar by moving party. This means the plaintiff (the moving party) withdrew the motion. Subsequent notes show that a summary judgment was granted on October 5, 2001. A summary judgment denotes the fact that the case was adjudicated (closed) without a trial.

In my experience, cases are withdrawn and dismissed because they get settled. It is an enduring frustration that my theory cannot really be proven, and more so, that settlement figures are not made clear in court records. The court's view, however, is that the public's right to know is not as important as the court's desire to move cases through the system. Settlements are encouraged as a means of unclogging the court's calendar; in order to effectuate settlements, confidentiality regarding their terms is needed, as otherwise many litigants would not settle because doing so could then look like an admission of guilt.

THE COMPLAINT

Okay, now we get to the nitty gritty of the suit. The complaint is at least written using words, rather than cockamamie abbreviations, and is clear about who is charging whom with what offense. The primary trouble with complaints is that they are excruciatingly repetitive; this can be handled, of course, by familiarizing yourself with the language used in common complaints, thereby teaching yourself how to ignore passages that may be legally necessary but that do nothing to add to your edification of the suit at hand.

Recall from the Ehee case study that a suit was filed in July 2000 by Senyon Kim. Named as defendants, as the complaint makes clear, were "Edward S. Ehee, an individual; Viper Investment Group, a business entity form unknown; Global Equity Partners, a business entity form unknown; [and] Does 1-100, inclusive."

A "business entity form unknown" simply is saying that the plaintiff does not know whether the defendant entity is a corporation, partnership or sole proprietorship.

Does 1-100 is shorthand for John Does, not the word "does" as in "to do" or a female deer. The reason for this entry is to put forth the idea that the plaintiff does not know all the possible participants in the matter that has prompted the suit, and thus needs to use fictitious names to represent these "unknown" other parties, such that the statute of limitations will not run against the plaintiff. When the identities of the John Doe defendants are learned, the caption and complaint are then amended to reflect the more specific information, converting the John Does to named defendants.

The first thing you'll notice in complaints is that for the first few pages, they don't tell you what the suit is actually about. In this instance, on page two, at the end of paragraph one, we are alerted to the fact that the plaintiff is suing because monies given to the defendants have not been returned, despite demands for that money. The story, however, is not spelled out here. Rather, this complaint follows a typical pattern, first laying out the parties; in this case page one and almost all of page two are devoted to describing who is suing whom. It is only after this that the story gets told.

Looking for this story is ultimately the most efficient means of quickly ascertaining what a suit is about and how serious the charges are (of course what adds to your analysis of relative seriousness is the pattern of behavior idea hammered home throughout this book). Here, points four and five, which are the last paragraph on page two and continue on through the second paragraph on page three, is what you really need to know. Let's pick it apart.

Point 4. " ... beginning in 1994, and continuing to the present date, Defendants, Edward S. Ehee, an individual; Viper Investment Group, a business entity form unknown; Global Equity Partners, a business entity form unknown; solicited plaintiff to entrust monies with defendants ... for investment. Defendants ... further represented that they would use their best efforts to obtain a favorable return on plaintiff's monies together with additional monies earned by way of any profits, gains, and increment thereon, and that said monies would promptly be returned to Plaintiff on demand. Plaintiff has made demand for the return of all monies entrusted to defendants.... To date, defendants have refused to return said monies."

A bit wordy, but the root of this suit is clear: Mr. Kim invested money with Mr. Ehee and Mr. Ehee's entities beginning in 1994. In March 2000, Mr. Ehee and his entities signed a promissory note indicating they owed

Mr. Kim $300,000. When Mr. Ehee was asked to return Mr. Kim's money, he refused, in contravention of the note.

Point 5, Sentence One: "On or about March 30, 2000, defendants, Edward S. Ehee, an individual in his capacity as an agent for defendants; Viper Investment Group, a business entity form unknown; Global Equity Partners, a business entity form unknown; signed a promissory note acknowledging that Defendants hold funds on account of plaintiff in the approximate amount of $300,000." The skinny? Allegedly, Mr. Kim invested $300,000 in Mr. Ehee and Mr. Ehee's companies, with Mr. Ehee signing a document confirming that this money was to be repaid by a certain date.

Sentences Two, Three, and Four: "Under the terms of said promissory note, Defendants agreed to pay Plaintiff the sum of $200,000 on or before June 30, 2000. Defendants further agreed in said promissory note (misspelled in the complaint as not) to pay plaintiff the sum of $100,000 on or before December 31, 2000. A copy of said promissory note is attached to this complaint and listed as Exhibit 1." These sentences are self-explanatory.

Sentence Five: "To date, defendants have failed to tender the payment due on or before June 30, 2000." This sentence is the crux of the suit: the plaintiff lent the defendant money, asked for the payment according to the contract, but was not repaid. You now have at least the framework for why the suit was filed, though reading the rest of complaint can and does, in this instance, flesh out particulars that help you gauge whether the hedge fund manager is reputable.

At this point, the complaint goes on to list, and then detail, 11 separate charges, or counts, for which Mr. Kim, the plaintiff, is seeking a ruling by the court and more specifically, monetary redress. As noted earlier, the delineation of these charges, which takes place beginning at the end of page three and is marked "First cause of action," can be somewhat repetitive. This section will hopefully teach you tricks you can use to get past the recurring themes (sort of like the fake crab sushi restaurants stuff in nearly every roll) and move directly to the meat.

The 11 charges in this complaint are Conversion, Breach of covenant of good faith and fair dealing, Breach of fiduciary duties, Deceit, General Negligence, Negligent Infliction of Emotional Distress, Negligent Misrepresentation, Intentional Infliction of Emotional Distress, Breach of Contract, Conspiracy, and Fraud (the granddaddy of them all).

As with the docket sheet analysis, I'll describe what these charges really mean, in this case and in general, while also marking with an asterisk those charges that I consider to be somewhat standard and not as important, frankly, in your review of future complaints. Conversely, charges like fraud as well as some others that will be explained below are quite significant though the names for these charges (conversion is a good example) may seemingly imply that they are relatively innocuous.

Conversion. Recall that the 'Lectric Law Library definition of *conversion* is "the unlawful turning or applying the personal goods of another to the use of the taker, or of some other person than the owner. . . ."). Mr. Kim's basic contention, as spelled out in points 8–13, over pages three and all of page four, is that the defendants took his money, and instead of returning it, used it for their own personal benefit, causing Mr. Kim a host of ills, for which he sought various damages. As you can see, this took over one page of lawyerly lingo to describe; what follows is a breakdown of this section, designed to help you skim the charges presented after conversion and cut to the quick in a reasonable amount of time.

* Point 8. "Plaintiff hereby repeats, re-alleges and repleads paragraphs 1 through 7, inclusive and by this reference incorporates the same as though fully set forth herein." This sentence is utilized at the outset of each new cause of action (though the number of paragraphs considered to be inclusive increases with each passing charge), and serves to tell the court that everything said in the part of the complaint that comes before the causes of action is considered repeated for each cause of action.

What does it tell you? Nothing. So ignore it.

Point 9. "On or before July 1, 2000 Defendants and each of them, took the monies entrusted to them by Plaintiff and converted the same for their own use." This is a little wordy, but generally gets to the heart of the charge.

Point 10. "On or about June 1, 2000 Plaintiff made a written demand for the return of the monies on or before June 30, 2000. Defendants and each of them have continued to fail and/or refuse to return the monies to plaintiff." A copy of said written demand is hereby attached to this complaint and listed as Exhibit 2. Translation: Plaintiff can prove that it asked for its money back, to no avail.

Point 11. "Defendants' refusal to pay plaintiff the monies entrusted to defendants have compelled plaintiff to engage legal counsel, incur costs, and to initiate litigation to recover such monies." Part of every lawsuit is the idea that the defendants' actions somehow caused damages to the plaintiffs. No damages, no suit. This point is setting up the damages idea.

Point 12. "As a direct and proximate cause of the conduct of defendants and each of them, plaintiff has sustained damages according to proof, including benefits claimed and other economic losses, including attorney's fees, loss of credit, interest on borrowed money, the value of the plaintiff's time in prosecuting this action, travel and other incidental expenses and costs, and has suffered embarrassment and humiliation, physical and severe mental and emotional distress and discomfort, all to Plaintiff's detriment and damage in amounts not fully ascertained within the jurisdiction of this court and according to proof."

Though not laying out specific numbers, this point naturally follows what I mentioned above, that is, for a case to proceed, the plaintiff has to be able to show it was actually harmed by the defendant's actions, not just that those actions were wrong. "According to proof" refers to what the plaintiff can and will prove, while benefits claimed is a mystery (possibly referring to the idea that the plaintiff suffered economic damages beyond just the money he lost). All in all, this term is not important.

Point 13. "At all material times and in doing the things alleged herein, defendants and each of them, knew that plaintiff relied on the assistance as promised by Defendants in their fiduciary capacity as investment counselors. Nevertheless, acting fraudulently, oppressively, maliciously, and outrageously toward the plaintiff with conscious disregard for plaintiff's known rights and with the intention of wrongfully interfering with Plaintiff's prospective economic advantage and property interest in such benefits and of intentionally causing or willfully disregarding the probability of causing unjust and cruel hardship and severe emotional and physical distress to plaintiff, defendants and each of them, withheld benefits as alleged. The aforementioned acts of defendants and each of them, were willful, malicious, and oppressive and justify the awarding of exemplary and punitive damages."

Quite a mouthful. The key phrases here? "Fiduciary capacity as investment counselors," "acting fraudulently," and "justify the awarding of exemplary and punitive damages." By asserting that the defendants had fiduciary capacity, the plaintiff is saying that he engendered special trust to the defendant; www.onlinewbc.gov/docs/starting/glossary.html defines a fiduciary as a "Person or company entrusted with assets owned by another party (beneficiary), and is responsible for investing the assets until they are turned over to the beneficiary." Acting fraudulently needs no further explanation. *Exemplary and punitive damages* are synonymous, and refer to damages awarded for particularly egregious behavior and in amounts that exceed the plaintiff's actual loss.

Breach of covenant of good faith and fair dealing. The free dictionary provides a lucid description of this covenant: "a general assumption of the law of contracts, that people will act in good faith and deal fairly without breaking their word, using shifty means to avoid obligations, or denying what the other party obviously understood. ..."[15]

Looking at the complaint, we find in Point 18 that the Plaintiff claims to have a "limited ability to speak the English language" and is not versed in U.S. customs or investment methods, all of which led him to rely on the defendants to invest his money. Points 14–21, excluding Point 18, either entirely or substantively repeat statements made in the previous cause of action, and thus can be overlooked. Note that a trick to quickly seeing this is to let your eyes wander and eventually focus on spotting the very over-lawyered language you will otherwise hope to avoid in your life. For example, Point 20 contains multiple phrases that are duplicated throughout the complaint, from "direct and proximate result ..." to vast descriptions of the harms suffered by the plaintiff. Once you see these, you'll know that unless any specific numbers appear, you need not read this section as if it were a contract you were entering into regarding a $10 million deal, where every word counts, but rather can skim it as you might a memo from a wordy colleague.

Breach of fiduciary duties. The website http://fiduciary.legalview.com/ defines this as follows: "Fiduciary duties" are held by people legally responsible for handling the money of others; for example, brokers authorized to make investments for clients without first notifying them. A fiduciary is generally held to a high standard of ethics in order to ensure clients' money is not mismanaged. Breach of duty is not determined by the performance of investments. Instead, actions of the fiduciary are scrutinized to ensure responsible investing practices were followed. When determining if a broker bears legal responsibility for a client's loss, it must be determined if prudent advice was given, if the broker, in fact, was a fiduciary, and if actions taken were in the best interest of the client."[16]

Point 23 of this lawsuit asserts that the defendants were investment brokers for the plaintiff, and failed to live up to the trust granted to them by not returning plaintiff's funds "despite repeated promises to do so." While ordinarily I'd argue that this is a serious charge, in this suit it seems to be more just more of the same, albeit with a twist. This is not to suggest the plaintiff was not harmed by the defendant's actions, but rather to explain that in other suits this charge has far more of an adverse effect on the plaintiff's reputation than it seems to here.

Note, as well, that Point 25 is practically a word-for-word copy of Point 20.

Deceit. Unsurprisingly, the plaintiff here is charging the defendants with lying. Specifically, the defendants stated that they would invest the plaintiff's money with "due care" and would return that money upon demand. According to this charge, the plaintiff knew these representations were untrue.

The relevance of this, in my mind, is the character issue. If the plaintiff's allegation is true, he is not saying that Mr. Ehee and Mr. Ehee's companies suffered some kind of reversal and just couldn't pay the defendant back; no, he is averring that they had no intention of doing so, which is clearly far worse.

Here again, you'll see that Point 31 is, for all intents and purposes, Point 25 and Point 20. Meanwhile, Point 32 introduces a new monetary demand (for $1 million). As you can see, this is more than the $300,000 owed to the plaintiff, and is thus properly characterized as "punitive and exemplary damages."

* *General Negligence.* This claim replicates much of the language presented in the deceit cause directly above. The primary difference is that here, the plaintiff is simply accusing the defendants of failing to act with due care, rather than intentionally telling mistruths.

* *Negligent Infliction of Emotional Distress.* According to http://www.personal-injury-info.net/infliction-emotional-distress.htm, "Negligent infliction of emotional distress is a claim that is not widely accepted by many states and jurisdictions. The legal concept is that Person A owes a duty of care to Person B to take reasonable care to avoid causing emotional distress or injury. Many states have shunned the theory of negligent infliction of emotional distress since it is difficult to define and quantify."

Agreed. When you see this claim, unless it is the only one made, ignore it.

* *Negligent Misrepresentation.* A negligent misrepresentation claim requires there to have been a duty of care (see above), a false claim made negligently by the claimant, then relied upon by the plaintiff to the plaintiff's detriment (http://www.aicanada.ca/e/pdfs/2004-spring-17.pdf). Sure sounds like an amalgamation of the causes brought before this one.

* *Intentional Infliction of Emotional Distress.* LSU's Law Center website (http://biotech.law.lsu.edu/Courses/tortsF01/IIEM.htm) states, "The tort of intentional infliction of emotional distress has four elements: (1) the defendant must act intentionally or recklessly; (2) the defendant's conduct must be extreme and outrageous; and (3) the conduct must be the cause (4) of severe emotional distress."

As with the claim for negligent infliction of emotional distress, ultimately this is a claim without a lot of relevance to your analysis, given that it focuses more on the impact to the plaintiff's emotional state, rather than specifying other actions of the defendant, your hedge fund manager prospect, not heretofore described.

Breach of Contract. Point 53 asserts that this cause is being brought because the defendants refused to return the plaintiff's money. Here, too, a breach of contract can be a significant charge, but in this matter the charge is not adding any substantive information to your decision-making process.

Conspiracy. Point 56 says that "[d]efendants ... knowingly and willfully conspired and agreed among themselves to induce Plaintiff into entrusting his monies with defendants, and to thereafter refuse to return said funds to plaintiff." The word *conspiracy* certainly conjures up images of John F. Kennedy, Watergate, the Iraqi invasion, and other landmark historical events. In a business lawsuit context, a conspiracy could be serious, as well. Except that here, the defendants are, in actuality, simply Mr. Ehee; the corporate defendants, companies Viper and Global, are turning out to be really no more than Mr. Ehee, and so a conspiracy, though plausibly a valid legal cause of action, is not very important to you.

Fraud. Fraud is another buzzword that will give any institution the heebie-jeebies. Reading this complaint, however, it seems that the fraud here was again a reclassification of the other causes of action, rather than something dealing with a separate action or actions of Mr. Ehee. Nevertheless, the fact remains that the plaintiff did claim that Mr. Ehee and the corporate defendants "never had any intention of returning Plaintiff's funds to him upon demand" and knew the representations they were making about investing the plaintiff's money with "due care" were "false." These are stern accusations, not found in the run-of-the-mill breach of contract case, thus warranting, at least, further analysis.

As mentioned above, this suit was eventually dismissed, likely due to some type of settlement. Though settlements are often contingent on the participants not discussing their details, it can be fruitful to contact the plaintiff. While specific details will not be given, with proper questioning (to be discussed below and more completely in Chapter 12 on Interviewing) you can gain an understanding of who won the suit and even whether the two parties would do business together again (believe it or not, this happens, and is an indicator that some suits get filed as a matter of necessity rather than vitriol).

One final thought. When reviewing court cases, do not be intimidated if you are not an attorney. Yes, attorneys file suits, and are therefore more naturally able to decipher their own wind-baggery. But with practice and guidance you too can gain an understanding of the items you need to know, while avoiding the minutiae that you don't.

DOES THIS SUIT NAME MY HEDGE FUND MANAGER?

Any court search conducted on a hedge fund manager whose name is not extremely uncommon will almost always reveal the existence of lawsuits citing people with that name. The person handling your court search, whether an internal staffer or an external entity, must be alerting you to this fact, or they are doing you a greater harm than any you'd suffer by doing nothing. They also must then be able to tell you whether the suits found are relevant to the subject or not.

Some of the mechanics involved in learning how to decipher whether news stories, corporate records, regulatory actions, or lawsuits relate to the subject hedge fund manager, or just another person

(continued)

DOES THIS SUIT NAME MY HEDGE FUND MANAGER? (*Continued*)

with the same or a similar name, were discussed in Chapter 5. Still, since this is perhaps the most important tactic for you to possess, indulge me in a review and explication of some critical identification techniques:

1. *Purge the unimportant.* Certain suits can be ignored based solely on their nature, so that it is unimportant whether they relate to the subject or not. These include, but are not limited to, suits focused on personal injuries, negligence-torts, clear title/mortgage foreclosures (in which the subject is named merely to clear title and not accused of any malfeasance), and even small claims actions (unless there are many of these, and you care about the subject's personality, in which case these could be relevant).

2. *Work backwards.* By this, I mean that trying to determine whether the suit names your subject by tying information found to that subject can be fruitless and frustrating. Instead, focus on ascertaining whom the lawsuit actually names, something that is often far easier to do. How? The magic of identifiers:

   - *Middle names or initials.* Clearly, a suit naming a Robert A. Thompson is not likely to relate to your subject, Robert V. Thompson. But what happens when the suit simply names a Robert Thompson? Is the middle initial classifier now of no use to you? On the surface, it may seem so, but a little digging can sometimes uncover nuggets of value. Suppose the suit gives an address for the litigant. You know from the previous chapter that with a name and home or business address, sources like LocatePlus, IRB, Choicepoint or Merlin will lead you to a middle name, among other things. Most suits, unfortunately, will not have an address. But they might connect the individual litigant to a business name; remember, secretary of state records and Dun & Bradstreet files also often contain middle names. Or they might name a spouse or a relative; here, property records, identification sources or even news stories will lead you to a middle initial for the person cited.

   - *Spouse's names.* A spouse shown on a court case should be enough, via property records and LocatePlus, et al., to help you ascertain who the litigant is. Be careful, though, because it is not impossible, although rare, for two married couples with similar names to reside in one small geographic area. Thus, assuming a suit relates to the subject because it names as a co-defendant a woman matching the subject's wife's name can, in the immortal words of Felix Unger, make an ass out of you and me. To avoid this embarrassment, first check identification sources to see if another couple with the same names live in the area in question, then look for other corroborating or refuting data, using all the ideas expressed above and below.

- *Addresses/Age/Context.* If a suit was filed in 1988, and involves a dispute dating back to 1982, it obviously does not relate to a subject manager born in 1966. If you have already confirmed that the subject manager was working in New York City in 1995, it is extremely unlikely that he got divorced in Massachusetts in that year. If a suit names a person who was licensed as a CPA, find the CPA, rather than spending time wondering whether your subject was a CPA. A suit filed in San Francisco cannot automatically be eliminated from consideration if your manager has lived only in Southern California, but the odds of it naming the subject are greatly diminished. Finding another person with that name in San Francisco makes an even stronger case. Finally, sometimes you'll get lucky and a suit or a corresponding judgment will contain an actual home address; here, your job is simply to find a social security number for that person and compare the number to your subject's.

- *Corporate affiliations.* As mentioned, this data on a court case can be tested against that found in various corporate sources to lead to information on the litigant. Example: a Robert Thompson cited as an officer or agent of a certain company, at a certain address, not currently known to be the subject's, but located in the subject's home town. Through LocatePlus et al., you should be able to find whether the questionable Robert Thompson (the litigant) and the listed business address are linked with a social security number different from or the same as the subject's number. If this fails, corporate records might have a biography or other details relating to the litigant, details that can tell you who this person is.

(continued)

DOES THIS SUIT NAME MY HEDGE FUND MANAGER? (*Continued*)

■ *Signatures.* These can be compared to one you may have for the subject on, say, a release or other document the subject may have sent to you.

■ *Precise corporate names and locales.* If you find 10 suits naming a Master Capital LP in New York, and the subject entity is Master Capital Inc. in Boston, checking corporate and regulatory records may make it clear that these entities are entirely distinct, thus saving you time and dollars in pursuing actions that do not relate to your target.

In these examples, as with others using the aforementioned identifiers, use deductive reasoning, to determine that a suit *does not* name the subject by showing *it does* name someone else.

3. *Universality of name.* Establish how common a name the defendant actually has. Identification sources like LocatePlus and IRB offer another feature besides the ability to develop an address history, and so forth for your manager: they can develop that same information for other people with your manager's name. Why would this matter? Sometimes, as noted above, it is more efficient to establish who a litigant is, rather than start by seeking to ascertain whether that litigant is the subject. One way of learning the probability that a suit names the subject is by seeing how many people with the subject's name reside in a certain area; identification sources allow you to search, remember, by a combination of fields, so here you'd use name and state to establish some odds. The natural limit of this approach is that a suit filed six years ago on a person who lived in Boston might have nothing to do with the fact that 3 or 300 people with that name currently live in Boston; still, you can at least get some idea, in most instances, how common a name is in an area, and at times you can do better than that by actually finding the exact person named in the suit.

INTERVIEWS OF LITIGANTS

At first blush, interviewing an individual involved in litigation with the subject manager sounds as though it might yield a goldmine of information. And at times it can. If executed properly, this interview can lead you to the discovery of other lawsuits, questionable and dishonorable business practices, and a host of other impressions that did not make it into the complaint of the lawsuit itself. Tempering this, however, are a few points. Rarely is it ever worth contacting the lawyers, as they will give nothing more than name, rank and serial number, in most instances, and in fact will hurt you, oftentimes, by then contacting their client with the advice to clam up as well.

If you absolutely have to call the lawyer (to me, this should be done only when you just cannot find the litigant, or the litigant absolutely refuses to say anything, in which case calling the attorney can't hurt), try this as an introduction. "My name is ___. I represent a party who is considering a business transaction with Mr. Smith. My client wished me to speak with people that are familiar with Mr. Smith to get a better understanding of exactly whom they are dealing with." Hearing this, a lawyer may assume you are a lawyer as well and treat you as such. (Of course, you should not say you are, and if asked, should be honest that you are not.) Avoid terms like "background report," "due diligence," "business biography," and so forth. Finally, recognize what it is that you hope to gain here; at times, if the lawyer stonewalls you too, your best hope can be to have him clarify the outcome of the suit for you, if documents were not clear, or even send you documents rather than offering commentary on them.

As for contacting the plaintiff directly, do not even bother doing so in an ongoing suit against a subject; litigants will not speak about pending litigation since doing so can do nothing but jeopardize the case.

Even in cases that have been closed, litigants are typically bound by confidentiality agreements forbidding them from discussing the terms of a settlement of the case. This notwithstanding, litigants are not generally prevented from discussing the subject manager, and it is here where you should focus your efforts. One place to start is by asking the plaintiff what prompted the suit, meaning how did the situation reach the point where a lawsuit was the only means left to resolve the differences between the source and the subject manager? (You are trying to determine whether the source has sued many people, and if not, what made this matter so egregious that a suit became necessary.) This question alone may lead you down quite a meandering path; follow whatever offshoot sounds as though it might be the most relevant to an analysis of the subject's business conduct.

During an interview with a litigant, it may be necessary for you to empathize, even to the point of subtle obsequiousness, with the litigant's tirade. This does not mean you have to fuel the litigant's fire by saying things you know to be untrue. Instead, react as a therapist or trusted friend might, by consciously interjecting with an "I see what you mean" or "That sounds painful." To the extent that these gestures make the litigant feel comfortable in opening to you, a stranger, the more the better.

On the issue of calling litigants, the elephant on the table is that litigants frequently have an axe to grind. Acknowledging this, however, does not render what they say less important or less likely to be accurate. Hear them out, add what they say to other things you have learned, and go from there. Finally, as always but especially here, get the names of other people who can authenticate the litigant's comments, and interview these folks as well.

What about interviewing the subject about the litigation? Since most institutions would say that court cases in which the manager is involved are one of their biggest, if not the biggest, worries, asking the subject to describe why a suit occurred and its outcome is critical. However, after doing this a few times you'll find that everyone has what seems to be a plausible explanation for lawsuits naming them. What you really glean from these conversations then is whether a subject would admit to a suit without your asking about it; toward that end, ask a question like this, first: "Are there any lawsuits involving you or your companies that we should be aware of?" If the answer is yes, ask simply, "What happened?" These two queries will not only help answer the specific question about the suit in question but will also provide a measure of how forthright a manager is, something that will frequently prove more illuminating than the initial legal action.

WARNING SIGNS: YELLOW AND RED FLAGS FROM LITIGATION RESEARCH

As is outlined in Chapter 16, not all court cases are perceived equally. This is true both because of factors relating to hedge fund investing itself, as well as factors relating to the court cases (and frequently due to a combination of the two). An institution considering investing in a hedge fund has a lot of choices. Although the 9,000+ hedge fund number that is bandied about clearly is not representative of the number of funds in which an institution would invest (the number is probably closer to 3,000, based mostly on asset size), and even though many quality hedge funds are periodically or even permanently closed to new investors, institutional hedge fund investors still have far more choices of places to put their money than, say, a venture capitalist. (This is certainly not meant to excuse venture capitalists from due diligence.) Given this, an institutional investor looking at a hedge fund might very well be, and often is, far more likely to have a negative reaction to a court case that might hardly concern a venture capitalist. One example that almost certainly would be perceived as a red flag by an institution is a personal bankruptcy filed by a hedge fund manager. For an institution, the theory here is blatant: "If the manager can't manage his own money, why give him yours?" An entrepreneur seeking venture capital, conversely, might be viewed almost positively for having a personal bankruptcy, as this can convey a sense of risk-taking that is desired by a VC in the people it backs.

As for factors involving the court cases themselves, an institutional investor is best served by analyzing the following:

1. How central was the subject manager's role in the suit in question?
2. How many suits name the subject as a defendant?
3. What type of investing does the subject do?
4. What types of suits were found? How serious and specific were the allegations?
5. What type of investor are you?
6. How old was the subject at the time of the incident?
7. When was the suit filed?
8. Is the suit ongoing? Could it be a distraction to the manager?
9. What was the result of the suit?
10. Did the manager admit to the suit when asked an open-ended question about his legal history?

How Central Was the Subject Manager's Role in the Suit in Question?

Clearly, the closer to the heart of the suit the defendant is, the more concern you should have. A subject manager named simply because the manager was a director of a firm that is itself being sued, even for a serious charge, might be a yellow flag worthy of examination but would not rise to the red flag status unless further review demonstrated some reason to make it so. More often, in fact, additional research would render this type of action to the "no need to be concerned" pile.

How Many Suits Name the Subject as a Defendant?

The more the merrier does not apply here. Multiple suits citing the subject manager as an individual defendant are often a yellow flag, even if those suits by themselves are considered relatively unimportant. One divorce, for example, would scarcely merit a second look; three or four divorces, however, might give an institution some pause. Similarly, a suit in which a hedge fund manager has sued his gardener would undoubtedly be ignored; if that same hedge fund manager also has sued his painter, fence installer, and tree man, or has sued two or three ex-employers, now you might have an indication of a personality trait or way of conducting oneself that could merit a second look.

Other factors that weigh in here, of course, relate to the type of investing in which the manager is involved, the types of suits found, and the type of investor you are (see below).

What Type of Investing Does the Subject Do?

A distressed investor, an activist investor, a short-specialist, will sue or be sued. In fact, I'd argue that hedge fund managers in these categories who are not part of lawsuits with companies they target, as either a plaintiff or defendant, are not really doing the type of investing they claim to be handling. Like a New York City real estate developer, distressed, activists and shorts will sue and be sued.

On the other hand, the CFO of a hedge fund with four suits filed against him and accusing him of some contractual mis-steps would certainly be troubling.

What Types of Suits Were Found? How Serious and Specific Were the Allegations?

Red flags would be felony criminal matters or a misdemeanor with aggravated circumstances, particularly if subject is found or pleads guilty to these charges. Civil cases that allege fraud are sure to raise an institution's hackles; if the allegations spell out specific actions committed by the subject, rather than, as was discussed in the Ehee example, actions that are more simply described as fraud using legal lingo, the alert level should be pushed up. Finally, actions that name the subject manager individually and are outside of the province of that manager's investment philosophy, or are extremely unique to hedge fund managers, period (like the John Whittier, CSFB action) should be deemed more serious.

What Type of Investor Are You?

Are you an investor primarily focused on returns? In that case, suits speaking to a subject manager's personality will probably not affect you. Conversely, an investor seeking to reduce his stress-level, while achieving steady returns, might very well be concerned by these actions, even if they are not business-related. Still another example is an investor who is desirous of avoiding bad publicity. To this investor, a manager with a history of personal problems, even one who has shown the ability to make money, might be passed over if those problems are thought to be things that might generate bad press at some point. Finally we come to investors that are public institutions, like public school endowments; these investors are rightfully concerned with all of the above, as well as with any indication that a manager has something in his history that the institution is simply unable to overlook, given the fact that it accepts government funding.

How Old Was the Subject at the Time of the Incident?

The same issue filed at different times in a manager's life may be yield a different feeling on behalf of the institution. A DUI filed against a manager when that manager was 22 years old is still serious, especially to other people on the road at the time of the incident. But a DUI against a manager at 40 years old is arguably much worse, since this dramatically speaks to one's judgment, and possibly, to a current problem that easily can be seen to adversely affect the manager's behavior and results, to say nothing of the negative publicity that might result from a public incident.

When Was the Suit Filed?

The more recent a suit was filed, the more troublesome it may be. This does not mean, however, that a suit making specific, negative allegations, especially one that resulted in a major judgment against the manager, should be ignored. Similarly, if multiple suits name a manager over a period of decades, even if none are within the last few years, further discussion is merited.

Is the Suit Ongoing? Could It Be a Distraction to the Manager?

Here we'd return to the divorce example as a good one to demonstrate this line of reasoning. A divorce filed and closed 15 years ago, unless it was followed by two or three more divorces, is not likely to even be read by most institutions. But an ongoing divorce, and surely a publicly messy or bitter ongoing divorce, could be a distraction to the manager, and therefore would need to be monitored, even if the thought of doing so is distasteful.

Speaking of divorces, one view, and one with a lot of value, is that all states should treat divorce records as New York does: the existence of a divorce is public, but the complaint regarding that divorce is not. Yes, this is antithetical to my earlier stated belief that in principle, documentation should be available, with investors entrusted with, and deserving of, using their judgment to decide whether materials they are reviewing are important or not. Somehow, divorces seem more personal, and the thought of someone reviewing a divorce in which one might be involved is a bit of a turn-off to many people. Having said this, the laws are what they are. Divorce records can yield a treasure trove of information, from behavioral issues/abuse allegations, to other business interests, to whether a soon to be ex-wife has a piece of the subject's hedge fund, to financial pressures the subject might be under. This latter point, in fact, might then mean the manager is more prone, possibly, to shenanigans, or high risk moves, a fact that again points to the value of information being available for public review.

What Was the Result of the Suit?

A suit clearly decided in favor of the subject manager is not a concern. A suit dismissed, but without a clear idea as to why (too common a phenomenon) could be an issue. And a suit or certainly multiple suits resulting in six-figure plus judgments or settlements against the subject manager would be scary.

Did the Manager Admit to the Suit When Asked an Open-Ended Question about his Legal History?

At this point you'll have observed that although court searches are possible the most critical component of manager due diligence, there are certain limits to what you can find:

- Cases can be and often are filed outside of the main jurisdiction searches and/or at branch locations of a company.
- Available court records sometimes date back only 10 years.
- Some criminal records have been officially expunged.
- Matters can be filed in jurisdictions where the subjects have not been reported to live or work.
- Some states destroy documents.

For these reasons, we suggest asking all subjects for a complete listing of present and past litigation involving them and/or their companies. We also recommend this because it can serve as an important measure of how forthright a manager is; a manager asked to discuss his litigation history and who omits certain court cases from the discussion is someone who may very well pull the same thing the next time you ask a question he doesn't want you to know the answer to. The best approach for testing the manager, then, is to either have a brief questionnaire, or a similarly brief direct conversation, with a very open-ended lawsuit question: "Please note any lawsuits that have named you or entities in which you have been an officer, director, principal, agent or otherwise associated." Note the omission of the word "material" prior to the word "lawsuits" is intentional; most people will sprint through any opening you leave them, and by creating a debate as to the importance of a legal action you are creating a door that would allow a football offensive line to squeeze through. Do yourself a favor and keep your wording as broad as possible, since this will lead to more insight than any other means.

RECAP

This chapter, hopefully, leaves you with the following takeaways:

1. Broad-based searches are best.
2. Though number one is true, it is only true to the extent that broad searches are supplemented with targeted searches of the regions where the subject manager has lived and worked.
3. Search state and federal courts, as far back as economically feasible.
4. Search courts either online, or manually, for those courts not covered online.
5. There is no online source, or even combination of online sources, that completely covers every state or federal court in the country. *You must conduct manual searches to fill in gaps left by online resources.* New York state-level criminal searches, for example, are not available via an online database service.
6. *You must obtain actual documents.* This is to determine the import of a suit (and often, even what it was about; the Paul Westervelt Bayou whistleblower action is an incredible example of this), to learn the outcome of the suit, as well as to ascertain, most vitally, whether it relates to your subject manager or simply someone else with the same name. Not doing this is the single biggest failing of most people's due diligence efforts and is simply unacceptable (boy, does that sound like a lecture, but so be it).

   Any description of a suit should describe how the suit involves the subject, indicate the amount in question, describe what happened, and explain the status of the suit (open, closed, judgment, settled, etc.). If this is not occurring, you are missing out.
7. Ways to determine that a suit does not name your subject focus primarily on comparing identifiers, such as middle name/initial, spouse, age (meaning a suit was filed when your subject would have been a minor), addresses, and sometimes, social security numbers (though civil cases will not have this "magic pill").

(continued)

RECAP (*Continued*)

8. Reviewing documents can be time consuming and confusing at first, but it gets easier with experience.

9. Cases will be either pending (also known as active or open), closed/dismissed/discontinued, or settled. There can be some overlap; that is, a suit can be closed, based on a settlement or based on one side definitively winning, in which case a monetary judgment will typically result.

10. Because a suit is dismissed does not mean it had no merit. Most suits are settled out of court, and do not result in judgments; *this does not mean the defense did nothing wrong.* (Of course, the argument can be made that people settle nuisance suits. This always has to be taken into account, and measured against the next point, that is, the Pattern.)

11. Always, always, look for a pattern of behavior. Was a single suit filed? Or numerous actions? Was a subject repeatedly accused of the same type of behavior, over a significant amount of time? Does the manager invest using strategies that naturally lend themselves to suits, such as distressed deals or activist investments, or is the subject a straight long/short or other type of investor? Are the suits filed unusual for a hedge fund manager?

12. Know what you are looking to accomplish. Do you care mostly about making returns, or avoiding bad press? Are you concerned with a manager's personality? Are you a public institution, beholden to rules not affecting private institutions?

13. Ask for help. Good investigators will be able to answer the above questions. They won't be able to tell you what to do, nor should they, but you'll be armed with information to add to your other analyses, information that is both critical but often not presented.

CHAPTER 7

News Media: Is Nexis Your Only Option?

Alex Foster

Rather than write this chapter myself, I turned it over to Alex Foster, an expert in news media and other background investigation research. Alex has worked with BackTrack/FADV since October 2000, and has demonstrated an uncanny ability to cut to the heart of the research material while also searching as broadly as possible to ensure nothing is missed. I can think of few people more uniquely qualified to guide you in this critical portion of hedge fund manager due diligence. Finally, what Alex will not say about himself but which bears mention is that searching databases is not simply a key-punch endeavor. For those old enough to remember the Batman series, picture Adam West and Burt Ward at the Bat Computer, reading the latest plot by the Joker to destroy Gotham City after merely typing in the phrase, "Joker's latest scheme." Now return to the present and realize that this was as nonsensical for Batman and Robin as it is for a present-day researcher. Tremendous skill in utilizing databases separates those who are typists from those who are investigators. Don't get sucked in by the former.

A comprehensive review of archived media is one of the most fruitful components of public records research. Someone checking out a prospective manager now has available a few sources aggregating content from literally tens of thousands of national and local newspapers, trade journals, specialty publications, wire services, press release delivery vehicles, and assorted newsletters and academic periodicals. These database sources have powerful interfaces that allow the input of search strings of great complexity. The advantage is awesome when compared to just dropping someone's name into Google and hoping to find something amid the tangled results a search engine customarily returns.

In addition to usability and scope, there are added advantages in searching old news articles. While a tax lien, judgment, or lawsuit can be mightily damning, there are any number of steps required to get to that lien, judgment, or complaint. In the instance of a civil judgment, say, a wrong has to be committed, the wronged party has to realize same, draft a complaint and acquire standing before a court, and have a judge or jury find in their favor. You then have to trust court clerks to record the judgment in a timely manner without horribly misspelling everybody's name. You are relying on a long chain of others to recognize and redress wrongs, and obviously few spats make it as far as the courtroom door. With news searches, you only need a heads-up as it were from one of the hundreds of thousands of reporters writing about all manner of esoterica. It becomes a numbers game, and someone searching press clippings needs only an insinuation by a reporter or an ability to read between the lines to uncover a matter of potential concern. An overview of the database scene and the relevant mechanics is first in order.

THE SERVICES

There are over two dozen so-called aggregator products—the names of several of which are likely already familiar to you—that pull together the full text of more than 30,000 subsidiary publications. Dates of coverage vary by publication, but some sources have uploaded the full text of articles dating back to the 1970s and abstracts of pieces published earlier.

There is a great deal of overlap when you look at what exactly is covered by each aggregator. For instance, according to the aggregator directory service Full Text Sources Online, the *New York Times* is covered more or less by LexisNexis, Dialog, ProQuest, DataStar, and a handful of others. *Global Money Management* is covered by, among others, Westlaw and Dialog. However, Westlaw's coverage extends only as far back as 2001. Dialog gives you coverage extending a further year and change, from August 1999 to present. Meanwhile, some of the aggregators focus on matters decidedly unrelated to finance. ScienceDirect covers some academic economics names but can probably be safely ignored. Given the overlap of coverage of some sources, the better coverage of some sources by one aggregator over another, and the essential irrelevance of other aggregators, we can see that it's a good idea to concentrate one's attention.

While no one source is totally comprehensive, we have found that the following four, when used together, approximate comprehensiveness while offering a favorable legwork-to-results profile:

LexisNexis. You probably recognize this one (if not subscribe to it) as it's the granddaddy of database services. The number of publications covered by its news library—which is just a small piece of the service—is truly staggering, and its coverage of those publications is often more complete than competitors. It is not without its unique annoyances though. For instance, certain newswire services play Cain with Lexis. Not only do you get a dozen far-flung local papers running the same *AP* story with more or less modification, you have certain "news" wires aimed mainly at day-trader types rerunning the same items every couple of hours (minutes, in some cases). You often find yourself happily chugging along in a Lexis review when you hit upon 75 consecutive FlyOnTheWall.com briefs posted at 15-minute intervals saying that activist investor so-and-so has taken a 5.2 stake in company such-and-such. We'll get back to overcoming these annoyances as part of the abbreviated tutorials on Lexis and the other three services that follow. For now, just know that Lexis is key and that the dividends paid on the time invested in familiarizing yourself with it are handsome.

LexisNexis offers a heap of different subscription and payment plans. Call 1 (800) 227-4908 for details.

Westlaw. Another powerhouse. While many of the other services seem content to serve as hole-plugging companions to LexisNexis, Westlaw seems as if it's trying to position itself as an outright substitute. It's got a *long* way to go, but it does have the virtue of aggregating some local papers and oddball journals not covered by Lexis. In addition, many find its interface a bit more intuitive, and you can easily exempt wire services from your searches.

Again, there are several pricing options here. Representatives at 1 (800) 227-0721 will discuss them with you.

Dialog. Somewhere in Cary, North Carolina, Dialog's corporate headquarters, I imagine that an array of old Commodore VIC-20s hum away powering this service. Its interface is extremely poor, requiring you to compose terms with funky building blocks and wait ages for retrieval of your results. Still, enough specialty finance pieces pop up here (and not on Lexis or Westlaw) to make it worth searching.

You can fill out the form at the below URL and someone will get back to you to discuss your requirements: http://www.dialog.com/contacts/forms/member.shtml

Factiva. An expensive necessity, this was originally founded as a Reuters-Dow Jones content delivery service. When you want to see exactly how badly your hedge fund manager's stock picks fared from that mid-90s

Barron's roundtable they participated in, you'll probably find yourself using Factiva.

Factiva promises to get back to you within 48 hours. 1 (800) 369-0166.

In addition to these services, there are some industry rags not covered by any aggregator at all. In these instances, you really have no choice but to plunk down the often outrageous subscription costs and search their websites directly. *Hedge Fund Alert*, for instance, is a fairly indispensable source. Unless your buddy has a stack of back issues in his basement, you'll have to pay the $2,300 cost of a subscription if you want to do this diligence component correctly.

Lastly, it's quite likely many readers already have Bloomberg subscriptions and terminals. This is an excellent, albeit very costly, complementary resource, but if you're already subscribed, by all means use what you have at your disposal.

SOME CHEAT SHEETS

Comprehensive tutorials are quite beyond the scope of the present volume. The various aggregator services hold periodic training sessions around the country. Further, they're quite mindful of their respective price points and provide customer service at a level that supports them. This book's price point gets you only the following cheat sheets listing a few of the more useful terms, their meanings, and an example of each. Hopefully the concluding discussion on general process and mindset adds a bit of value.

LexisNexis

Lexis is fairly sprawling collection of separate databases. The syntax used in composing search strings is common to each, more or less. We are focusing here on the news libraries. When you log on there, you will probably see a bunch of tabs toward the top of the page. You will probably have the option of clicking on "News." This will bring you to a page with a few input boxes for the terms you wish to search for, as well as a bunch of drop down boxes that can be used to limit things a bit and focus your searches. This lends a certain ease to things, but I would instead suggest clicking the "General" tab instead, which gets you to a stripped-down page dominated by one large box for inputting your search terms. This forces you to script a proper search string ahead of time, but the string you compose can be of great complexity. The time spent in putting that string together should be repaid when fewer irrelevant documents are returned. Plus you'll have a written record afterward showing exactly what you searched. Similarly,

TABLE 7.1 Lexis Search String Menu

()	Used to set terms apart	
AND	Must contain both terms	Marino AND Bayou
AND NOT	Excludes subsequent words from	
results	(Bayou Management) AND NOT (Army Corps of Engineers)	
OR	Can contain either term	Marino OR Bayou
PRE/N	Must be positioned no more than N number of words before	Bayou PRE/2 Management
W/N	As above but order unimportant	Management W/2 Bayou
W/P	Terms within the same paragraph	(Bayou Management) W/P Marino
HLEAD	Terms in headline or first paragraph	HLEAD(Bayou Management)
BYLINE	Articles authored by so-and-so; used in conjunction with 'NOT' when subject shares name with a journalist	(Daniel PRE/2 Marino) AND NOT(BYLINE(Marino))
!	Root expander	(Dan! Marino) would return Dan Marino, Daniel Marino, dancing Marino, etc.
*	Wildcard	Br*an would get both Brian and Bryan
CAPS	Capitalizes first letter of word(s)	
ALLCAPS	Word in all capitals	
AND DATE	Followed by BEF or AFT and actual dates to limit search	(Bayou Management) AND DATE AFT 01/01/2005 returns all Bayou articles datelined after January 1, 2005.
AND LOAD-DATE	Similar to above but goes by date when articles were updated to Lexis—useful when updating old searches	(Bayou Management) AND LOAD-DATE AFT 01/01/2005

you should be capturing the text of any articles you see that seem at all important for later reference. Those wire items noting someone has reached the Rule 8.3 1 percent ownership threshold for a UK security are probably not the most important articles you will find. Something showing a large redemption or the departure of senior staff just may be. See Table 7.1.

TABLE 7.2   Westlaw Search String Menu

&	Equivalent to AND in Lexis
%	AND NOT
+N	N number of words before (PRE/N as in Lexis)
/N	Within N number of words, order unimportant
/P	Within the same paragraph
DA()	Limits by date; for instance & DA(AFT 10/10/2001) would give you everything after October 10, 2001

Westlaw

It's actually quite easy to create search strings directly on the Westlaw site if you're a drop down menu kind of person. The key thing to remember here is that Westlaw is not as forgiving as Lexis when constructing phrases and applying terms. Phrases have to be designated by quotes, as a blank space between words is interpreted as 'OR.' For instance, *red apple* would be read by Lexis as (red apple) whereas Westlaw would understand it as (red OR apple). In Westlaw, you would isolate it with quotation marks: "red apple." Parentheses are still used to separate multipart terms. The root-expander and wildcard characters are the same as in Lexis. See Table 7.2.

Dialog

After reading this section and contacting a Dialog rep but before attempting to actually use the service, I suggest placing bottles of gin and Advil at the ready. You will be making frequent resort to both as a result of Dialog's needlessly poor interface. This is an extremely abbreviated cheat sheet. Proper documentation—hundreds of pages of it—is available in the Blue Sheets section of Dialog's website. The AND and OR operators are the same as in Lexis. Multiword constructs have to be set apart with parentheses, and spaces between words are substituted with open and closed parentheses—(such()as()this). Wildcards and truncating characters exist, but using them can send Dialog into spasms, effectively derailing your search. I would urge against using them.

One of the oddities of Dialog is that you are able/forced to choose from a set of particular data files before completing your search. Basically, you will enter your terms and Dialog will spit names back out at you. Some of these names are single sources—*PR Newswire* or the *Boulder Daily Camera*—others collect articles from multiple sources. We'd recommend, generally, keeping all the multisource sets and applicable local media. The remainder can probably be ignored safely. See Table 7.3.

TABLE 7.3   Dialog Search String Menu

Nn	Within N number of words—(Bayou(2n)(Management OR affiliates))—order unimportant
Nw	As above but preceding by N number of words
Pd=, pd>, pd<	Limits by date, with date entered as YYYMMDD. For instance, (Bayou()Management) AND pd=>20051010 returns stories naming Bayou published on or after October 10, 2005
Py=, py>, py<	As above but denotes year of publication

Factiva

Factiva, like Westlaw, has a number of drop down boxes on the page from which you perform your searches. These can be used to remove duplicate articles, limit your searches to particular journals or groups of journals that you yourself define, restrict your search by date, and so on. In consequence, you really only have to remember the basic operators for proximity searches. See Table 7.4.

ORDER OF OPERATION

Lexis is the ideal starting point when doing this sort of research. In 9 out of 10 instances, you'd be in pretty good shape if it were also your end point. Unfortunately there's no real way to tell in advance whether you're looking at the 1 in 10 where supplementary excavation in the likes of Dialog and Westlaw will yield any treasure. You therefore really need to look at everything available.

Do enough of these, and patterns will emerge. The heavy lifting will be accomplished with the aid of Lexis. Dialog is useful in patching holes of particular types. For instance, some of the publications covered there but not elsewhere mean articles with a fixed income focus will turn up. Westlaw is easy, and has truly respectable coverage of many local papers.

TABLE 7.4   Factiva Search String Menu

nearN	Within N number of words—(Bayou near2 (Management OR affiliates))—order unimportant
adjN	As above but preceding by N number of words—i.e., ((Sam OR Samuel) adj2 Israel)

You often find the earliest record of a manager's achievement: high school honors, collegiate scholarships, academic awards, and the like. With less frequency (but to greater personal amusement) I sometimes find record of early distinction of a negative sort. While youthful offender records are often sealed, and documents to arrests expunged, the news record endures. And lastly we have Factiva. Its stranglehold on *Wall Street Journal* and *Barron's* content makes it indispensable.

THE MECHANICS

Common to all the above services is the basic methodology of searches. Your first order of business is composing your search string. You basically use Boolean logic and terms indicating proximity to connect a few words. The aggregator then checks your string of terms against its data horde and returns articles with text meeting your parameters. We'll run through a few sample Lexis searches to illustrate. While this doesn't pretend to be anything like a comprehensive Lexis tutorial, it should show you in advance what kind of hardships you're likely to encounter as well as a few ways to navigate around them. A few words on the particularities of Westlaw, Dialog and Factiva will follow.

Let's take me for example. While only a few people call me Al, someone searching me on Lexis would reasonably assume that it's possible I go by that name. Nobody calls me Alexander that I know of, but it's probably certain that if I was arrested and my name appeared in the local paper's police blotter, it would be under my full name. The terms in Lexis—and we're using the "News, All" library here—would therefore look like this:

$$((Alexander\ OR\ Alex\ OR\ Al)PRE/2\ Foster)$$

The "PRE/2" means I want all articles in which the words Alexander, Alex or Al appear two words or fewer before Foster. If I run the above in Lexis I would come quickly enough to grief as an avalanche of 3,755 articles is unleashed. My name is surprisingly common. The chairman of a public company in the UK called Universal Salvage shares the name. I do not lead the Al Foster Quartet, nor am I the Alex Foster who plays in the American Hockey League. Oh, and there's been an awful lot of talk about the efforts of Iraqi Prime Minister Nuri *al*-Maliki to *foster* national reconciliation.

I am all for Iraqi national unity, but we can get rid of the prime minister as far as it concerns this search. If we merely capitalize the search terms, we'll eliminate instances of "foster" as a verb (unless leading a sentence) and

Arabic prefixes in one quick stroke. We would therefore search:

CAPS((Alexander OR Alex OR Al)PRE/2 Foster)

That gets us down to 3,400 "hits," which is still entirely too unwieldy. What to do now?

Well, we want to spread our traps as widely as possible while keeping results manageable. Your first thought might be to keep the above string but tack on a series of words that would identify negatives. Something like:

CAPS((Alexander OR Alex OR Al)PRE/2 Foster)AND(fraudOR arrest OR swindle OR theft OR misappropriate)

But that would be a really bad idea.

Some time back, a bulge bracket client sent us one of their internal due diligence reports on a manager, instead of the customary subscription documents and memoranda. Most interesting was the annexed news clip file. It was a straight screen capture from Westlaw, and had all the search terms bolded throughout the text. It was plain to see they had searched Manager X plus various catchwords (bankruptcy, sentence, defendant, gang, lawsuit, arrest), but hadn't included obvious identifying information among those catchwords (the name of the fund complex was not bolded, nor were the names of his former employers).

I have seen a fair bit of this. When it's done in-house, it seems like it's an artifact of the compliance department checklist mindset. Do we have their Form ADV on file? Check. Did we see if they were on the OFAC list? Check. Was there an absence of articles showing the manager caught in outright criminality? Check. When I see a third-party provider doing the same, it's more obviously a time- and/or money-saving device. Whoever it is that's responsible, they are both squandering a chance to develop insight as to where a manager has been in addition to possibly failing to detect what they are so monomaniacally trying to pursue.

I remember once reading an article written by someone with a great facility for euphemism and apparent unfettered access to a thesaurus. It reported that a certain money manager (and it gave the name of his former management company) had been arrested for DWI in a state in which he did not live. At the time, I believe that state's courts were not catalogued electronically. There was no way court searches would have revealed the arrest. As the manager's name was very common, a search like the above would have yielded all articles showing persons by Manager X's name being arrested. However, the article in question said that the manger, an employee of Fund Complex Y, had "been found by law enforcement operating his motorcar while in a state of advanced refreshment" or something very similar. You really have no idea how a reporter will phrase something, so it's a far better bet to do the hard work of slogging through *all* the things that likely involve a given subject than the *few* things that might involve the subject specifically doing something bad.

Your better bet then is to cram your search string as full as possible with information specific to a given subject that we already know: addresses, names of former employers or business partners, spouse's name, middle names and initials, schools the subject has attended. Let's have another look at our old friend "Fantastic Dan" Marino, hero of Chapter 6. You are likely familiar with another person sharing that august name: legendary Miami Dolphin, gridiron Susan Lucci, Nutrisystem pitchman, and failed restaurateur Daniel Constantine Marino. We would clearly have a superfluity of football news. Had Marino been a lesser player who faded into anonymity after his playing days were done, we could possibly use the following:

> (((Dan OR Daniel) PRE/2 Marino) AND NOT (Dolphins or
> University of Pittsburgh))

The "NOT" would exclude all articles from further consideration that name either the pro team or college where Marino played. This would leave us with over 10,000 articles, reviewing all of which being just a bit outside the realm of possibility. We would have to get more specific. From marketing materials supplied by Bayou in advance, we would have a fair amount on accountant Marino to start:

> ((Daniel OR Dan) PRE/2 Marino) AND ((Daniel E! Marino) OR
> Bayou OR Wagner College OR Coopers Lybrand OR JGM))

The "!" above is a root expanding character, which would catch anything on Daniel E. Marino; Daniel Elias Marino; Daniels, Elway, Marino; and sentence fragments such as "... disappointed Daniel. Eventually, Marino returned ..." Obviously it would be best to replace that with the name, middle initial and last name, and the name middle name and last name (if available) to reduce irrelevant results. We also would have generated his address history by this point, so we would add what we could. Names of towns, sections of towns, and street addresses should all go in. And note that when inputting addresses, it's often best to simply plug in just the street name. For example, had Marino lived at 5201 Elm Street, we would miss an article that mentioned a Dan Marino of the 5200 block of Elm Street had we used the exact address.

If pruning away excess in advance is one of the bigger problems Lexis will make you face, make sure you don't yourself create any problems by making your search strings *too* selective. Always include the names of all funds and entities connected with the fund. Back to Bayou, for instance:

(Bayou PRE/1 (Management OR No Leverage OR Accredited OR Superfund OR Super Fund OR Affiliates))

This will ensure performance data for the subfunds is picked up. In addition, journalists aren't omnicompetent. Sometimes, someone writing for a popular audience might mention, say, the feeder fund instead of the main management company. It happens. And you should likewise include all those "personal entities," the significance of which seemed totally irrelevant when you initially found them. If you learned that your manager lives on Magnolia Street and registered something called Magnolia Property Investors with the secretary of state, you might conclude it's something he incorporated for tax purposes to hold or transfer his home. But what if the property transfer notices in his local paper show Magnolia Property Investors buying a series of pricey homes on Birch Street, Sycamore Drive, and Maple Avenue—even though the private placement memorandum he supplied says that substantially all his net worth is invested in the fund he manages.

A SECOND CAUTION AGAINST A BAD IDEA

As noted above—and as cannot be stressed enough—freighting your search strings with "red flag words" so that you'll quickly catch only articles detailing malfeasance is an incredibly bad decision (this is often termed a "negative news" search). As you have no real idea what it is you're fishing for when you start, it makes sense to trawl greater distances with as wide a net as possible. I can't tell you each and every thing to look out for in advance, but if you yourself are looking at *everything*, you won't need to be told. Permit me a few examples, both general and specific.

As I go through the depressing entirety of whatever text I find, I keep a pen in my right hand. I write down the names and titles of everybody I see connected to the fund, from the lowliest junior analyst on up. Some titles are unambiguously the possession of one person (there's probably only one chief investment officer, while the number of risk arbitrage VPs is theoretically limitless). When I see a title change hands, I pay closer attention. Often there will be a press release or brief in a trade paper announcing the succession and perhaps elaborating on the reasons for it. Sometimes there is no such announcement, which makes contextualization important: was the strategy for which the replaced manager underperforming at that particular shop? Am I finding articles indicating that the strategy was underperforming generally across the market? And what about the person who was replaced? If he is immediately announced as joining another firm, it's a pretty safe bet that he jumped and was not pushed.

In addition to that pen, I try to keep handy whatever materials I have from the fund under consideration. Placement memoranda, Form ADV IIs, Power Point presentations, due diligence questionnaires all help. I'm constantly trying to square what I'm seeing with what the fund itself puts forward. Similar to the above example, we recently reviewed a manager who ran a rather concentrated portfolio from a small office composed of just a few professionals. He had founded his fund maybe four or five years ago, which resulted in no small amount of news. As I trudged through it, I was writing down the names of everyone I saw: a telecom analyst, a cell phone handset analyst, two unspecified "tech analysts," three different enterprise software analysts, a person someone from the *Times* thought was an authority on personal computers, a full five analysts studying the art and mystery of semiconductor manufacturing. I believe I already mentioned that this was a very small fund. How are they able to retain so many specialty analysts when the fund itself wasn't even tech-themed? It turns out they weren't. Their placement memorandum was particularly helpful in that it named everybody currently employed there. Only one of the people whose names I recorded when going through the news appeared in the memoranda as a current employee. The fund had apparently been suffering from massive employee turnover as long as it had been in business. This is where you would want to reread the chapter on interviews and make some calls to determine what exactly is driving junior employees out the door.

There were probably no gotcha-type words in any of the prior two examples that would have flagged them as revealing possible negatives at the funds in question. Indeed, it was the longitudinal study of a fund via a series of dull and un-illuminating articles in the second example that clued us in to a matter of concern. And sometimes such clues are to be found in downright laudatory pieces. Not long ago I was looking at yet another manager who enjoyed a reputation in his local press as his homeland's equivalent of Warren Buffett. I guess the humility didn't translate across cultures as this particular fellow never challenged the extremely flattering comparison. Anyway, the article stressed how like Buffett this manager was, sharing Buffett's grounding and humble nature. In his downtime, we read, the manager in question enjoyed meditating and spending time with his kids. Oh, and he enjoyed that most Buffetesque of diversions: high stakes casino gambling! Buffett does bet several hundred grand when he plays his online bridge, right? Doesn't he?

Remember, so-called negative news searches are done not to protect you, but to limit what the searcher finds, thus saving time and money. You get to keep all the risk of missing crucial information, though, if that's any consolation. If this doesn't sound like a fair deal, make sure you don't make it going forward.

CONTEXT IS KEY

You obviously want to look at the entirety of the published record on your particular subject. Confining yourself to the most recent five years, say, is arbitrary and foolish. The person who puts in Zelig-like appearances over the years—working on something vaguely REIT-related until the late 1990s, at which time he fetches up bringing West Coast tech companies to market for a few years before emerging in 2005 with a natural resources fund—is probably not going to finally distinguish himself after so many reinventions. Even for someone with a more conventional past, the whole of that past is important. Past performance is not necessarily indicative of future results, as the familiar caution goes, but it is a fitting yardstick to measure someone. There are few things more indisputably your own than your track record.

Beyond the individual, it is important to see what was happening at that individual's employer around the time the individual was there. With judicious use of the date restrictions in Lexis, you can see pretty quickly what was happening at a previous job. This is easier with smaller funds and managers, which may be the subject of just a few dozen articles. Larger managers and the bulge bracket firms that often wind up supplying those managers with staff are trickier because you will have to limit your searches to, say, articles naming the particular desk the subject worked on or articles naming, perhaps, Highbridge Capital (a particularly large entity) in the headline or first sentence of the article. If someone leaves on the eve of a merger with another firm, that potentially tells you one thing (was she forced out when the other firm proved it had a superior analog to the subject?). If she arrived someplace immediately after that place experienced a managerial exodus, you might wonder if your subject was a desirable hire or merely a warm body. Most important, did any of the firms she formerly worked for implode or uncover irregularities within a reasonably short period of time after the subject left? This is all suggestive and not definitive, but it should at least give you an idea of the sorts of things to look out for.

I just want to stress that you should be looking at everything, thinking about and contextualizing what you're looking at, and comparing your thoughts to what other materials you have, be they supplied by the manager or generated by yourself in earlier phases of your research. The context will help connect otherwise fragmentary records, and any variances between management's representation and the public record will come into sharp relief.

RECAP

1. Use multiple databases.
2. Avail yourself of whatever free training and tutorials those database providers offer.
3. Read everything you can, not just those things you think will reveal prior or continued wrongdoing. After all, this is a means of acquiring insight, which is far more valuable a thing to have than a checked-off box indicating you did not find any unflattering news.
4. Cross-check, compare, and contextualize.
5. Look for inconsistencies in biographical assertions versus what the news is reporting.
6. Seek sources for independent interviews.
7. And try not to let your eyes cross and your spirit flag as you suffer through the hundreds and thousands of kilobytes of raw ASCII text that comprise your search results.

CHAPTER 8

Regulatory Bodies

The securities industry regulatory apparatus, contrary to popular belief, is not set up to serve the public, in my view. If this sounds controversial, and elicits a tart response from any of the various regulatory agencies, so be it. For as long as I have been involved in due diligence investigations (going on 20 years) the regulatory bodies have been ineffectual at best, and directly and almost deliberately harmful at worst.

Let's start with the Securities and Exchange Commission (SEC). To be fair, it has to be acknowledged that the SEC is overwhelmed; it is impossible for any clear-headed person to believe that the SEC could have any hope of really keeping track of the comings and goings of the entire mutual fund industry as well as the world of hedge funds. If I was a betting man (and I am), I'd wager, too, that if you asked an SEC enforcement person, he would concede this immediately. Of course, this also leads us to the inevitable question: if the SEC cannot really expect to efficiently oversee such a vast financial territory, then what exactly are they protecting the public from? (This very issue is being raised now in regulatory circles, as hedge funds are questioning the value of the nonsolicitation, nonmarketing rules that make any public comments made by hedge funds fraught with danger, and contribute (possibly) to their secretive nature. Watch for this rule to be abolished as it relates to hedge funds; it will be curious to see whether the hedge funds really become open at that point, or whether it turns into a case of "you have to be careful what you wish for.")

Operating within the constraints set out below, at least, you say, the SEC must provide the public with information about the investigations it is or has conducted. But if you said this, or thought it, you'd be wrong. And this is the crux of my invective: by not opening up, pretty much at all, about the funds it has looked at, the SEC serves very little function to the common investor. And, yes, I certainly respect the-innocent-until-proven-guilty theory: for instance, consider the news of an SEC inquiry (something that clearly could adversely affect a fund) that turns out to have uncovered nothing wrong. That said, by the time the public learns of an SEC check, indeed often by the time the SEC even gets involved, the horse has left the barn, the barn is burning, and the only thing that remains is the SEC holding a very hot pitchfork. Think of the well-known hedge fund blow-ups; in any of these, can you recall the SEC coming out and saying something first, thus potentially saving people who might have invested from losing their money? I can't.

But let's grant the SEC a pass here, accepting that it is almost impossible for a regulatory body to get ahead of fraud. In fact, how does the SEC, absent an informer (typically a disgruntled former employee or a whistleblower) even know where to look, where to concentrate its very finite resources? In case it seems as though I am piling on, or making this up, it might be prudent to hear the SEC itself. According to a recent *Dow Jones Newswire*, the SEC's enforcement division is "focused on ferreting out fraudulent activity in hedge funds, the director of the commission's enforcement division ensured attendees at a hedge fund forum.... The division is focusing on two fundamental types of fraud—fraud against the investor, *which it will ultimately learn about through whistleblowers* (emphasis mine), and fraud such as insider trading and market manipulation, which may create systemic risk, and which is much more difficult to ferret out, said Linda Thomsen, director of enforcement at the SEC."[1]

Ms. Thomsen described a frequent occurrence as when "things start going south and people start lying and things just get worse." She averred, "In such situations, investors ultimately become aware that something is wrong and notify regulators. The danger, she said, is that *such fraud may not be noticed 'until it's a little too late to actually recover investments* (emphasis mine, again).'"

Fast forwarding to postfraud scenarios, the question I'd pose is whether the SEC helps investors get their money back, to the extent that such money still exists? Given the above admission, as well as anecdotal evidence, it is almost certain that the SEC is not doing this better than the court system, which already serves this purpose as well as could be expected.

According to an *InvestmentNews.com* piece on the recent proposals to increase the minimum net worth an investor must possess to invest in a hedge fund, it was noted that another proposal "would make it illegal for hedge fund advisers to defraud, deceive or mislead investors, regardless of whether the advisers are registered under the Advisers Act."[2] Hmmm. Isn't it already illegal for anyone to defraud anyone else? Yet this was described in the article as a proposal securities regulators believe is "aimed at better protecting hedge fund investors."

Even when the SEC wins, it is not clear to me what benefit this serves. Take our man Kirk Wright, discussed at length in Chapter 4. You may recall that the SEC's suit produced a big victory;[3] it was announced on February 9, 2007, that the U.S. District Court, Northern District of Georgia entered a default judgment against Mr. Wright, "restraining and enjoining him from future violations of Sections 17(a) of the Securities Act of 1933 and Section 10(b) of the Securities Exchange Act of 1934 and Rule 10b-5 thereunder, and from future violations or aiding and abetting violations of Sections 206(1) and 206(2) of the Investment Advisers Act of 1940." Once again, it sure seems to me that these are things one is not supposed to do in the first place, so telling a violator not to do them again and considering this beneficial to investors is mystifying. As for the massive judgment entered against Mr. Wright, the chance of collecting is near zero, and the suit itself could easily have been brought by an investor directly.

So why bother with all of this? Why not just let the courts handle events that are already illegal by law and which they are already equipped to punish? Why not avoid the almost inevitable turf battles, the waste of public dollars, and the waste of the regulators' precious time?

My suggestions? First, the SEC should shift its focus from enforcement and concentrate entirely on regulation, so that regulators and the courts agree on the type of registration that will be lawful and in and of itself valuable. Within this shift, the SEC should also consider the idea that it is often the smaller funds, the very funds that do not attract institutional attention, that end up blowing up. And these funds, because they are marketed to individuals, are more apt to damage the "public" the SEC is charged with protecting. Given this, the registration rules as they have been proposed, with smaller funds being exempted, turn logic on its ear. I'd suggest that these rules therefore be reversed (though the Libertarian in me recognizes that regulation in theory stifles creativity, here the public outrage over getting bitten by small funds outweighs this concern). Full disclosure, by the way: this is not a position I am just recently advocating. Refer to Amanda Cantrell's August 5, 2005, *CNN/Money* story entitled Hedge Funds: A $25 Million Loophole (http://money.cnn.com/2005/08/05/markets/hedge_regulation/) for more.

I'd also strongly suggest that the SEC lift the ban on advertising, marketing, or solicitation, or however it is phrased; it is always better to allow conversation to exist, then shine bright lights, rather than make labyrinthian rules designed to limit speech and here possibly doing that job too well, ultimately contributing to the very secrecy shrouding hedge funds that so many people complain about. (A must read on this theory was penned by the *New York Times*' superb business reporter, Jenny Anderson, http://www.nytimes.com/2007/02/09/business/09insider.html?_r=1&ref=business&oref=slogin.)

For more on the various points raised in the regulation vs. nonregulation debate, see the following:

http://www.dailyii.com/article.asp?ArticleID=1241986&LS=EMS120 251—In this February 2007 *Hedge Fund Daily* piece on the President's Working Group on Financial Markets (PWG), Micah Green, co-CEO of the Securities Industry and Financial Markets Association, asserted, "Too often, regulators reach immediately for new laws or rules which can have the unintended consequence of stifling innovation or smothering markets."[4]

http://www.treasury.gov/press/releases/reports/hp272_principles.pdf— Mentioned in the above piece, *The Agreement Among PWG and U.S. Agency Principals on Principles and Guidelines Regarding Private Pools of Capital* avers that "Public policies that support market discipline, participant awareness of risk, and prudent risk management are the best means of protecting investors and limiting system risk."[5]

http://www.dailyii.com/article.asp?ArticleID=1126684&LS=EMS117 593—In January 2007, according to *Hedge Fund Daily*, former SEC Chairman William Donaldson argues that the SEC's proposals are misguided. "'The rulemaking doesn't address the ongoing problem of the rapid growth of hedge funds and the lack of knowledge that regulators have,' Donaldson said in an interview with *Bloomberg News*."[6]

A February 28, 2007, story in *Marketwatch*, reported that Robert Steel, under secretary of the U.S. Treasury for domestic finance, stated in a speech that "changing the currently regulatory structure is not the best way to tackle new risks posed by the rapid growth of the hedge fund industry." Mr. Steel added, "We reject calling for more regulation just for regulation's sake."[7]

ARE HEDGE FUNDS REALLY UNREGULATED?

SMU professor Ed Easterling, referred to at various points in this book, has an interesting take on this oft-parroted tenet. According to Professor Easterling,[8]

Hedge funds often are said to be unregulated or lightly regulated. The perception is that hedge funds are cowboys taking advantage of the wild-west financial markets without a sheriff in town.

Hedge funds are required to comply with every rule, regulation, and law that affects virtually all investors in the public and private financial markets. Further, hedge funds are subjected to a variety of investor-related laws and regulations that impact who can qualify to invest with hedge funds. Additionally, there are a variety of state and federal laws that can require some managers to register as investment advisors—thereby invoking a series of additional regulations and requirements, including periodic regulatory examinations and filings. When the topic of regulation arises in the hedge fund industry, managers are far from being cavalier about the existing and continually proposed regulatory requirements.

For all of the SEC's issues, the National Association of Securities Dealers (NASD) is even worse. It is helpful to understand, contextually, that the NASD is essentially there not for investors, but for its constituents, the member firms in which you might have an interest. This is an important distinction that cannot be overstated, for it guides the NASD's behavior and helps explain its information road blocking. The most egregious example of this was a 1998 decision to in effect delete records in a broker/dealer's past if that person has not been registered for two years or more. Robert Brennan of First Jersey Securities infamy, for example, does not show up in Broker Check; Mr. Brennan, you may know, is a penny-stock broker who in 2001 was sentenced to more than nine years in federal prison for bankruptcy fraud and obstructing justice. In the 1980s and 1990s it was difficult to find a newspaper story discussing penny stocks that didn't mention Mr. Brennan's battles with federal and state securities regulators. Finally, in 1995, according to an August 30, 2000, story in Knowledge@Wharton, a federal judge concluded that Mr. Brennan had masterminded a "massive" fraud, and ordered Mr. Brennan to "disgorge" more than $70 million.[9] Mr. Brennan remained free as a result of a civil suit brought by the Securities and Exchange Commission. And the indictments that led to his aforementioned criminal conviction "did not directly involve securities fraud," (a function having to do with, among other things, prison sentences being so uncommon, then, for white collar crimes), instead charging that Mr. Brennan, who had filed for personal bankruptcy after the 1995 verdict, had concealed assets that should have been used to satisfy the judgment in the SEC case.

According to a 1997 New York State Attorney General report on "Micro-cap stock fraud," "The modern history of micro-cap stock fraud probably began with Mayflower Securities, Broadchild Securities, Robert E. Brennan's . . . First Jersey Securities, Inc., and Randy Pace's . . . firm, Rooney, Pace Inc."[10]

It strikes me that this would be the kind of information an institutional investor seeking to invest in a fund headed by Robert Brennan, should he decide to become a hedge fund manager (and I wouldn't put it past him) would want to know. So sorry. It's just not there.

Okay, time for me to put away the soap box and describe what these agencies do provide. First, a snapshot:

SEC, NASD, AND NFA NAMES AND NUMBERS

SEC: (212) 748-8000
(202) 942-8090 Washington DC
(202) 942-0649 Provides a good standing letter for investment advisors
(202) 628-9001 Fax—SEC—attn: disciplinary information http://www.sec.gov/
IARD: (202) 551-6999 (SEC number)
www.iard.com/
NASD:(800) 289-9999
(301) 590-6500 option 2
www.nasdr.com
NASAA: (202) 737-0900
www.nasaa.org/home/index.cfm
NFA: (800) 621-3570
www.nfa.futures.org

DETAILS

Securities and Exchange Commission (SEC)

http://www.sec.gov/

For all its limitations, the SEC is a must site when reviewing hedge fund managers (that is, the funds and organizations, for the SEC focuses its efforts on companies, not people). Even though as of this writing funds are not required to register as investment advisers, many still do. The SEC will indicate whether the company is registered (and if so, indicate the dates of registration), if the company has any previous registration (dates once again), and where the company conducts business.

Searching for registered advisers is as simple as clicking on http://www.adviserinfo.sec.gov/IAPD/Content/Search/iapd_OrgSearch.aspx. Though the process is simple and menu driven, here is an explanation of how it works (you know when people tell you something is simple but it really isn't, like programming your TV remote, or finding out why your computer is frozen? Well, this site is very simple, for real.):

1. Enter the company name, and click on "Contains" as this will broaden the search.
2. Click "Go."
3. You will see a list of entities with addresses; click on the one that matches the one in which you are interested.
4. Click on any of the hyperlinked states in which the entity is registered.
5. You will now be viewing the Form ADV, the Uniform Application for Investment Adviser Registration.

The Form ADV asks a series of questions designed to reveal who runs the entity, where it is based, its phone number, its Central Registration Depository (CRD) number (if it has one) and other similar identifiers. The Form ADV also asks whether the firm or its key personnel have had any disciplinary history (see below for more on this); in my experience this is actually a useful way to uncover disciplinary history as for whatever reason, firms are unduly frightened about lying to regulatory bodies.

INVESTMENT ADVISER REGISTRATION DEPOSITORY* (IARD)

http://www.adviserinfo.sec.gov/IAPD/Content/Search/iapd_OrgSearch .aspx
From IARD.com:

The Investment Adviser Registration Depository (IARD) is an electronic filing system that facilitates Investment Adviser registration, regulatory review, and the public disclosure information of Investment Adviser firms. [The] NASD is the developer and operator of the IARD system. The system has been developed according to the requirements of its sponsors, the Securities and Exchange Commission (SEC) and the North American Securities Administrators Association (NASAA), along with those of an Industry Advisory Council representing the Investment Adviser firms."[11]

(continued)

INVESTMENT ADVISER REGISTRATION
DEPOSITORY* (IARD) (*Continued*)

The IAPD (Investment Adviser Public Disclosure) system referred to above is what you'll use to check public IARD information and is part of the SEC's web page. A few notes:

1. The ADV form is filled out by the company; it is a self-reported document. That said, in my experience companies are typically forthright with regulatory forms.
2. The search is conducted on a company, not an individual. An individual can certainly be listed under the company's information, but that is the only way the individual will show up.
3. According to the IARD website, currently some investment advisers do not register through the IARD electronic registration system. These investment advisers generally file via paper filings with the states and cannot be found on this IAPD system. Therefore, it is possible that an investment adviser is legally registered with a state but a search on this system will return a "not found" response. If you want to check on an investment adviser's registration status, you should contact the SEC at (202) 942-7820 or contact the appropriate state securities authority through http://www.nasaa.org."

SEC EDGAR

Electronic Data Gathering, Analysis, and Retrieval system http://www.sec.gov/edgar/searchedgar/companysearch.html.

According to its website, "EDGAR, the Electronic Data Gathering, Analysis, and Retrieval system, performs automated collection, validation, indexing, acceptance, and forwarding of submissions by companies and others who are required by law to file forms with the U.S. Securities and Exchange Commission (SEC). Its primary purpose is to increase the efficiency and fairness of the securities market for the benefit of investors, corporations, and the economy by accelerating the receipt, acceptance, dissemination, and analysis of time-sensitive corporate information filed with the agency."

In English, this means that EDGAR collects the various forms the SEC requires entities to file when they are investing in (or selling) or invested in public stocks. For the purposes of this discussion, this information is not nearly as useful as whether the firm is itself registered as an investment adviser; it is not providing background information on the company or on the manager, per se, but is instead describing, to some degree, the firm's investment history. (Note that this information can be informative, but is more in the area of operational due diligence, something that falls outside the scope of this book.)

National Association of Securities Dealers (NASD)

http://pdpi.nasdr.com/pdpi/disclaimer_frame.htm The NASD (now known as Financial Industry Regulatory Authority, or FINRA, but referred to here still as NASD) is perhaps the most important of the regulatory agencies because it can provide you with an extensive educational and employment history for the manager, something that can then be compared to what the manager has provided, as well as being independently verified. The NASD indicates whether the persons and companies are registered (as broker/dealers; remember the SEC covers investment advisers), dates of current registration (in addition to title: broker/dealer, etc.), dates and titles involved with previous registration, CRD number, and disciplinary info.

From their website:

> [The] NASD has long served as the primary private-sector regulator of America's securities industry. We oversee the activities of more than 5,100 brokerage firms, approximately 109,300 branch offices and more than 657,690 registered securities representatives. In addition, we provide outsourced regulatory products and services to a number of stock markets and exchanges.
>
> From oversight to education, we touch virtually every aspect of the securities industry. NASD licenses individuals and admits firms to the industry, writes rules to govern their behavior, examines them for regulatory compliance and disciplines those who fail to comply. We oversee and regulate trading in equities, corporate bonds, securities futures and options. And we provide education and qualification examinations to industry professionals while supporting securities firms in their compliance activities. We also operate the largest securities dispute resolution forum in the

world, processing over 8,000 arbitrations and 1,000 mediations a year. With a staff of nearly 2,000 and an annual budget of more than $500 million, NASD is a world leader in capital markets regulation.[12]

The NASD's Broker Check service (http://pdpi.nasdr.com/pdpi/disclaimer_frame.htm) is the mechanism used to determine whether your manager is registered now or has been registered as a broker/dealer at any point within the last two years (again, this is a serious limitation, as "bad apples" who simply stop registering have their histories wiped out). Before you proceed, you'll need to agree to certain terms and conditions described by the NASD. Once done, for individuals, you must search by Last Name, First Name *and*, crucially, part of the company name. You must use these three search criteria to get a result; you can search by just the person's name only if you have the individual's CRD number, but that is something of a Catch-22, in that the CRD number is typically what you're looking to obtain in the first place. As it happens, there is a function of the company name search form where you can mark it as "Contained In", and just plug in vowels: A, E, I and so on. If you're having trouble finding a subject you know or suspect should be found here, make sure you're effectively using the Company Name portion of the search. For company searches only a company name is required.

As an aside, this database will not show any results if your search yields more than ten matches. If you look up "J Smith" who worked at a company containing the vowel "A", the database will inform you that it has more than ten matches and require you to narrow down your search terms.

As noted above, the NASD Broker Check database contains information on brokers, not investment advisers; the reason this still has value is that many people in the former category have become part of the latter due to, among other factors, the "hotness" of the hedge fund field. Here's what the NASD says on this topic:

1. **"What is the difference between a stockbroker and an investment adviser?** A stockbroker is paid a commission for buy and sell transactions. An investment adviser is paid a fee for the counseling services they provide.
2. **Who regulates Investment Advisers?** The SEC along with the state securities regulators.
3. **Where can I get regulatory information about an Investment Adviser?** You should contact your state securities commission. You can find a listing of all the state securities offices here on the NASD Web Site."

Broker Check records contain the person's CRD Number (as mentioned earlier), past and current registrations as well as past and current employment. If there is any disciplinary history, this search will return an answer of "maybe." If you see a Maybe, click on an option called "Deliver Report." and it typically will be e-mailed to you almost immediately. Note that what you will receive is usually a plain text copy of the person's CRD information, with the disciplinary measures cited toward the end of the document.

Reading the above, you'd really be tempted to believe that the NASD is a super-regulatory body, capable of leaping tall buildings in a single bound, or at least capable of providing information on the worst of the worst broker/dealers. But as noted earlier, there is a catch. If there is a period of two years of inactivity for an individual or an entity, the record of that individual or entity is removed from the NASD website. Now an organization whose mission is to be "a world leader in capital markets regulation" could hardly hope to achieve this worthy goal by deleting data. Yet they do.

When confronted with lemons, as my father always used to say, freeze them, and throw them as hard as you can at the NASD building. If this fails to get you the information on a broker who is no longer in the NASD system, you can try calling a state securities representative, who might be able and willing to access the legacy information using the CRD number you provide.

State Securities Agencies

http://www.nasaa.org/about_nasaa/2062.cfm

For the most part, State Security Agencies (SSAs) provide similar information to the NASD, only in greater detail and without the attitude. (Having a CRD number is helpful, but hardly necessary.) Along with the information normally found in NASD records, the SSAs will list exams taken and passed (like the Series 7, Series 22, etc.). All State Security Agencies have the same information because they access the NASD database (although they are able to retrieve more information than is available to you and me via the NASD website), so call *any* state office if you are unsure as to where a company or individual is located. That said, some states are stricter than others regarding what they will report, and on whom. This notwithstanding, calling a SSA is often your only hope of obtaining information that has been erased from the NASD Broker Check system.

From NASAA's website:

> *Organized in 1919, the North American Securities Administrators Association (NASAA) is the oldest international organization devoted to investor protection. NASAA is a voluntary association*

whose membership consists of 67 state, provincial, and territorial securities administrators in the 50 states, the District of Columbia, Puerto Rico, the U.S. Virgin Islands, Canada, and Mexico.

In the United States, NASAA is the voice of state securities agencies responsible for efficient capital formation and grass-roots investor protection. Their fundamental mission is protecting consumers who purchase securities or investment advice, and their jurisdiction extends to a wide variety of issuers and intermediaries who offer and sell securities to the public.

NASAA members license firms and their agents, investigate violations of state and provincial law, file enforcement actions when appropriate, and educate the public about investment fraud."[13]

State securities regulators serve the investing public in your state and play a unique role in their protection. For example, the securities administrator in your state is responsible for licensing securities firms and investment professionals, such as broker-dealers and investment advisers, registering certain securities offerings, reviewing financial offerings of small companies, auditing branch office sales practices and record keeping, promoting investor education, and most important, enforcing state securities laws. In addition to protecting investors, many state regulators also help small businesses raise money and comply with securities laws.

Okay, now we're getting somewhere. This organization's "fundamental mission is protecting consumers who purchase securities or investment advice." Unfortunately, though the SSAs are typically more helpful than the NASD when it comes to "out-of-date" information, they themselves are not uniform in what they provide, or even whether or how often they will respond. New York's securities office, located in the attorney general's office is, stereotypically but predictably, by far the most difficult to deal with; it will search only three names at once and will cut you off if you call too often. Connecticut is part of the Department of Banking and does everything through e-mail. California won't furnish series exam results, but other states will. All in all, it's a hit and miss process.

The National Futures Association (NFA)

http://www.nfa.futures.org/BasicNet/

The National Futures Association (NFA) provides registration information as well as disciplinary history on those involved in the world of futures (Commodity Trading Advisors, or CTAs and Commodity Pool Operators, or CPOs to name a few). NFA records will show with which entity a person is currently registered (in addition to her dates of registration with that company and her position, such as principal, or associated person), previous registration information (with dates and position), the company's address, related entity names, and lastly, the disciplinary history associated with the person or entity (below).

The NFA search site is http://www.nfa.futures.org/BasicNet/. BASIC, or Background Affiliation Status Information Center, provides information on both individuals and companies and contains current and past registrations. Valuable documents to order are 7-r or 8-r forms; the 8-r is the form filed by an individual, with the 7-r being used by the firm. (Refer to http://www.nfa.futures.org/registration/8-rform.pdf for an 8-r template and to http://www.nfa.futures.org/registration/7-rForm.pdf for the 7-r.) These forms are chock full of information, including home address history, early employment history, as well as periods of unemployment, the kind of data that is often omitted from a current biography. The individual filer also is required to answer questions regarding disciplinary and legal actions.

From their Website:[14]

"What is NFA?

National Futures Association (NFA) is the industrywide self-regulatory organization for the U.S. futures industry. NFA's mission is to provide innovative regulatory programs and services that ensure futures industry integrity, protect market participants and help its Members meet their regulatory responsibilities. NFA's activities are overseen by the Commodity Futures Trading Commission (CFTC), the government agency responsible for regulating the U.S. futures industry.

Who are NFA's members?

Virtually every firm or individual who conducts futures or options on futures business with the public, must be registered with the CFTC and a Member of NFA. NFA performs the registration process on behalf of the CFTC. NFA Member categories include: Commodity Trading Advisors (CTA), Commodity Pool Operators (CPO), Futures Commission Merchants (FCM) and Introducing Brokers (IB). Definitions of each of these terms can be found in the Glossary. There are approximately 4,000 NFA Member firms. There also are about 55,000 NFA Associate Members, individuals who are Associated Persons of these NFA Member firms.

Where does the information in BASIC come from and how far back does it go?

In addition to NFA, the information contained in BASIC is contributed by the CFTC and the U.S. futures exchanges. NFA's and the CFTC's regulatory information dates back to when they each began operations, 1982 and 1975 respectively. Data contributed by the exchanges dates back to at least January 1990.

What information is not available in BASIC?

The system does not include information about civil actions between parties (other than summary information concerning CFTC reparations or NFA arbitrations), criminal proceedings or actions taken by other federal or state regulatory agencies or self-regulatory organizations in other industries. Information about pending arbitration cases or cases that were settled, withdrawn, rejected or closed prior to January 1, 1990 is not included. Regulatory actions taken by futures exchanges prior to 1990 may not be included, because while some exchange contributors have entered them, others have not. Finally, pending exchange complaints that have not been adjudicated are not included."

REGULATORY DISCIPLINARY ACTIONS

Now we get down to the stuff that investors really talk about: disciplinary actions. If you are considering investing in a manager who has several infractions noted by one of the above-referenced state or federal regulatory bodies, but with no single action resulting in a fine of more than, say, $10,000 or so, and you conclude that these matters are "insignificant," well, you are not alone. Most institutions, in my experience, believe this; most, in my opinion, are also wrong. It is certainly understandable to reach this belief based on a comparison of the amount the subject managers trade every day, or manage in total, versus the then negligible amount of the fine. Where this conclusion jumps off the rails, however, is by failing to take into account why the fine amounts are so small. This, crucially, has almost everything to do with our regulatory bodies simply not being set up to reduce recidivism by doling out fines that could actually affect the way managers, well, manage. (For those familiar with professional sports, who face a similar conundrum now that players make boatloads of money, this theme will resonate.) The mere fact, therefore, that a fine is small in relation to the numbers otherwise being tossed around in hedge fund conversations is not, by itself, particularly relevant to whether the charge against that manager had merit, or was important. As is pointed out in the chapter on warning signs, red and yellow flags, you should again be looking for a pattern of behavior, rather than a monetary amount, when examining disciplinary records. A manager who has been fined, censured, or otherwise disciplined more than three or four times, even if these occurred over a multidecade period of time, and even if each action resulted in a nominal fine, should warrant further inspection.

Now, some specifics.

NFA

The NFA's BASIC search, referred to above, details disciplinary actions (on both firms and individuals) as well as other regulatory information.

Anywhere you see a number, simply click on the hyperlink marked "details" and further information will be revealed. At times, these disciplinary actions have little documentation aside from a mention of the occurrence and the fine paid. In other instances more details, including a description of the event at hand, will be provided. In either case, it is always suggested that you ask subject managers first whether they have had any disciplinary matters filed against them, and then, if so, to describe what happened. (As noted earlier, if you simply ask people what happened with a specific matter, they will have a story, and one that usually sounds credible. By not asking them initially to state whether they have had any been subject to any disciplinary actions, you lose the opportunity, forever, to gauge a measure of their truthfulness.)

NASD

Using the BrokerCheck database allows you to see whether a person is registered, and simultaneously if he has had any disciplinary actions filed against him. Once you have gone through the process of searching and finding the record for your manager, you will see, on the left hand side of the screen, an item marked "Disclosure Events." A hyperlinked "No" or "Maybe" follows; clicking on a "Maybe" results in the following, somewhat frustrating message, "Disclosure information may exist for this individual broker," along with an instruction to click on the "Deliver Report" option, located at the top of the screen. Results are then forwarded within two days, according to the NASD BrokerCheck site, and within a day, most of the time, according to our experience.

Some disclosure events may have multiple reporting sources. For example, some information required to be reported by an individual broker via Form U-4 may also be reported on the individual broker's record by a brokerage firm via Form U-5 (Uniform Termination Notice for Securities Industry Registration) and/or by a regulator via Form U-6 (Uniform Disciplinary Action Reporting Form). If a disclosure event is reported by multiple sources, all versions of the reported event will be disclosed on the individual broker's NASD BrokerCheck report. Similarly, some information required to be reported by a brokerage firm via Form BD may also be reported on the brokerage firm's record via Form U-6. If a disclosure event is reported by multiple sources, all versions of the reported event will be disclosed on the brokerage firm's NASD BrokerCheck report.

Unlike the arbitration information required to be reported by individual brokers via Form U-4, brokerage firm arbitration information is not required to be reported on Form BD and is therefore disclosed through NASD BrokerCheck via a slightly different mechanism. Summary information regarding NASD arbitration awards involving securities and commodity disputes between public customers and NASD member firms is updated and disclosed on brokerage firms' NASD BrokerCheck reports, generally within 10–15 days after the arbitration award is signed and served to all parties.

The full text of arbitration awards issued by arbitrators at NASD and at other forums is available online as a cooperative arrangement between NASD Dispute Resolution and the Securities Arbitration Commentator (SAC) at www.nasdadr.com. The awards are generally available within one month after the arbitration award is signed and served to all parties. To access the arbitration award information it is suggested that you first view the summary information available via the NASD BrokerCheck, and then use the case number included in the NASD BrokerCheck report to access the full text of the award at www.nasdadr.com.

Types of disclosure information include, but are not limited to:

- Criminal events (e.g., felony convictions, certain misdemeanor charges and convictions, such as theft of money, bribery, etc.).
- Financial disclosure events (e.g., bankruptcies, unsatisfied judgments and liens).
- Regulatory actions (e.g., suspensions, bars).
- Customer complaints/certain consumer-initiated arbitrations.
- Civil judicial events (e.g., injunctions).

As you can see, several of the items on this list, including "criminal events" as well as "financial disclosure events" are covered by court records searches (which in fact cover these items far better, and of course more independently, than they could ever be by the regulatory agency, which is relying on either the subject to self-report or others to report data that they come across).

Note, too, that a shortcut to arbitration awards is http://nasdawards online.nasd.com/. Also note that you can search these records not only by case number, as outlined above, but also by name.

The records discussed above are primarily self-reported, and are thus unidirectional. In the case of the NASD, contacting its enforcement office at (202) 974-2800 can at times reveal information that came from the NASD itself, such as a letter to an employer of a broker about charges filed against that broker. Also, some forms describing disciplinary actions, such as a U-4, are available only to NASD members, and thus if you don't fit that bill, you'll need to have someone who does obtain the records for you.

You'll recall that the NASD site drops records of individuals who are not registered for two years; this includes, unfortunately, records of any sanctions. A Lexis library, Docket;sanctn, thankfully does retain docket numbers, which can be used to retrieve documents relating to the action in question, documents you wouldn't otherwise even know existed. The specific records covered in this library, according to Lexis, are "Disciplinary actions and sanctions collected from various Federal and State Agencies, including":

- National Association of Securities Dealers (NASD)
- Securities and Exchange Commission (SEC)
- HUD (actions through Mortgage Review Board)
- Stock Exchanges
- State Mortgage Regulators
- State Real Estate Regulators
- Other Federal and State Agencies

SEC/IARD

SEC disciplinary information is found on the IARD site discussed above (http://www.adviserinfo.sec.gov/IAPD/Content/Search/iapd_OrgSearch. aspx). Once you have learned that the subject firm indeed is registered as an investment adviser, a tab on the left hand side of the screen, entitled, cleverly, "Disclosure Information," directs you to the section in the ADV form where the entity has been asked various questions about its disciplinary history; these questions are asked of the entity and its "advisory affiliates," defined, in part, as "all of your current *employees* (other than *employees* performing only clerical, administrative, support or similar functions)." The upside here, for the institution, is that this is worded very broadly, and forces entities, hopefully, to disclose everything that might be of concern rather than picking and choosing.

Any answers marked yes require the entity to fill out a Disclosure Reporting Page (DRP). This form is available to an investor online as well.

Note that SEC disciplinary history relating to individuals is retrieved via the full CRD reports, themselves found in State Securities Agencies' records. As noted earlier, each state has a different policy regarding how it releases this data, with some requiring a fax request, others an e-mail, and so forth.

Tangentially, another Lexis library, Fedsec;admin, provides the full text to SEC administrative releases. Though often you'll have to wend through a fair amount of verbose text drawn from general testimony to the SEC, at times a narrative to an episode that drew SEC enforcement is found.

One final note here. The SEC segments its administrative proceedings, trading suspensions, litigations releases and other similar filings at http://www.sec.gov/litigation.shtml. The way to effectively use this section of the site is to first discover that an action has taken place, as the site itself merely presents a chronological list of actions that have occurred, and is not readily searchable by company or individual. Still, if you know that an action occurred, this can be a quick and easy way of reading the genesis of that action and the decision that was rendered.

Stock Exchange

Disciplinary decisions for individual exchanges are generally available on the Exchange's website, on Lexis and on Westlaw. Westlaw offers a combined database of decisions from the NYSE Hearing Panel, the Amex Disciplinary Panel and the NASD National Adjudicatory Council (formerly the National Business Conduct Committee).

Tip. You will often see a manager accept a fine and/or some other punishment while asserting that he "neither admits nor denies" the allegations in question. It is important to understand that the phrase "neither admitting nor denying" guilt is commonplace in securities parlance and does not speak, at all, to the merits of the charges.

Final Tip. Lexis has several libraries containing regulatory disciplinary actions. Docket (Sanctn) is Lexis's national financial sanctions and legal actions library. It contains records of sanctions—SEC, NASD, various state agencies, stock exchanges, and so forth—but does not go into details. Fedsec; admin, short for the federal securities library, contains the actual SEC and CFTC releases and decisions. If a record is found in Docket (Sanctn) of someone being fined by the SEC, you locate specific details in fedsec.

RECAP

1. Always search the alphabet: NFA, NASD, SEC/IARD, SSAs.
2. Most regulatory searches can be done online.
3. Many hedge funds are registered as investment advisers, through the SEC, though currently they do not have to do so.
4. Many hedge fund managers came from a broker/dealer background; this is searched via the NASD.
5. Futures records are found with the NFA.
6. Disciplinary actions, or disclosure events, are available on most websites.

CHAPTER 9

Credentials Verifications

One of the hallmarks of hedge fund blow-ups has been mistruths regarding the hedge fund manager's credentials. It may seem surprising, but a review of a number of high profile blow-ups demonstrates this. Even if you believe this is accurate, you might be tempted to overlook what could be considered a minor transgression. So what if a manager said he graduated in 1983 and it really was 1984? Who cares if he left a job in March, not August?

Recall from the Chapter 6 that Sam Israel was something of a poster boy for warning signs that a fund might have trouble at some point (a little like saying, I suppose, that Anna Kournikova had a pretty big Internet following at one time). One particular signal was his claim to have been the head trader at Omega, a job he purportedly held for four years. Interviews with various Omega executives revealed that he instead had been there for approximately 18 months, a far cry from four years, and had not, in fact, been anything approaching a "head trader."

While the Israel case is an egregious example that would likely not be termed minor by most people examining it, other instances of so-called resume padding are equally as troubling if not as profound as this one. Managers who fudge dates and titles are telling you that they are okay with, well, not being truthful. The question then becomes whether you think this is merely a societal issue; that is, everyone does it, so who cares, or whether it is meaningful. Let's review a brief hall of shame and then decide.

- Sam Israel did not lie about school, but left out that he attended only briefly; lied about title and time spent at the position immediately prior to the formation of Bayou.
- Scott Sacane—various publications, including his wedding announcement in a local newspaper (and subsequently picked up in other news stories, like Matthew Goldstein's article on TheStreet.com[1]), indicated he graduated when school records showed he did not. Mr. Sacane headed Durus Capital Management and in December 2005 pleaded

guilty to violating the Investment Advisers Act of 1940 (another way of saying stock market manipulation). On January 30, 2007, he was sentenced to three years in prison.

- Michael Berger claimed he was 27, when he was only 21. Now on the lam, Mr. Berger pleaded guilty to securities fraud charges in November 2000; at the time of his sentencing in March 2002, he had disappeared like a Christmas ham at Walter Hudson's house.

As discussed in the Bayou sidebar, the idea that people willing to exaggerate, obfuscate, or just outright lie about "unimportant" items in their history would then be completely forthright when faced with a potentially devastating blow to their business is simply ridiculous. The "everyone does it" theory just doesn't hold up to scrutiny in the hedge fund industry; not only does fudging reflect poorly on people's character, it also shows they are not who they say they are, a combination punch that institutions would be best to slip.

WHAT TO ASK MANAGERS/QUESTIONNAIRES

Biographies. Releases. Questionnaires. The holy trinity of credentials verifications, these three documents should be the standard institutions have managers provide.

Biographies are a cinch; it is already common practice for managers to have these as part of various forms they fill out, either for regulatory or marketing purposes. The more specific the biography is, the more useful it will be as a tool of comparison between what it presents and what is found.

A biography furnished to you by the subject manager can also serve as a yardstick vis-à-vis other biographies your research uncovers. Coming under the heading of "do not overlook the obvious," comparing the biography that's been given to you by the manager to one that has been given to regulatory agencies can be quite revealing. Often, glaring omissions are found; at one time, an internal audit showed that in nearly 10 percent of the reports we had conducted, a misrepresentation or a significant omission from someone's biography was present.

Releases get a little trickier; here the idea is to make a release so benign that it will meet with no resistance from the manager.* (Attached at

---

*It must be stressed here while some managers may indeed get their dander up when asked to sign a release, most won't, and none should. You are the investor. You have every right to check that what has been expressed about someone's credentials is accurate. You don't control the fact that schools and employers ask for releases;

Addendum 9.1 is an example of just such a release.) As will be treated further below, most schools and many employers now require a release prior to verifying information regarding a former student or employee. No release, no verification. As this trend will only increase in the future, the sooner obtaining a release from managers becomes common practice, the better.

As for questionnaires, saying they are "necessary" is a bit of an overstatement. However, they can prove quite valuable, though only if they are worded correctly. It is critical to phrase the questions broadly. Do not, for example, ask if people have had "material" lawsuits filed against them. Instead, ask simply: "Have you ever been sued?" This way, you are the one to decide whether a suit that is mentioned is material, while getting, more importantly, a measure of how forthright the subject is. (See Addendum 9.2 for a sample questionnaire.) A subject who has been divorced yet answers "no" to this question could be troublesome for you, whereas your knowing about the divorce itself is often irrelevant.

Past incidents are not always as banal as divorces, however. Though not relating to a hedge fund manager, a headline-making event occurred in February 2004, when Smith & Wesson acknowledged that it had hired James Minder as its chairman of the board without realizing that he had spent almost 15 years in prison for various offenses, including a number of armed robberies. Yes, we are talking about a huge company, hiring someone for a huge job, without knowing about a huge blot in his past. The relevance to this discussion is found in a February 27, 2004 *AP* story which reported, "Asked why he [Mr. Minder] didn't disclose his past to Smith & Wesson earlier, he said, 'Nobody asked.' 'No one asked the question, so I guess I never answered it. The only thing that would have disqualified me was if I had committed securities fraud in the last 20 years, and I didn't.'"[2] The long and the short of it is clear: don't ask, don't tell might work (debatably) for the military, but it won't work for you.

And as might be expected, our old friend Sam Israel was also kind enough to be illustrative here, too. Evidently being charged with driving under the influence of alcohol, along with a charge of illicit drugs in the vehicle, was not something Mr. Israel thought merited inclusion on a questionnaire asking him, according to a possible investor, to list civil or criminal actions with which he had been involved. So with questionnaires, it's really a matter of whether you believe managers will fill them out willingly; the value of having them do so, however, is indisputable.

---

in fact, this is done to protect the manager, not you. Managers want your money (and truth be told, it is often not even really yours, per se), they should meet your conditions. Refusal to do so may not be a red flag in and of itself, but it may speak to a certain arrogance or secretiveness in the manager, and therefore should be judged accordingly by whatever standards you yourself have set.

WHAT TO VERIFY

Verification efforts should help you establish the veracity of a person's claims regarding his business history, beginning with schools attended, proceeding through employment stints held, and ending with any professional licenses held. Memberships in country clubs, directorships and other posts that are current and/or not business-related can be ignored, given the low cost/benefit ratio of spending time seeking to corroborate this type of information.

From a background due diligence perspective, the first step you'll take is to work off the biography the managers of that fund have provided. Do the representations on the biography (or biographies, as it were) check out? Verify that the managers worked where they say they did, when they claim they did, and at the stated positions. One of the first things perpetrators of fraud are going to do is make investors feel comfortable with their past professional experiences, even those that are fabricated.

There are also those managers who do not intend to commit financial fraud, but nonetheless misrepresent themselves in their biography. A manager may state that he was vice president at a particular entity, when in fact he was an associate. As a result, this manager may very well not have the skill sets and experience his biography touts, not to mention what it takes to make his current fund a success.

When looking at a manager's biography, ask yourself whether the credentials in the manager's background make sense in relation to what you are expecting the manager to deliver. Claiming a PhD in chemistry or having worked at a venture capital firm can be accurate, but that does not necessarily make the manager qualified to run a convertible arbitrage fund. Is a manager who graduated with a BA in English five years ago the right person to be running a hedge fund? Note that the aforementioned Michael Berger wrote a "Wall Street" newsletter at 21, when he had no Wall Street experience to speak of. How had he earned the right to make insightful Wall Street commentary? These are the types of questions to consider when examining someone's educational and employment history.

HOW TO VERIFY SCHOOLING

When verifying degrees, the first stop is the web. Once you have located the school's web page, find the registrar page. This can be accomplished by finding a link to a campus directory, a list of departments, or by using the school's own search function. If you cannot find any registrar information, use the school's main number, typically found on the front page or in the "contact us" section, and ask the switchboard operator to connect you. When you contact the registrar, tell them you are seeking to verify a degree.

Make sure you have the subject's Social Security number handy because it will yield faster results. The older the record, the more time it might take to verify the degree, as some older records are stored on microfilm or in a remote location. Either way, when the registrar has located the subject, be sure to obtain the type of degree awarded, the date it was awarded, the start date, and whether any honors have been awarded.

Sounds easy, right? The problem with the above is that most schools now outsource their verification efforts to one of two independent entities: the National Student Clearinghouse or Credentials Inc.

National Student Clearinghouse (NSC)

This third-party company (http://www.studentclearinghouse.com/) verifies degrees for the vast majority of schools in the U.S. (at the time I am writing this, almost 3,000 schools are covered by the NSC system; in the 2004–2005 school year, according to infoplease.com, approximately 4,200 two and four-year schools were accredited in the U.S.).[3]

To use the NSC system, you'll need to set up an account. Go to http://degreeverify.com/dvev/dv_how_to_signup.htm. According to the site, "Each of your users will receive an individual ID and password, enabling you to track activity by user. To join, contact the Clearinghouse at 703-742-4200 or degreeverify@studentclearinghouse.org."

Each time you receive verification regarding a student's academic career, you will be assessed a fee; there is no fee for simply signing up to use the system. Similarly, if there is no record found for a student at a school, you will not be charged.

Once you have an account, you will log in by entering your username and password. The process is pretty simple after that:

1. Click on "Verify Degree" or "Past Attendance"—top, center of screen.
2. The required fields info should already be entered; click on next.
3. Enter the name of the school, the person's name, and click on whether you are verifying the degree or just attendance.
4. Click on "Submit Request."
5. Verify that you have a release.
6. Enter the address for the credit card you are using if it does not already appear.
7. Click on place order (the fee for checking a student at the University of Michigan was $6.50; other fees are similar to this).
8. Once all information is entered into the website, you will receive verification within a minute. If the record is old, you will then be alerted to the fact that NSC is sending a response to your inquiry "offline." Typically, you will then receive an emailed response within 1–2 days.

Like Credentials, Inc. (below), NSC requires a release from the subject to verify information regarding that individual. Although neither entity insists that you provide the actual release prior to the confirmation, both conduct random audits to ensure that releases do in fact exist. Moreover, if a student has placed what is termed as a "block" on his records, then a release will need to be produced. As an aside, if you do not have a release, your efforts to verify schooling will be severely curtailed, but not stopped completely. Approximately 25 percent of schools, especially smaller ones, will verify information directly via the registrar even when they also are part of the NSC system. Still, obtaining the release is preferred, since the number of schools that will not confirm over the phone and require a release is still staggering.

Credentials Inc.

Credentials Inc. is another third-party entity that verifies degrees, albeit for considerably fewer schools than those handled by NSC (considerably less does not begin to describe it, really, as Credentials Inc has a bit more than 100 schools in its system). Their website is http://www.degreechk.com/. Here again, you will need to first establish an account by calling (800) 646-1858 (the set-up is incredibly fast, so don't be alarmed). According to the site:[4]

> In general, degree and enrollment verification services offered by Credentials are available only to "registered users." Before using these services you must first register yourself. This process results in the creation of a User ID with an associated password that you will use to access our services. During the registration process you provide us with basic information about yourself and your company, credit card information to be used in billing your transactions, and e-mail or fax addresses for delivery of your results. During registration, you must also review our Service Agreement and indicate that you accept its Terms and Conditions. We consider the personal information you provide us during registration to be confidential information. If you have any questions as to our policies regarding this information, please review our Privacy Policy on our home page.
>
> Transcript ordering services do not require user registration and are normally accessed via the college or university web sites. Our home page also contains a link to the transcript ordering process for all of the schools that we serve.

The walk-through:

1. Click on "Degree and Past Attendance Verification."
2. Enter your user name and password.

3. Click on "sign on."
4. Click on "Start a degree/past attendance verification."
5. Select the school in question.
6. Select how fast you want the information (one day, two days, etc.). and click on "Continue."
7. Enter the required data and hit "Submit."
8. Wait.

A third, far more obscure system can be used to verify a subject's PhD (regardless of the school). Proquest Company, an educational publishing company that was formerly known as Bell & Howell, has a Dissertation Abstracts section that can be contacted at (800) 521-0600 and reportedly has information on over 2 million individuals. According to Denise, a Customer Service representative, this organization will verify if a student has published a dissertation as well as a student's PhD (if the school has given them that information).

HOW TO VERIFY PREVIOUS EMPLOYMENT

When verifying employment, again, your first stop should be the web (until you have created a spreadsheet of sorts). If you cannot find any human resources information, try the company's main number and ask the switchboard operator to connect you. When you contact the company, tell them you are trying to verify past employment. Here again, have the subject's Social Security number at hand. Also remember that the older the record, the more time it may take to verify the employment; in fact, many employers simply do not have data dating back past 710 years or so (you'll want them to be specific about this if they tell you they have not found a record of the subject). Finally, be persistent; you likely will have to leave some combination of voice mails, e-mails and faxes to get your answer, and only rarely will receive one on the first try.

When the representative has located the subject, obtain the subject's title and his complete dates of employment; be clear in your mind that unless otherwise indicated, this is merely the subject's final listed title. (A 35-year-old hedge fund manager who worked for Goldman Sachs for four years just out of college did not start as a vice president, though he may have ended as one.) Also note that large investment houses often maintain generic-sounding titles in their records, so do not be alarmed if someone is described as a mgr.-tech.avr or some other mostly nonsensical series of letters.

Indicate how the record was found (by Social Security Number, date of birth, name only, etc.) Try to use as much identifying information as possible to avoid errors. Again, get the representative's full name and title, particularly if there is a discrepancy between what was given to you by the subject and that which the representative provided.

As with the educational outsourcing described above, many companies now farm out their verification efforts to an entity known as The Work Number.

THE WORK NUMBER

The Work Number, found at http://www.theworknumber.com/, likewise requires an account prior to its use. Several pricing models exist, based, naturally, on volume. An institution that might be verifying data for a fair number of managers every month would probably choose the "frequent users" plan   http://www.theworknumber.com/Verifiers/serviceagreement_CC.asp; our firm, conversely, is charged less as we fall into the "high-volume users" segment, as a company that performs hundreds or thousands of verifications a month. General pricing information can be found at http://www .theworknumber.com/ProductsServices/Verifiers/.

When confirming employment information on The Work Number, you need to enter a company code (corresponding to the company where the subject worked) along with the subject's Social Security number. After this is submitted, the verification is processed. Note, too, that at times on the top of the verification will be a message stating, "Additional Records Available, View Now." This allows you to obtain all of the employment records (every employer) for that Social Security number on The Work Number, and will sometimes lead you to uncover positions you did not know the manager had. If these posts held prior to the biographical data presented (meaning the manager has detailed only the past 15 years of his career and this record was from a post held 16 years ago), you may decide that no further action on your part is warranted. If, however, the position took place during the time covered by the biography, yet was omitted from that biography, contacting the subject directly, along with representatives of the firm that was absent, is a must.

The walk-through:

1. Click on "Enter Verifier Section."
2. Enter your user name and password, click "Go."
3. Enter Social Security number.
4. Enter a company code. This code can be found by conducting a search on the website by clicking "Find Company."
5. Enter a reference number. Submit.
6. Voila.

Note that the Work Number's records, at times, do not cover an extensive period of time. In these instances, they may have no record of a subject, in which case you can contact the employer directly (recognizing that the employer, too, may no longer maintain records for the time period in question).

Tip 1. NASD and other regulatory agency records don't always accurately reflect someone's dates of employment, just the dates during which they were registered with that agency.

Tip 2. Managers frequently have worked for entities that have either gone defunct, merged with another entity, or are otherwise not immediately available in a search of standard phone directories (http://www. superpages.com, for example). After exhausting the obvious methods, including the aforementioned phone directories, news searches, wikipedia (which can be quite effective, oddly), Hoover's Online (http://www.hoovers .com/free/), and the like, a particularly helpful site is corporate affiliations.com (http://www.corporateaffiliations.com/). This site, which is actually a Lexis product, has a tremendous database of information regarding merged entities, family trees and other similar data. The site states:[5]

> *Our database provides current, accurate corporate linkage information and company profiles on nearly 200,000 of the most prominent global public and private parent companies and their affiliates, subsidiaries and divisions—down to the seventh level of corporate linkage.*
>
> *Not only does Corporate Affiliations publish corporate family trees, the database also contains over 700,000 corporate contacts, 110,000 board members, 150,000 brand names and 140,000 competitors.*
>
> *Find the details you need on mergers, name changes and companies that went out of business. Our M&A records are available from present day all the way back to 1976.*

Try it. You might just get attached to it.

HOW TO VERIFY MILITARY ACTIVITY

Military verifications are relatively straightforward. Send either a traditional verification release (described above) along with a specific military release form (attached at Addendum 9.3) or just the latter form to the following entity:

National Personnel Records Center
(Military Personnel Records)
9700 Page Avenue
St. Louis, MO 63132-5100

Now, simply wait 6 to 12 weeks or more, pray the forms were filled out correctly, try to remember why you bothered to send this in the first place (see, I told you this was simple), and you should, might, may, possibly get an answer.

Is it possible to obtain military information with no release? The National Archives (NARA) website has this to say about the public's access to military records, sans release:[6]

Limited information from Official Military Personnel Files is releasable to the general public without the consent of the veteran or the next-of-kin. You are considered a member of the general public if you are asking about a veteran who is no relation to you, or a veteran who is a relative but you are not the next-of-kin. Next-of-kin is defined as the unremarried widow or widower, son or daughter, father or mother, brother or sister of the deceased veteran.

The type of information releasable is intended to strike a balance between the public's right to obtain information from federal records, as outlined in the Freedom of Information Act (FOIA), and the veteran's right to privacy as defined by the Privacy Act. Information will not be released if requested for unethical purposes.

The type of information releasable to the general public is dependent upon the veteran's authorization.

With the Veteran's Authorization

The veteran (or next-of-kin if the veteran is deceased) must authorize release of information which is not available to the public under the Freedom of Information Act (FOIA). (In some cases the veteran may already possess military documents that contain the information you are seeking.) The authorization must 1) be in writing; 2) specify what additional information or copies that NPRC (MPR) may release to you; and 3) include the signature of the veteran or next-of-kin. (A sample authorization is included for your review.)

Without the Veteran's Authorization

Limited amounts of information can be released from a record to a member of the general public. This is the information available under the provisions of the Freedom of Information Act. Please review the list of releasable items under that topic.

Freedom of Information Act and the Privacy Act (FOIA)

The public has access to certain military service information without the veteran's authorization (or that of the next-of-kin of deceased veterans). Examples of information which may be available from Official Military Personnel Files without an unwarranted invasion of privacy include:

- Name
- Service Number
- Dates of Service
- Branch of Service
- Rank and Date of Rank
- Salary*
- Assignments and Geographical Locations
- Source of Commission*
- Military Education
- Promotion Sequence Number*
- Awards and decorations (Eligibility only, not actual medals)
- Duty Status
- Photograph
- Transcript of Court-Martial Trial
- Place of entrance and separation

If the Veteran Is Deceased

- Place of birth
- Date and geographical location of death
- Place of burial

Note. Items marked with an asterisk are rarely available in the records we maintain.

So what does all this mean? Without a release, you need to file a FOIA. Filing a FOIA, in theory, will yield limited data. In practice, by the time you receive this information, the fund could have shown a year's worth of performance tables. So my advice here is that if you care about military credentials, get a release.

Tip. Military service mentioned on a biography invariably discusses some form of "Special Forces" service. For some reason, almost no one has been in the not-so-special forces, which seems odd given that this represents most of the military, and is clearly nothing to be ashamed of. It may be that the results are skewed, in that people who have been in the Special Forces are more likely to emphasize this credential on a biography than those who have not. Additionally, or alternatively, if I were a cynic (actually, I am), I might argue that people recognize the difficulty in quickly verifying this data, and thus reason that the upside of placing it on a biography outweighs any possible downside of it being discovered to be untrue.

HOW TO VERIFY LICENSES

Hedge fund managers no longer have the same pedigree, as has been stressed throughout this book. Increasingly, we're seeing people from all walks of professional life, from pharmacists to accountants, from lawyers to doctors. Below are some of the common mechanisms for confirming whether the hedge fund manager actually held the stated license for the dates in question (again, whether this is the case is not nearly as relevant as whether the stated information is simply true) and whether any disciplinary actions were filed against the manager in question.

Certified Public Accountant (CPA)

The website http://www.aicpa.org/yellow/ypsboa.htm lists all state accountancy boards. Locate the state in question and go to their website. Most states allow you to run a license check on the website. For those that don't have this option, you'll need to call the accountancy board to obtain this information.

Separately, the http://www.cpe-tracker.com/financial/reqstate.htm site provides links for the CPA boards of each U.S. state, in the event you are interested in knowing the various requirements a CPA must meet in a particular state.

Also, like a CPA, the CMA (http://www.imanet.org/content/About_IMA/Overview/AboutIMAOverview.htm) is a professional certification for accountants working internally for a single corporation, as opposed to the CPA designation, which is for public accountants working for numerous external clients. A single accountant can and frequently does attain both designations. It can be verified by the Institute of Management Accountants, (800) 638-4427, X 173. As with many certifying boards, you can at times also obtain current or previous employment and/or educational history.

Certified Financial Analyst (CFA)

Being a CFA is something that is not so uncommon for hedge fund managers (though it is more of a mutual fund manager-type background). To verify that a person is a CFA, contact the Association for Investment Management and Research (AIMR) http://www.cfainstitute.org/support/contacting/ at (800) 247-8132. This organization will verify dates and standing; note that the CFA is earned in stages, and thus someone may have passed two of the three tests but not yet be an active CFA. Note, too, that international CFA designations can also be verified at the U.S. number; simply inform the representative of the country at the onset of the call.

Attorneys

The website http://www.findlaw.com/06associations/state.html lists all state Bar Associations. Most states allow you to run a license check on the website. For those that don't have this option, call either the Bar Association, or in those states where Bar membership is voluntary or where the Bar does not confirm that someone is licensed to practice law, another agency like the New York State Unified Court System (https://iapps.courts. state.ny.us/attorney/AttorneySearch).

A secondary, valuable site for attorney information is Martindale Hubbell, whose lawyer locater service is found at http://www.martindale. com/xp/Martindale/home.xml. This site has a listing for every actively licensed lawyer and law firm in the U.S., and includes biographical data such as educational history (you'll still want to independently confirm this, but if you did not have it already, this is a nice bonus) and date of birth. This site is also useful for furnishing the names of prior colleagues as well as licensing information (in what states someone is licensed, when the license expires, what kind of law the person practices, and so on).

Tip. Confirming biographical data is only one phase of the verifications effort. The second, more difficult part is being proactive in identifying those things in managers' backgrounds that have been omitted from biographies. This is achieved by first observing where the dates you have been given don't quite add up to a seamless transition between positions the manager has held. Next, you'll broadly search public records, such as news, court, regulatory, and corporate records, all discussed at length in their respective chapters. Obviously, certain managers' names are common, making it difficult to determine whether the John Thompson mentioned as the fired investment banker in an article from 10 years ago is in fact the subject; this is where cross-referencing of information becomes vital. Based upon the pieces of information discovered about the manager from the preliminary research, including his middle initial, home address or wife's name, you will seek to deduce in a step-by-step process whether important facts regard the manager in whom you are interested.

Proactively identifying these nondisclosed entities is extremely important because perpetrators of fraud naturally will seek to hide a checkered past. In fact, it is rare that someone with a spotless background will commit fraud. People demonstrate patterns of behavior throughout their careers and lives. A manager who has ran two funds in which at two separate times it has been alleged that returns were misrepresented is more likely evidencing a modus operandi than bad luck or mere happenstance. Though it can obviously happen that someone with no prior issues will commit fraud, a pattern of behavior is telling.

One final item here: you won't always be able to fill in the gaps verification research has revealed. Just learning the fact that a gap exists, however, can be almost as important as filling it. Note, too, that for some reason the biographical writing consultants are evidently no longer advocating using months and years, as most biographies we see these days have just years. This is odd, because almost no one has held jobs for a whole career beginning in January and ending in December. Consequently, you may find gaps of a month or so, about which you may not be concerned, all the way up to 17–18 months, which indeed will raise your neck hairs a bit. (Also, in my book working from December 31 of one year to late February of the next does not qualify as one year, as one manager's biography recently implied.) In those latter cases, the subjects themselves should be pressed to educate you as to what they were doing during this time; the information they present should then itself be independently confirmed.

EXAMPLES FROM THE ARCHIVES

- A manager indicated that a former partner had departed, without noting that this partner had actually sued the firm, alleging that he had wanted to leave, was convinced to stay, then just before he was to leave he was fired and not paid the bonus and other monies he was owed.
- A manager's biography stated that he "started his investment career" five years after research revealed he had worked for a notorious boiler room broker dealer firm. Although you might sympathize with his desire

to leave this off his biography, as he clearly was a bit player in the bucket shop, it is harder to ignore the choice of language in the biography.

- A manager who claimed to be a bond trader was ticketed for illegal vending out of his car during the time his bond trading career purportedly was taking place.
- A manager who claimed to have been a financial advisor to a government later conceded to the press to having been a low-level employee for an organization working on an account for the said government.
- A manager claimed to have attended a school overseas from August 1995 to June 1998 and received a master's equivalent as well as a bachelor's degree. The school reported that the manager attended the university from 1993 to 1997 (note the difference in attendance dates) and did not receive the advanced degree due to a lower than necessary average score.
- A manager stated that he earned an MBA but turned out to have attended before he simply "stopped attending."

CREATING A TEMPLATE

I'd suggest completing a template of sorts by entering the information from the biographies and so forth into a document. You can always simply scribble the information you find directly onto the biography, but visually this may lead to missing the gaps mentioned immediately above. A simple template appears below.

Education
BIO:

    Degree:

    Dates of Attendance:

    Notes:

Verification Information:

    Degree:

    Dates of Attendance:

    Verification through SSN / DOB / NAME:

    Verifier's full name/department/title:

    Notes:

Business History

BIO:

> Job Title:
>
> Dates of employment:
>
> Notes:

Verification information:

> Job Title:
>
> Dates of Employment:
>
> Verification through SSN / DOB / NAME:
>
> Verifier's full name/department/title:
>
> Notes:

RECAP

1. Biographical errors of omission or commission can be a powerful indicator of future problems.
2. Obtain at least a biography and a release from every manager; a questionnaire can also be useful.
3. Verify precise dates, since this is how gaps are revealed.
4. Most schools and large firms now require a release to verify data.
5. Make the release you use as nonthreatening as possible.
6. Write down the name of the person who verifies data, particularly if a discrepancy is found.
7. Be persistent.
8. Ask the subject to explain any discrepancies or gaps. Verify additional information you are given.
9. Look for a pattern of mistruths, half-truths, or untruths.

CHAPTER 10

Corporate Records: Not Just D&B Anymore

Sean Leadem

As with Chapter 7, which discussed news media searches, I opted to turn over the chapter on corporate records research to an expert, Sean Leadem. Sean has worked with BackTrack/FADV off and on since December 1998, and has demonstrated both the ability to process copious amounts of research material as well as the demeanor and skill to teach the mechanics and the thought processes behind the searches to countless new hires. As I previously mentioned it's worth repeating that searching databases is easy, but searching databases well is not. The expertise Sean is sharing below will help turn your research from data entry mode into a superior investigative process. Always remember that a tool only has value for someone who knows how to use it.

The term *corporate record*, as you no doubt know, refers to any of a variety of filings made by corporate entities or about companies by regulatory bodies. For our purposes, a corporate record is any available record filed by or about a business entity that contains information helpful in determining the background of an individual or fund or company. Examples include a Dun & Bradstreet report, a state incorporation record, an 8-K filed with the SEC, an analyst report, and so forth.

This chapter deals primarily with an outline of what corporate records are available and how to search them intelligently and effectively. Before we begin, however, some discussion is in order of the value of searching these records.

First, searching corporate records will help you verify and gain more robust information about your subject's business history as compared to the information that appeared in a biography, resume, or a fund's PPM. Secretary of State filings and documents submitted to the SEC will help confirm (or contradict) dates as presented in a biography, and help you build a basic third-party/independent account of what your subject has been doing career-wise. A basic example: You will always want to compare dates provided with dates recorded in various database filings you collect. Do the dates of incorporation listed in the subject's PPM match those given in secretary of state records? If these dates do not correspond, you obviously will have questions for your subject.

Furthermore, when the subject has provided no background information, your search of corporate records—together with the address history you generated early in your research, news searches, and information from regulatory bodies—can enable you to get a picture of where the subject has been and what he or she has been doing. Simple biography checking is a major reason to conduct these searches.

Second, you can't assume your subject is providing you with the information that you need. Corroboration of what you already know (from a biography) is valuable, of course, and a search of corporate records will enrich your understanding of the companies or funds already provided. But just as important to any investigation is the search for information that you *don't* already know. It is vital to get the details on a company listed on the subject's biography; it is just as crucial to discover what he or she hasn't mentioned or doesn't want you to know. Depending on how you run your searches, you can plug in terms that will only pull out information already provided. That's what data miners do, and it is a terrible miscarriage of investigative technique. (The sections below will discuss how to avoid this.) You have done less than half the job if you haven't searched in such a way as to collect information—associations, incorporations, and so forth—that you didn't already know was there.

When it comes to hedge fund managers, two things you are seeking to uncover are omissions and distractions. Searching corporate databases correctly will allow you to find records of companies linked to the subject's name or address that do not appear in any of his or her printed biographical materials. Discovery of these is fundamental, for they raise one of two important questions (if not both): Why did the subject refrain from mentioning his association with Company X in his biography? And will the subject's association with this company, not mentioned on the biography, distract him from focusing on the active management of his fund?

There are extreme examples. In the course of one investigation, we located a record of a fictitious name filing for an entity called CraterFade

[This and all names and corporate entities in this chapter are inventions and do not, to my knowledge, represent any real entities, corporate or personal.] Records showed this entity linked to the subject's fund and his home address. Subsequent searches on CraterFade revealed that it was a tradename for an online gaming and pornography site or set of sites. This side business may not interrupt or impinge upon the subject's capacity to run your target fund, but this is exactly the kind of information you do *not* want to discover in a *Wall Street Journal* article a year after you have already invested with the subject.

You will also find the simple omission. Your subject's biography lists Smith Barney and Citigroup as former employers but is vague about the dates. Why? Corporate records show that in addition to these entities he also served as a partner (or employee, or analyst, or co-incorporator) of two smaller companies/funds before launching his current one. Why don't they appear on the biography? We don't know; we didn't even know about them until we searched corporate records. But investigators in this field have countless examples of learning about these associations through corporate records, following up through more targeted searches or phone calls, and learning that the subject was fired, or the company went bankrupt, or any one of several other unsavory events occurred. As you have read elsewhere in this book, the vague biography is itself a yellow flag. Corporate records searches help you fill in gaps and ask questions—questions that you didn't know you needed to ask until you searched.

More innocuous, but no less important, are possible distractions. As Randy Shain noted in a recent publication, paraphrasing client feedback: "Unlike your friends, who you want to be Renaissance men, in a hedge-fund manager you're looking for the guy that doesn't have a personality. People who have spent a lot of time doing a lot of other things, like auto racing, means that they're away from a computer screen." News articles are helpful but haphazard in revealing activities that may divert the subject from what is supposed to be his principal work, namely, the management of the fund in which you are about to invest. Corporate records can provide essential information of this kind, and although it's not always auto racing that you find, other associations can be no less distracting.

Consider the following examples. One subject was raising capital for his fund. Corporate searches revealed that at the same time as he was supposedly working full-tilt to get his new fund off the ground he was also working for another firm. Calls then revealed that he was not merely a silent partner or board member, but was actually working full-time for this other entity. There's nothing inherently wrong with making ends meet while trying to get a start up off the ground, but an investor should know about it, at a minimum. More troubling here was the fact that the subject essentially was pretending to be managing a fund, when in fact he hadn't really even started it.

Similarly, a biography may make an oblique reference to a charitable organization on whose board the subject sits. Corporate records searches have more than once revealed that the subject not only sits on the board but in fact is the president of the organization, which incidentally is listed at his current fund's address. At this point two questions arise: will your subject have sufficient time to devote to the management of the fund in which you are investing? And second: are you investing in his fund, or his charity, or some odd amalgamation of the two?

Corporate searches will also help you learn that companies listed as active are no longer active; conversely, start-ups listed as past employments are at times found to be still active. In an age when everyone with half a degree from Wharton is supposedly a hedge fund manager, it is imperative to know your subject's work history and present, and corporate record searches are integral to achieving this through your investigation.

Last, and by no means least in importance, corporate records give you access to the names of individuals who can provide information about and comment intelligently on your subject's background, performance, and character. The value of collecting the names of these independent references cannot be overstated. Former partners know things that never appear in the news or in the public record, and there is an entire chapter of this book devoted to the discussion of how best to interview individuals in order to persuade them to share their insights. You can't interview them, however, if you don't know who they are. In the course of your investigation, you will find the names of individuals listed as partners in incorporation records. You may find stock analyst reports coauthored by the subject and another individual. You will find business biographies of people who once worked for your subject's current entity but have since moved on. Write them down. These people are gold.

Here are two very different instances of corporate searches leading to valuable interviews. Secretary of State records listed a subject as a partner in an entity with a Robert Jones. This concerned the client, who was aware that Mr. Jones was a convicted felon who had at one time or another been incarcerated for fraud. When confronted with this information, the subject noted that his association with Mr. Jones was very brief—though they had incorporated an entity together, that company never actually conducted business and he quickly terminated his association with Mr. Jones upon realizing that he was dealing with an unsavory character. This is a plausible explanation: The record was filed years ago, and Mr. Jones was known for duping people into partnerships (hence the fraud charge). Mr. Jones, it turned out, was currently serving time in prison and therefore could not be contacted for comment. Thankfully, however, a third party was also listed in the incorporation record, a James Smith. By cross-referencing incorporation records with property records we were able to find Mr. Smith and get him on the telephone; this conversation revealed that the subject's association with Mr. Jones was substantially more involved than he had lead us to believe. Now, we and our client were more than ready to believe that the subject had been taken for a ride with Mr. Jones; our interviews with Mr. Smith, however, showed that the subject minimized in his retelling of events, which called into question his candor.

Perhaps more common is the following example. The subject worked for Citigroup, and we want to know more about his role there. Did his work on the convertible arbitrage desk prepare him to manage his own hedge fund, as he claims? Citigroup is vast, as you know. Searches of corporate records, however, can bring up stock analyst reports coauthored by the subject and another individual while both were working at Citigroup. Here, within a vast corporate organization, a simple corporate record search has plucked the name of an individual who worked closely with the subject. In some cases, of course, the subject will have provided a list of references for you to call, and these can be valuable. Nothing, however, beats an interview with someone familiar with the subject who does *not* appear on the list your subject has provided. Corporate records—as well as news articles—can provide these invaluable names.

CORPORATE RECORDS: THE LIBRARIES

We will focus our attention on Lexis for, while there are other ways to access secretary of state incorporation records, Dun & Bradstreet, and the SEC, we are unaware of a service as comprehensive as Lexis's that enables you to search combined arenas/states and combined libraries. Remember that when you are beginning your search, you probably know where your subject has lived, but you *don't* know where he *may have* worked or incorporated his business(es). The organization of Lexis's libraries enables you to search combined records. You can troubleshoot and target searches later by contacting a particular state's department of incorporation, or by going to the SEC's EDGAR site (also covered on Lexis).

Before trumpeting Lexis any further, however, a warning: LexisNexis may contain the most comprehensive collection of libraries for the purpose of corporate records research, but its web interface can be very confusing with respect to what you are searching. Lexis offers a vast array of libraries, and access varies depending on the subscription you have, which in turn is driven by, of course, the price you are willing to pay. Lexis offers specific libraries, "combined sources" libraries, secretary of state records broken up by state, SEC Filings, Directories of Corporate Affiliations, each of which can be searched individually (depending on your subscription). This near infinitude of options is not particularly helpful to background research, where the purpose in searching corporate records is to collect all records that pertain to a person or a business entity. It doesn't serve you as a researcher bent on learning all you can about a certain individual to be forced to contain your search to *only* California secretary of state incorporation records, for example. You may know your subject worked and lived in California and Oregon; there's nothing stopping him, however, from having done business in Illinois.

Luckily, in addition to the myriad libraries offered, Lexis has several aggregate or combined libraries, two of which are sufficiently vast for your purposes. The first of these is "All Company Information (excluding Investext and D&B)," or Compny;Compny. The second is "Combined Business & Corporation Records," or Incorp;Allbiz. We include the shortened names here—compny;compny and Incorp;allbiz—because these are actually keys to finding these libraries in the veritable minefield of options that Lexis' Website offers. Here's how. Once signed into Lexis, choose the "Search" tab at the top of the screen. You will see a field of recently used sources at the top. Ignore it. Below that there appear four tabs, *Legal, News & Business, Public Records, Find a Source.* You can navigate to "All Company Information (excluding Investext and D&B)," Compny;compny, from *News & Business* tab, or you can select "Find a Source." Here, a field appears in which you can search for a source or a library. Beneath this field there appears a choice between "Match Terms in Long Names" and "Short Name." Select "Short Name," and then type in Compny;compny. This will lead you to a page of links from which you can select "All Company Information" as your search library. Likewise with "Combined Business," or Incorp;allbiz. See below for reasons to locate and employ these vast and magnificent clusters of data libraries.

As noted in Chapter 7, News Media, LexisNexis offers a variety of subscription plans, available by calling (800) 227-4908.

INCORP;ALLBIZ

This aggregate library allows you to search the following libraries at the same time, a key resource when you are hoping to be comprehensive: Corporation and Ltd Partnership Filings, "Doing Business As" Filings, and a few others.

You have no doubt seen incorporation or corporate registration records file with a secretary of state or department of state before. The following is a very typical one, pulled directly from incorp;allbiz.

NEW YORK DEPARTMENT OF STATE

Company Name: BACKTRACK REPORTS, INC.

Process Address:
 THE CORPORATION
 45 WEST 21ST STREET, 4TH FLOOR
 NEW YORK, NY 10010
Business Address:
 THE CORPORATION
 45 WEST 21ST STREET
 4TH FLOOR
 NEW YORK, NY 10010
Type: DOMESTIC BUSINESS
Status: INACTIVE
Filing Date: 6/30/2005
County: NEW YORK
Date of Incorporation/Qualification: 10/20/1993
Corporation Number: 1765587
Microfilm Number: 931020000147
Officers, Directors:
 RANDY SHAIN

This is a basic boiler-plate incorporation record. It shows the company's name, address, date of qualification/incorporation with the state of New York, its status as currently inactive, and in this case the name of one officer. Some records contain more information, including the name of a registered agent, prior names, other officers, alternative addresses, and out-of-state incorporations or registrations. Some contain *less* information. Either way, these files can help you confirm or contradict contents of a biography. For example, if the PPM states that the company began in 1998, and several corporate records show a later date, you've got to wonder. Be careful not to jump to conclusions, though. A firm can be active well before it files with a particular state. Likewise, it can remain active after it is listed as inactive. These type of filings are necessary to cover your search, but not sufficient to show all that a subject or entity has been doing. For example, one untrained in these matters might assume from this listing that because BackTrack Reports is listed as inactive, it is no longer in business. In fact the company could be active in another state (it is) or have been merged with another corporation but have continued all its activities (it has). You can see from this file that BackTrack Reports Inc. is no longer active in the State of New York under this specific corporate identity. That does not mean that your entity has not been doing business elsewhere, possibly under a very similar named entity. Be mindful of what these records tell you, and do not assume they tell you more than they really do. This is why you need an expansive search and a comparative review of as many sources as are available

It is very common in these records to list a company's status as "dissolved." This term means the firm is no longer considered active by the secretary of state. It does not imply insolvency.

Companies can be incorporated/registered in more than one state, as you probably know. Many companies will incorporate in Delaware for tax purposes and then register in the state in which they actually conduct business. For these reasons it is invaluable to search the broadest libraries available and to collect all corporate records pertaining to your subject or his or entities. (*Side note:* Delaware incorporation records occupy their own, separate library, outside of Incorp;allbiz.)

Incorp;Allbiz also contains "doing business as" and fictitious names filings. A person or corporation may choose to register under a more descriptive name for marketing purposes. This is much less common with a fund manager, of course, than it is with an entrepreneur. That said, if your subject, head of TTTTT Tree Capital, also incorporates with the Secretary of State as TTTT Inc. in 1999, and TTTT Inc. later filed to do business as Top Taste Tease Theater, or Smugly's Bar & Grill, you'd want know about it. In all your research, you have to have an eye out for the odd and the unexpected. You cannot assess risk if you don't know what your subject has been doing.

Another important reason to search incorporation records (and those records available from Compny;compny, below) is that they also frequently contain the names of people with whom your subject has done business in the past. These people may be partners in your subject's current business, or they may be convicted felons whose affiliation with your subject would never appear in the most recent TTTTT Tree Capital memoranda. In most cases they are simply former colleagues; as you will read in the "Interviews" chapter of this book (Chapter 12), treated correctly an interview with a former colleague can yield more insight than the thousands of pages of news and corporate data available to you in databases. But you can't reach the colleagues that don't appear as references if you don't look for them. As you conduct your research, you'll want take note of any and all persons with whom your subject may have worked or otherwise been affiliated.

COMPNY;COMPNY

This combined library contains literally hundreds of sources, grouped and searchable in one place. This is probably the largest collection of sublibraries that you'll search in your investigation. (There may be more actual data in news libraries.) A list of all sources grouped in compny;compny is available at Lexis's website, and is also included at Addendum 10.1.

Most notably, Compny;Compny contains Bankruptcy Reports, Business Executive Biographies, U.S. Company Profiles, Non-U.S. Company profiles, Mergers & Acquisitions Reports, Industry Reports, numerous SEC filings, U.S. Insider Trading Database (note that this source tracks stock transactions made by executives involving their companies and should not be confused with illegal insider trading, which normally involves trading that uses non-public information), and more. With the right search strings, here you will find information about the investment activities of your subject company, biographies of your subjects (which you can compare to the information they have provided you), names of entities that your subject company has acquired or been merged with, some financial reporting, some mention of litigation initiated by or against your subject's company or a company for which he worked at the time, more names of individuals with whom your subject may have worked, and so forth.

Granted, the information contained in incorp;allbiz and compny; compny is almost never thrilling. But a thorough search of these libraries is essential to obtaining a comprehensive background search on your subject. You'll find a lot of noise in these records that needs to be filtered or discarded. There are many ways to search in Lexis, choosing only the sub-libraries you think are pertinent. If, however, you are seeking information that you may not know about your subject's background, in many cases you'll have to bite the proverbial bullet and search them all.

That said, you face two very serious risks. First, you need to conduct your search with a view toward obtaining any and all pertinent information; second, if your subject's name, or that of his company, is at all common, you will absolutely drown in false hits, worthless reams of mind-numbing data. For this reason you need an intelligent approach to searching.

THE SEARCH STRING

Leave Open the Possibility to Discover What You Don't Know

You had an introduction to the Boolean operators used in search strings earlier in this book (Chapter 7). The same rules apply in searching corporate databases as they do in news, though your emphasis may shift a bit. When searching any of the libraries discussed above in Lexis, select "Terms and Connectors" just above the search field. Your other options are "Natural Language" or "Easy Search," each of which employ algorithms to "guess" what you mean in your search and to retrieve generally something that you might want. Leave them alone; if you don't employ Boolean search strings that lay plain what you are searching (and what you are excluding), you cannot claim to really know what you have searched (and what you haven't). There is enough confusion in this research; you should have a very clear understanding of the parameters of your search. Conducting a search and only kind of knowing the parameters is quite possibly worse than not having searched at all: The people who are relying on you expect you to have covered some basics; if you are unaware of what your search included and excluded, you cannot feel comfortable with what you have and have not found. Half-cooked chicken, after all, is worse than none. For that reason you want an explicit search string. That's the investigator's obsession; it should likewise be yours.

Almost all corporate searches rely on the same basic model: *(principal's name) or (entity's name)*. A simple compound string. And in some cases your actual search will remain that simple. When searching the background of Don Varatomosa of Cyrrilty Capital, a basic string would be the following: (Donald w/2 varvatomosa) or (cyrrilty capital). Now, this subject has a very uncommon name and his fund's name is rare as well. Nonetheless you should not be comfortable with this search: While it *will* pull any record in which the word "Donald" appears within two words of the word "Varvatomosa," and any record in which the word "cyrrilty" occurs within two terms of "capital," it will never, ever, ever pull a record for Cyrrilty Offshore, or Cyrrilty Limited, or Don Varvatomosa, or any other variation of the subject's or fund's name that you might not know about but would not want to exclude. We'll address the more common problem of limiting searches for subjects with common names below, but here we want to stress a general principal that should guide you in your investigation and research. Do not assume you know what you are looking for. Whenever possible, leave open the possibility of finding pertinent information that you did not know was there.

Here is the search string that you might use in this case:

((Donald OR don OR Donnie OR donny W/2 varvatomosa) or (cyrrilty OR cyrilty PRE/1 capital OR partners OR offshore OR management OR limited OR inc!)

Notes on the above string:
The first string in the compound above will pull any records in which the terms don, Donald, Donnie or donny occur within two words of varvatomosa. This will pull "Don James Harold Varvatomosa," but it will also pull "Eric Varvatomosa, don of Princeton . . ." In the case of an uncommon name the false hits are still worth the trouble.

Note that the second string in the above example, (cyrrilty or cyrilty pre/1 capital . . . .) includes a misspelling of the fund's name. Including plausible misspellings is a luxury we can afford only in cases of uncommon terms, but they can yield fruit.

The second section of the "cyrrilty" string searches for possible subfunds of Cyrrilty Capital. In the case of such an uncommon name as Cyrrilty you might just as well have left off connectors and searched *just* the word Cyrrilty. You don't often have that option, as even funds with uncommon names are often pretty common words. For example, there doesn't appear (at the time of this publication) to be a fund called, for example, Cyrano Capital or Cyrano Partners, but try typing "Cyrano" into compny;compny. You get over 600 hits. (None of them is Cyrano Capital.) Now, very often you will have some idea of the names of subfunds (cyrrilty offshore partners, etc.) and you will want to include them. If you don't, you can speculate (*partners, offshore,* etc.).

Further, often the files pulled from the search on Mr. Varvotomosa's name will yield further information about his fund, so be ready to amend your search string. For example: (cyrrilty or cyrilty pre/1 capital or partners or offshore or management or limited or inc!) will not yield a record for Cyrrilty Asia Futures. But the search for records naming Don Varvotomosa may pull Cyrrilty Asia, because Mr. Varvotomosa appears as a partner of the fund. When this occurs, you want not only to capture and inspect that file, but to change your search string so as to capture any files naming Cyrrilty Asia that don't also name Mr. Varvotomosa. Hence you add "asia" to the list of terms to follow Cyrrilty. So, to repeat: be ready to amend your strings.

Here's a more concrete and valuable example of the above. You have entered the string above and retrieved a number of filings on Cyrrilty and a number of files on Mr. Varvotomosa. You discover that one of the files naming Mr. Varvotomosa is an incorporation record for Telekosos Partners. You compare address information in the filing and find that Telekosos is located at the same business address (or home address) as other entities with which Mr. Varvotomosa has been associated. It's a hit. Now, there may be other records for this company—your subject's company—that *don't* happen to name Mr. Varvotomosa. *You want these.* You especially want to know whether the company is active and what other officers are named. Elsewhere in the investigation you want to store this name so you can search for any matters of litigation or news items involving Telekosos. After the discovery of a whole new entity arising from a name-search, you want to search for that company on its own: (telekosos pre/1 capital Or partners OR . . . . etc.).

You need to be mindful and nimble in this process. Remember that you are seeking the broadest possible array of pertinent records, and that one piece of information can serve as an imperative to amend your search string or to follow up with new searches.

Limiting

The above is fine for searches in which names are uncommon. What about common names? Let's take the fictional example of John Jenkins of Balustrade Partners. John Jenkins is not the most common name, but searching his name in the manner outlined above (John w/2 Jenkins) yields over a thousand hits in Compny;Compny alone. Too many to view effectively. You have to limit the search. Your first impulse may be to write the following:

((John W/2 Jenkins) AND (balustrade capital))

Fine. The first string will pull *all* files that contain the term "john" within two words of the term "Jenkins" and also contain the term "balustrade capital." Great, if you're not interested in any other corporate affiliations he may have. If you've been reading along in this volume, however, you know already that this is no good. So here you have a situation in which you are unable to perform an unlimited search, but are loathe to limit to the point of irresponsibility. Here is where you will rely on your earlier research into Mr. Jenkins's address history, middle name, and any corporate affiliations you may already know from his biography or his fund's PPM. In these investigations you usually know something about the subject's former employment—from a biography or from regulatory agency records—and can include the names of those entities in the right hand side of the above string:

((John W/2 Jenkins) AND ((balustrade capital) OR (TTTT Tree Capital) OR (Tim, Oscar partners) OR (tiger management))

This expands your search considerably, but it remains overly restrictive. For example, what about that company Mr. Jenkins may have incorporated after he left Tiger? The one, for example, that he never mentions on his biography? *That's* a company you want to know about (in addition to all the others). Or you may not even have a biography for the subject. Regardless, the search above has not met the justifiable balance between inclusiveness sought and restriction necessary. Because remember: in search strings like the two listed above, (X AND (Y OR T OR M)), *anything* naming X *but not* Y, T, or M is wholly excluded. The search string above will not pull a secretary of state filing naming John Jenkins and Balustrade *Partners,* for example, unless it happens also to name "Balustrade Capital." It won't pull a record naming "Jonathan Jenkins." And it certainly won't bring us corporate information on a company the subject registered but that you have not heard of yet.

Here you will want to move on to addresses, middle initials, and—if available—personal affiliates. Whether or not you have a biography or regulatory records displaying former corporate affiliations or employers, by the time you are ready to search corporate records you have gathered address history information from available databases. (Refer to Chapter 5.) You have a collection of addresses, and can add these to the right-hand side of the search string above to *greatly* improve the likelihood of locating corporate affiliations that you don't already know about. Similarly, Balustrade's PPM probably contains the names of other Balustrade officers. You can use those, too. Lastly, by this time in your research process you are probably aware that Mr. Jenkins' middle name is Chancellor. Consider the following:

((john or Jonathan or Jon pre/1 c. or chancellor) w/1 Jenkins)

This string searches for three variants of the subject's first name immediately preceding his middle name or initial, and puts that cluster within one word of his last name.

John C. Jenkins, Jon Chancellor Jenkins. Now, it will also pull "Ruth Jenkins, John Chang ..." The advantage is obvious. The disadvantage is that it may pull far too many nonpertinent records.

((john or Jonathan or Jon w/2 Jenkins) and ((372 oak) or (33 park) or (14000 elm) or (7 eastern))

This will bring you the much coveted company that the subject incorporated at 14000 Elm Avenue but did not mention on his biography, if there is one. You'll have to use your judgment here. Depending on the address or the commonness of the subject's name, you may find that it is sufficiently limiting to put the towns, zip codes, or states in which he is known to have lived in the right-hand side of this search string. In the case of a Smith or Jenkins (probably), it behooves you to use the more specific addresses.

((john or Jonathan or Jon w/2 Jenkins) and ((Bartholomew or Bart w/2 smith) or (Jake or Jacob w/2 Dowd) or (Jessica or jess or Jessie w/2 Phillips or Philips)))

Here you have written a string that searches for any record containing John Jenkins and at least one of the people named in the right-hand side of the string (these being imagined partners in his current entity, Balustrade). You may find that Mr. Jenkins has been named in the corporate records along with one or more of these individuals in records not related to Balustrade.

The search strings above are separate to illustrate our various potential intentions, but they can be combined:

> *((john or Jonathan or Jon pre/1 c. or chancellor) w/1 Jenkins) or ((john or Jonathan or Jon w/2 Jenkins) and ((372 oak) or (33 park) or (14000 elm) or (7 eastern) or (Bartholomew or Bart w/2 smith) or (Jake or Jacob w/2 Dowd) or (Jessica or jess or Jessie w/2 Phillips or Philips) or (balustrade) OR (TTTT Tree Capital) OR (Tim, Oscar partners) OR (tiger management)))*

Now, as mentioned above, the degree of specificity required for terms in the right-hand side of a given search string is basically contingent upon the commonness of the subject's name and your willingness to tolerate tedious review of nonpertinent information. (Don't forget, you *could* just search the name and spend the day or week going through corporate files and SEC reports.) Basically, the more common the name, the more restrictions necessary. The less common, the more generalized the right side of your search string can and needs to be.

Get Creative

You are not restricted, when building search strings, to the types of searches outlined above. Keep in mind that you may enter *any* set of terms into a search string, and restrict in a number of ways. In a few instances, for example, we have searched databases using the telephone number of the subject's fund to reveal another, very different businesses. In some cases it will make sense to enter an address—*just* the address, unrestricted—into corporate databases to discover what corporate entities have been listed there.

There is also a great deal you can exclude with the use of such operators as "NOT," "SINGULAR," "PLURAL," and "CAPS." See Lexis' glossary of terms and connectors. Get creative.

DUN & BRADSTREET

We also collect Dun & Bradstreet (D&B) records, available through Lexis. (We sometimes also retrieve full reports from D&B directly.) If you know almost nothing about a company, D&B can help with information about its founding date, listed officers, and sometimes a biography that can be compared to information the subject has already provided you. Dun & Bradstreet is what it is: a vast database of self-reported information of limited value.

RECAP

1. Thorough and intelligent research of corporate records is essential to corroborating information received and discovering information concealed.
2. Pay attention to dates and addresses.
3. Know the parameters of your search strings.
4. Do not assume you know what you are looking for; do not search merely for data on corporate entities about which you already know.
5. Be nimble: amend your search strings as new information arises in your searches.
6. Record the names of individuals listed alongside your subject in corporate records; consider interviewing them.

CHAPTER 11

The Internet: What It Can Do and What It Can't

The proliferation of websites and Internet search engines has led to undoubtedly the largest misunderstanding of what constitutes an effective due diligence tool. Many institutions now question the value of so-called pay databases and completely ignore manual searches. Why? The power of Google, Yahoo, and other web-based products to convince people that everything can now be had on the web is incredible. It is no mystery why even sophisticated financial people may be led to believe that the Web harnesses previously unforeseen and now unsurpassed power. The real question that arises is whether this very real information source, or agglomeration of sources, has any value in hedge fund manager due diligence.

WHAT THE INTERNET CAN DO

1. *Finding biographies.* Recall from the chapter on verifying credentials that a crucial element to background due diligence is taking what a manager has said about his background and comparing it to what your research reveals is actually accurate. A way to supplement this analysis is to locate other biographies of the manager, then match these up against the one you were provided as well as the information provided directly by the schools and employers cited. You may find some surprises this way, both in terms of information that one biography features and another doesn't, as well as in information that one biography states that turns out to be simply untrue (the Scott Sacane web biographical claim of college graduation is an excellent example of this).

   The places these alternate biographies will appear are somewhat random. You might find that the subject was a speaker at an industry conference. Biographical data is also included when someone is an officer or director of another, typically public company. Or you may even see a biography when the manager had applied for a job. Regardless of where these documents are found, always remember that their value lies in determining whether what they say is consistent with what similar material claimed.

2. *Clarifying company mergers.* Your subject's biography states that he worked for an entity known as Pershing during the mid-1980s. You find a news story reporting that the manager was working for DLJ in 1984. Before you get alarmed, Internet research quickly reveals that Pershing was a division of DLJ at this time, explaining the seeming incongruity. Internet searches can also quickly show that DLJ, in turn, is now part of CSFB, where you would need to direct your verification efforts.

3. *Identifying potential interview sources.* News searches typically are the best way to find a manager's former colleagues, given the breadth of their coverage, time-wise, combined with the narrow focus afforded to you via search terms (allowing you to search via company all the way down to a unit of a division of a subsidiary of the overall company). As a means of augmenting these news searches, however, Web searches can be valuable. Googling the company for which the subject worked, and being as specific as possible regarding departments, divisions, groups, and the like, can yield a variety of mentions, some of which will include a former colleague who can then be located and contacted.

4. *Locating interview sources' current contact information.*

LIMITS/NOT SO GOOD FOR

1. *Historical data/news.* The Internet is not at all designed to be a replacement for Nexis, Factiva et al. It has a remarkable amount of recent, esoteric pieces of information but is in no way as comprehensive as a paid news database search, both in terms of its breadth (amount of sources covered) and reach (time period covered).

2. *Its very breadth is both a positive and a negative.* Broad searching can be very difficult precisely because so much data exists. Many searches yield so many "pages' of hits that culling through them is unproductive.

3. *Much better for lower-level people.* For hedge fund managers, sources like Lexis, Factiva and the courts are without question vastly superior to the Internet searches.

4. *Replacing court searches and retrievals.* Despite the proliferation of high energy advertisements screeching about free criminal records and

the like, there is absolutely no substitute for reviewing courts the way we discussed in Chapter 5. As for retrieving court documents, the Internet is worthless.

I tested several systems just to satisfy my curiosity. Search Systems (http://www.searchsystems.net/) claims to be "the original, largest, most up-to-date and reliable directory of public records on the Internet. Online since 1997, SearchSystems.net continues to be by far the best resource of business information, corporate filings, property records, deeds, mortgages, criminal and civil court filings, inmates, offenders, births, deaths, marriages, unclaimed property, professional licenses, and much more. Access billions of records!"

Wow. Where do I sign? It turns out the sign-in process is easy, too. By clicking on "**Sign up for DirectPass**" one gets "access [to] our directory **AND** get discounts on our **Premium** nationwide & statewide criminal record, bankruptcy, judgment, and tax lien databases."

Alas. The billions of records in here do not cover things like: Sam Israel's $2.2 million judgment in California (which it missed) and Louisiana federal courts (where the Westervelt/Israel matter was found). An institution searching for court cases naming hedge fund managers cannot rely on this site, which overall, is a general mess.

5. *Being a person.* The Internet cannot, for example, verify credentials because it can't pick up a phone and call a school, or an employer, or anyone else.
6. *Stay around.* For nearly 20 years an entity like Lexis-Nexis has done little more than add to its array of data sources. Internet sites, conversely, are here today, gone tomorrow.

SPECIFIC SITES

While skipping over Web versions of services already described in this book, what follows is a description of the utility of Web searches, as well as, more importantly, the limits of this search method.

Phone Records

When I first started in this industry, not only were websites not readily available, one couldn't simply dial 411 and ask for a phone number for a person anywhere in the country; no, dialing the area code and 555-1212 was the mechanism of the day, at that time. Now, even calling 411 seems hopelessly antiquated, what with the multitude of websites that provide phone numbers for businesses or individuals. So, instead of using directory assistance for people or businesses, try the following:

http://www.superpages.com

http://www.switchboard.com

http://www.411.com

http://www.anywho.com

The problem with the anywho.com site is it requires you to enter a state; oftentimes the reason you don't have the phone number in the first place is because you don't know what state to search.

And if you need to find an area code, try http://www.areadecoder.com.

Also, for an email address, you can try www.the-email-finder.com. This is not a free site; you must pay a one-time $19.95 fee to access these records.

Two other sites include http://www.people finders.com and http://www.whowhere.com and http://www.iaf.net. The upside of these sites occurs when you are looking for someone (often, say, an interview source) and you already know of at least one address connected to that person; otherwise, it does not afford you the ability to determine the difference between the person you are seeking to find and everyone else with the same name. The other advantage here is that you might come upon relatives of your source; these parties, in turn, can sometimes direct you to the source if all other avenues fail. As an aside, I have found the IAF site to be the most accurate of the three, as it often has both a clear, current home address along with previous address history.

Another site is http://www.ancestry.com/search/db.aspx?dbid=3693. Among other things, this site includes a social security death index. Frustrated interview source searches can sometimes be ended by a look-see here; although the result is bad, at least the search itself is over. The trick, naturally, is that this search is most effective with a social security number. While a name search does work, it does not tell you whether any of the people you have found are the person for which you were searching.

Corporate Records

In addition to Dun & Bradstreet and its derivatives, Secretary of State records, and other similar searches described in Chapter 10, certain websites can provide, at times, quirky but sometimes valuable results to your search efforts.

- *Lists of banks.* http://www.bankersmarket.com/alpha.html
- Most of the terms on the following site will undoubtedly be familiar to you already. However, for those junior members of your staff who

may be too embarrassed to admit their ignorance, this online business glossary could help them avoid having to ask you for definitions of certain terms, or nod blankly in a meeting when a word they don't know comes up. http://www.oasismanagement.com/glossary/

As for the Better Business Bureau, it may very well have a place for consumer complaints, but obviously hedge funds are not its strong suit. Searching Bayou does indeed pull up a record for the infamous fund, albeit a record of zero complaints filed. Wood River produces no matches at all. So much for the BBB.

Military Records

A military network source, http://www.military-network.com, is a bit of a reach for searching hedge fund managers. But for the few managers who do claim a military background, this site does have veteran records and contacts and might help you find a former military colleague to interview.

Blogs

Blogs, or weblogs, about hedge funds are fast becoming as popular as, well, hedge funds themselves. Although the impact of blogs is primarily felt by companies who are replacing their boring, static websites with a blog, which allows for actual, real-time interaction and feedback with and from customers, vendors and the others interested in that "community," for our discussion blogs serve another purpose: reporting about hedge funds and that which concerns hedge funds. While reviewing the below-mentioned blogs will not likely help with any particular hedge fund manager research you are conducting, it certainly can't hurt to keep yourself abreast of general trends and specific theorems posited by those parties specializing in what is obviously a very particular niche of the investment world.

By the way, blogs are more fluid than even websites. You'll want to review the blog-rolls of your favorite blogs and update your blog-roll continuously based on this review. For the uninitiated, blogs also have what are known as RSS feeds, which in nontechnical parlance allow you to easily learn when the blog has been updated with something new, obviating the need for you to constantly check in. A quickie lesson: signing up for RSS feeds is simple, as the sites that have them boldly feature a typically orange box labeled "sign up for RSS feed here," something even a technophobe like myself can master. After signing up for the various sites (see below for some suggested blogs to seed your roster), you'll need an RSS reader. This, too, is free and easy, with one such reader readily available on www.bloglines.com. Right now, winnowing the 100 articles a day you'll receive is a tad clunky:

instead of reading the stories, you search them, sort of like searching Google, by looking for certain, key words you'll develop (to start, of course "hedge fund" would be one such search) and then reviewing only those stories with those words present. I expect that this process will become more sophisticated as time marches on, but for now, the aforementioned method certainly works.

Now, for some suggested blogs.

http://www.allaboutalpha.com/blog/

No description of who is behind this site is made obvious but a spin through shows many items of interest. Worth adding to the blog-roll.

http://www.breakingviews.com/OuterHomepage.aspx

According to the home page, Breakingviews "is the leading international source of online financial commentary. We deliver real-time views on companies, markets and trends, giving clients clear insight into what's happening in business and finance.... Founded in 2000, breakingviews is now read daily by the world's leading investment banks, institutional investors, hedge fund managers, corporations, law firms, public relations advisors and media outlets.... breakingviews commentary ... reach[es] nearly four million readers."

The problem? This site is not really a blog, as it is not free. A free 21-day trial is offered, however.

http://www.businessweek.com/

The online version of *Business Week*, utilizing this blog efficiently will take some playing around with the parameters of your RSS feed. Like other search terms, you'll use certain words and phrases to narrow down the articles sent to you; you'll probably fiddle with these, but over time you should be able to develop something that yields stories of interest while eliminating the chaff.

http://www.corpct.com/index.php

This site is a bit broad, given its focus on business in all of Connecticut. That said, many hedge funds do operate there, and so a little RSS feed magic will once again go a long way toward making this a viable source of information.

http://joshilaa.wordpress.com/tag/markets-life/

A very new entrant to the blogosphere, Pool Commodities describes itself as "a window to the world of commodities and life as can be seen in India."

http://www.decheung.com/

Demonstrating the true power of the blogging universe, Dennis DeCheung is a regular guy, a Microsoft Program Manager in fact, who happens to write a bit about hedge funds. Granted, most of his stuff will fall outside your interests, but a targeted feed of his blog could prove useful at times.

http://www.dailyreckoning.com/

According the website, "The Daily Reckoning is a contrarian e-letter, brought to you by New York Times best-selling authors, Bill Bonner and Addison Wiggin, since 1999. The DR looks at the economic world-at-large and offers its major players—investors, politicians, economists and the average consumer—some much-needed constructive criticism."

They do comment a lot on hedge funds.

http://dealbook.blogs.nytimes.com/category/hedge-funds/

Dealbook, edited by Andrew Ross Sorkin, is brought to you by the *New York Times*. Above is the link that directs you to the blog's hedge fund category.

http://www.dealbreaker.com/

According to the homepage, "DealBreaker is an online business tabloid and Wall Street gossip site that covers the personalities and culture that shape the financial industry...." It by no means focuses exclusively on hedge funds but covers the financial industry.

http://hedgefund.blogspot.com/index.html

Veryan Allen describes himself as a global market investor who is based in Tokyo. His posts are not frequent enough to classify him as a prolific blogger, but the topics he discusses are very relevant to many institutional investor issues.

http://economistsview.typepad.com/economistsview/

Presented by a University of Oregon Economics Department professor, no further comments are necessary.

http://www.financeasia.com/

As its name implies, this blog focuses on Asian financial trends. According to the site, it was formed in 1996 and is now "Asia's leading financial publishing company based in Hong Kong. With additional bureaus in Singapore and Sydney we have over 15 journalists covering Asia...."

http://www.gurufocus.com/

A little offbeat, this site "tracks the Stock Picks and Portfolio Holdings of Warren Buffett, George Soros and other guru investors...."

http://www.informationarbitrage.com/hf_regulation/index.html

Roger Ehrenberg, a self-described 17-year Wall Street M&A, Derivatives and Trading veteran, now heads Monitor110, which the site describes as enabling "institutional investors to access, analyze and monetize information gleaned from the internet in a manner previously unthinkable." To boot, he writes a blog.

http://knowledge.wharton.upenn.edu/signup.cfm;jsessionid=9a30c03d620 751307049?CFID=3314021&CFTOKEN=14744634&jsessionid=9a30c 03d620751307049

You have to sign up to receive information from Wharton's site, though doing so is free.

http://www.marketwatch.com/blogs/

Marketwatch consists of a number of columnists and bloggers devoting substantial space to the various financial markets.

http://nakedshorts.typepad.com/

Greg Newton, who for nearly two decades was the president of Metal Bulletin Holdings Corp., according to his biography, opines here in a frequently cited financial blog that presents "alternative thoughts on alternative investments." A must read.

http://www.rgemonitor.com/blog/roubini/

This global economic blog is the provenance of Nouriel Roubini, chairman of Roubini Global Economics, and is a professor of economics at the Stern School of Business at New York University.

http://www.riskcenter.com/

A bit dry, this syndicated news service offers regular financial features, tutorials and the always impressive white papers, targeted to risk professionals.

http://seekingalpha.com/

Described by a fellow financial blogger as "a compendium of stock-market opinion and analysis from 200 contributors," SeekingAlpha is regularly mentioned in sites like Hedge Fund Daily.

http://old.institutionalinvestor.com/default.asp?page=65&lpid=385
&LS=hfd

Hedge Fund Daily is a subscription-based publication emailed to you by Institutional Investor. An agglomerater akin to Opalesque, it has articles, people moves (which can be quite enlightening, especially when someone big is leaving a fund unexpectedly) and other kernels of interest.

http://www.smartmoney.com/

This site feels a little hectic yet the reason for this appearance, the amount of pieces all on one page, is the same reason that the site has a lot to offer.

http://suddendebt.blogspot.com/

It is not entirely clear who is behind this blog, but the occasional item of interest pops up.

http://www.fool.com/

Best known as The Motley Fool, this site focuses more on stock analysis and investment tips than on hedge fund insight per se. Nonetheless, the occasional hedge fund nugget proffered here makes it worth a look-see.

http://www.peridotcapitalist.com/

This blog is the work of Chad Brand of Peridot Capital, an "active manager of personal and family investment assets since 1992." The blog purportedly "has been named one of the best investment blogs in the U.S. by several sources."

http://www.247wallst.com/

Penned by John C. Ogg, 24/7 Wall St. claims that it "has become famous for its coverage of small cap stocks that are overvalued or undervalued, its break-up analysis of larger companies, and its early look at buy-out candidates."

http://www.wallstreetfolly.com/

"Shining a bright light on and poking fun at the money, power and mind games of Wall Street and beyond." Wallstreetfolly is nothing if not prodigious in its postings.

http://worldbeta.blogspot.com/

This blog "focuses on a worldwide beta asset allocation program. It also tracks global alpha portfolios comprised of ETFs, mutual funds, and closed-end funds. Lastly, it follows portfolios based on the top value and activist hedge fund managers through their 13F filings." One of four blogs put out by Mr. Mebane Faber of Cambria Investment Management.

www.opalesque.com

This site is not free. That said, it is an excellent agglomerater of worldwide news regarding hedge funds and, less interesting to this conversation, private equity investments. Opalesque is certainly worth the very moderate fee it charges.

Then there are the blogs put out by major news organizations. Sites like http://economictimes.indiatimes.com/?, http://ftalphaville.ft.com/ (Financial Times' Alphaville), http://money.cnn.com/magazines/fortune/, http://www.nytimes.com/, http://nymag.com/, www.portfolio.com, http://business.guardian.co.uk/, http://www.economist.com/, http://blogs.guardian.co.uk/news/, http://online.wsj.com/public/us, fit into this category and should be added to your blog-roll.

Remember, above all else the list above should not remain static. Add by viewing other blogs' blog-rolls and checking those blogs out in turn; pare away those blogs not sending you enough useful information via the RSS feeder system.

RECAP

1. The Internet has its place in a background report, but is by no means a panacea.
2. Identifying and locating possible interview sources are a bonus of web searches.
3. Web-based court searches have no place for the institution.
4. The net cannot replace paid news searches.
5. Blogs are useful for industry knowledge and occasionally for juicy morsels of highly current information.

CHAPTER 12

Public Records—Is That All There Is?

So we have come to nearly the end of our show. Up to this chapter, this book has focused almost exclusively on a discussion of public records: from court documents to news files, from credentials verification to corporate records review. What is left to do? That is the question this chapter will answer.

Interviews. Most institutional investors, hearing this, conjure up an image of an interview with the hedge fund manager. But while this is certainly a valuable piece of due diligence, it is best done by the institution itself, given that most of the questions will be technical, performance, and/or strategy-related ones. No, what I am referring to here is not an interview with the manager, or even interviews with references the manager provides, but rather interviews with independently developed sources, individuals who may have or definitely have had a business relationship with the subject.

WHY DO INTERVIEWS AT ALL?

This is the question many institutional investors ask. Based on experiences they probably have had with calling a hedge fund manager's references, or talking to administrators, prime brokers, lenders, and others that service the hedge fund manager's accounts, they are rightly frustrated with the cost-benefit relationship of this effort. The key distinction—and if I had to pick the one item I'd hope every reader takes away from this chapter—is that speaking with people familiar with the subject, but not listed as a reference, will almost always (I hedge this only slightly, and am tempted to just say always, flat out) reveal information that is not available in any public record. Now it is clear that this information will not always be earth-shattering or nefarious, or lead the institution to immediately cancel its investment plans. Having said this, the insight gained from interviews is irreplaceable, not replicable by other methods, and without question adds to the texture of understanding the institution develops into a hedge fund manager's practices, peccadilloes, and likely future behavior.

Though I believe interviews are useful in all instances, some practically demand them.

1. The subject manager is very young so public records are scant.
2. An issue has arisen where public records point to a possible problem that interviews would help flesh out.
3. Litigation, regulatory, or other problem has occurred in an entity where the subject manager worked, but you have no clear idea how or whether the subject was personally involved.
4. Research has uncovered an entity the subject manager has omitted from his biography.

So why doesn't every institution rigorously pursue this line of research? I have already alluded to one possible reason above; that is, calling references has been proven to be, in many instances, a monumental waste of time, and institutions therefore are chastened by this process. Below are some other common objections, along with what I hope are answers that will refute these objections.

OBJECTIONS

1. "I don't have time."

Thinking about the lost time and opportunity cost incurred when calling a list of the hedge fund manager's closest friends and associates, from a reference list, is undoubtedly depressing and distressing, as Walt Frazier might say. But this same argument is no longer reasonable when considering the benefits of contacting independently developed sources. Moreover, this is something that you don't necessarily have to do yourself; a skilled investigative service will be able to offer this as part of an everyday report, and can thus augment your own interviewing efforts with a systematic method aimed at identifying, locating, and contacting people familiar with the hedge fund manager in a business context.

Another timing issue is one that is not discussed often, and is perhaps more troubling: as most institutions make investments on the first of every month, and as due diligence done correctly takes weeks to complete, inevitably a conflict occurs between how much due diligence should get done and how much can get done "on time." The third item to consider is the one that is the most critical, and to my mind, the most adjustable: when should the due diligence process begin? This book is not the first to draw the conclusion that due diligence, meaning, again, due care, is absolutely, fundamentally, necessary to every institutional investor's investment processes. Starting with this root belief, it is certain that doing proper due diligence is not the part of the equation that can or should be changed. Investing on the first of month is also not going to change. So that leaves only the initiation date. Though true that beginning the process earlier might lead to slightly higher costs, as you'll be researching more funds than those in which you ultimately invest, this cost is negligible when compared to the tremendous cost, both to your financial picture as well as to your reputation, that comes with investing in a hedge fund that blows up, particularly one that is subsequently proven to have emitted warning signs that should have been detected prior to the investment. Starting the investigative process earlier, and allowing for the time necessary to complete the process, is the way the smartest institutions operate, and will also allow for interviews, the focus of this chapter and an area that, given their nature, takes time, to conduct.

2. "The manager may get mad; he'll think I am checking up on him."

Well, you are. So what? The problem would be not that you are checking up on the manager, but that you aren't. Certainly managers check out the investments they make. So what's the difference?

I recognize that the above may sound cavalier. I assure you it's not to (well, only slightly). But few things are more personally aggravating than the theory that somehow the person who is receiving money has the power to dictate what the person giving the money does before they give it. Does this sound at all crazy?

The long and the short of it is that not only is it your right to check into the hedge fund manager, it is your duty, both as a fiduciary in some situations and, in others, to those who count on you to invest wisely. While this is not to say that you should be confrontational about discussing this with the manager, neither should you be fearful that doing interviews, and telling the manager about them, will lead him to go elsewhere (for frankly, if he does, this is probably telling you something anyway).

Also note that more and more, hedge fund managers are becoming familiar with the idea that they attract scrutiny, especially from those giving them money. Most hedge fund managers are secretive about their investment methods and competitive advantages, and may avoid publicity at all costs, but increasingly they are okay with the idea that to get, they must give.

3. "The public records are clear, —so, there is no need to do interviews."

I can hear Fred Gwynne now, saying something like this to Joe Pesci in *My Cousin Vinny*: "That objection is lucid, well-constructed and reasonable." As Pesci smiles, Gwynne then scowls and avers, "Overruled." The idea that if public records reveal nothing amiss, interviews are unnecessary is a common misconception, but one that is easy to understand because it is so logical. In fact, we probably subscribed to this school of thought at one time, too. But after seeing what interviews can do and although it sounds counterintuitive, it makes more sense to pursue interviews when nothing adverse is found than when it is. The expression "when there's smoke, there's fire" applies here; often, when public records indicate a subject manager has encountered some problems, conducting interviews will lead to the discovery that the problem was actually worse than reported, and that other, unreported problems also exist. (This is not always true, of course, and thus I am not suggesting that interviews not be done when public records reveal a spotty history.) The corollary, however, is just not true. Many times, newspapers will report what we might term as "fluff." Obviously, once a problem has come to light, many business reporters swoop on it like a seagull seeking dinner. But the absence of negative news and lawsuits does not always mean the subject manager is a good risk. Interviews, simply put, can often be the only way to discern someone's character, primarily because the information is derived from those who know the manager the best: former colleagues, bosses, underlings, and others with whom the manager has done business.

4. "It seems sleazy, and I think it may be against the law."

First and foremost, there is nothing illegal about interviewing former business associates of the subject manager. As will be discussed further in Chapter 14, which deals with laws affecting hedge fund investigations, unless you are hiring the manager (meaning you the institution are actually seeking to employ that person on your staff, as opposed to investing money in their fund, the more typical reason institutions look into managers and the focus of this book), not only can you talk to anyone you like, but the subject also has no legal right to see the information you develop. This is distinct from the so-called sleaze factor, which holds that talking to people about a hedge fund manager, without the manager's knowledge, is in general something to be frowned upon. One solution to this problem, if indeed you consider it one, is to be upfront with the manager. This has two positive effects. One, you eliminate any guilty feelings by explaining to the manager that due diligence on that manager is being done, as a matter of course, and that this is not reflective of how you perceive that manager individually. Two, some managers will, upon learning of your inquiries, reveal things about themselves that would otherwise almost certainly not have come up. So if you think it is improper to conduct interviews sans notice, provide that notice, and let the interview process begin.

WHO IS A SOURCE?

Simple answer: the hedge fund manager's former bosses, coworkers, underlings, and any other person familiar with the subject manager's business history. The best people to reach are those who have left the fund in which you, the institution, are seeking to invest; depending on when they departed, they could be critical to your review. Ranked in descending order of importance are people who worked with the subject at the subject's previous job, starting with his boss and progressing down through colleagues and people who may have reported to the subject. Next would be the same group of people, for each preceding position the subject held. Others might be lenders, heads of entities in which the fund has invested, litigants, and anyone else who has had a professional interaction with the subject. (Remember, I am not all suggesting that you act like the Secret Service and interview the subject's neighbors. Those interviews have a place, just not here.)

HOW DO YOU IDENTIFY SOURCES?

Mostly, via the public records searches I have harped on for chapter after chapter. (See, I bet you thought I was just being unnecessarily long-winded and didactic. Though true, I also had a reason.) Using news searches, corporate records, court cases, regulatory filings, and other similar records, you'll be able to find sources who know the subject manager. The keys to success here are two-fold:

1. You must be looking.
2. Your searches have to be designed to produce these results.

Okay, I know these above statements sound either ridiculous, ridiculously obvious, or both. But trust me, most people reviewing hedge fund managers are doing neither of these things. When I say you must be looking, I am referring to the idea that during your public records searches, you need to keep in one corner of your mind the fact that information you are developing could lead you to plausible interview sources. When reviewing news articles, look for names of former coworkers and bosses, even in stories that otherwise might be somewhat soporific. When looking at corporate records or regulatory filings, bear in mind that a person named as a co-officer/director/member/agent, alongside the subject, could prove to be a valuable source of first-hand insight. And when reviewing a complaint in a lawsuit, file away the idea that the litigants suing or being sued by your subject, though obviously bearing the proverbial axe to grind, might also be a worthwhile interview source.

Point two is trickier. The problem with conducting public records searches designed to reveal, among other things, possible interview sources, is similar to the problems one encounters in doing effective court searches: it is time-consuming, and expensive. But these two problems are merely costs of doing business, and the fact that they influence how due diligence is conducted is both a dirty secret and a public shame. Many of the actual mechanisms used to conduct searches the proper way were discussed in previous chapters. For those whose memory is no longer what it was (I can still remember my first telephone number but have forgotten what I had for breakfast), a brief refresher course follows.

NEWS SEARCHES

News searches are an especially fertile ground for identifying interview sources. The searches need to be both broad and, seemingly oxymoronically, concentrated. By broad, I am referring to the idea that the searches should cover the entities for which the manager has worked before, as well as the current fund, separate and distinct from searches on the individual hedge fund manager. (One of the most damaging hedge fund investigative business practices is searching just the individual manager; many PIs do so in an effort to provide a "cheaper" search, as they charge separately for the manager and the fund. This presumes, of course, that all relevant data will cite the manager, a presumption that is flat-out absurd. In reality, this type of search is offered, again, merely as a cost-cutting measure, and unfortunately those who buy it, unwittingly, have done nothing but cut their knowledge of the risks they are taking. Infuriating, but a fact. Searching the fund and the fund management company, as well as the fund manager's former employers, will turn up numerous stories, many of which will not only provide critical information about how these entities have fared, but will also lead to a contextual basis upon which rapport can be developed in the interview process. A news story mentioning that a fund has seen some turnover can be precisely the introduction needed to open a conversation with a person identified in that story as having left the fund. Meanwhile, that story very often does not mention the subject manager; by searching only the manager, you miss the opportunity to conduct the interview, and you miss knowing that the fund has had turnover.

During the process of reviewing news (or other) sources, one move is simply to search directly for possible independent interview sources. When searching news records regarding the current fund (again, this now presumes that you have seen the benefits of doing so), generally there will be no need to have specific search strings designed to find only interview sources and no other news. The exception is for those enormously public funds that generate tons of news; in these cases, where the search might have to be modified to be effective, specific terms relating to former employees would be added to your search.

Reviewing the news regarding a subject's former firms is an excellent way to illustrate the benefits of broad and concentrated searches. Here, broadening the search alludes to time, that is, extending your research to a short time before and after a subject manager has joined and left a specific firm. Here again, you'll achieve context for future interviews, by learning how the entities for which the manager has worked have fared around the time he was there. And by specifically searching for stories citing just the entities, not only the manager, and by extending the timeline, you may just pick up on a subject who is either the envy of John Edwards for his ability to see that his employers are failing, or is actually one of the reasons they failed. The articles, naturally, will point to this situation as having occurred, but they won't tell you why; interviews might.

Concentrating your search means burrowing down a search from the broadest corporate entity to the division, department, trading group, or other similar smaller entity within the huge conglomerate that employed your manager. Searching for news stories naming Goldman Sachs but not naming the subject manager is obviously a waste of time. Searching Goldman Sachs Global Alpha Fund is a different story. Targeting the appropriate specific area that housed your subject is important with most medium to large entities; the need to target is obviated when the subject has worked for a small firm.

Tip 1. Some entities have gotten so large that there is simply no cost-effective way to research them using broad search terms (this is not, I stress, an indictment of any kind of these entities, merely a statement of fact). If a subject hedge fund manager worked at Highbridge, for example, trying to identify former colleagues by searching news sources for articles naming Highbridge would be pointless. Instead, we would run a search string that looks something like this:

((FUNDNAME) w/20 (former! OR previous! OR join!
OR prior OR subsequent!))

Tip 2. Business wires, believe it or not, often are a good resource for both for interview sources as well as their contact numbers.

CORPORATE/REGULATORY RECORDS

Recall from Chapter 10 that corporate records are derived typically from Secretary of State records, or Dun & Bradstreet (D&B) and its derivatives. In either case, finding interview sources via corporate records is more a matter of paying attention than it is to any special search technique. In entities citing the subject as an officer, director, member or manager, but of which you were previously unaware and which are not disclosed on a biography, contacting the other parties cited as officers, directors, members, or managers can help you understand the hedge fund manager's role in the organization, how much time, if any, he dedicates to it, and what these parties think of the manager's acumen, behavior, and reputation. More typically, these corporate records, like the news sources discussed above, will help you identify former coworkers of the subject manager. Dun & Bradstreet is renowned for its financial reports into businesses; these reports are not what you need to access here. Rather, as discussed in Chapter 10, you'll search D&B market identifier documents,* which are quite helpful in pinpointing interview sources. If a subject manager worked for Lehman Brothers in London, for example, a search of D&B files will often turn up two dozen executives, the subject being one of them. Or if the subject was, say, the CFO of a smaller company, D&B, unlike secretary of state records, will list the rest of the management team. Following news searches, D&B may just be the best single place to identify interview sources.

Much less helpful are Secretary of State records, which all too frequently list only registered agents (this is not really the fault of the databases themselves, but rather is the result of the secretary of state filings themselves not requiring, in many states, officers to be identified). In exceptions, a company's founder, president, or other officer might be cited, but again, this is not typically the case.

Another technique is reviewing SEC files. As noted in Chapter 8 on regulatory searches, these records are available on EDGAR, which in turn is found in a search of a Lexis library (under the "Company" tab on the web-based version; the menu directs you to EDGARPlus).

As with some of the searches described above, this works best when you are trying to spot former colleagues at entities that are public and sizeable.

---

*Through Lexis' gduns library you can access all of D&B's market identifier documents. Gduns is a global file containing company records for both domestic U.S. and international companies. While using this library does not reveal as much information as ordering directly through D&B (something I'd suggest you do on the subject company, for instance), it does list executives, making it perfectly acceptable for the purposes of identifying possible interview sources.

Also understand that coverage here is spottier the further you go back. However, the SEC site now has full-text searching covering the last four years (previously, you could only search by the filer).

DIRECTORIES

The computer era has relegated the common hard-cover directories to the dusty shelves of history, next to the Bananarama albums and IBM Selectrix parts. Still, aside from reminiscing about the good old days, learning what certain directories are surprisingly might prove useful one day. In fact, some of these sources are now available online, further proving their merits; what's more, if you are looking to identify a source who worked with the subject many years ago, suddenly a crusty old book may be your only chance. So here goes.

- *Standard & Poor's Security Dealers of North America.* What we used to call "that little red book" is now described by S&P as "today's most comprehensive guide to brokerage and investment banking firms in the U.S. and Canada." Okay, I will go with their vision. Most important for you is that this directory lists key executives *and* departments, and in today's era of investment bankers reinventing themselves as hedge fund managers, many hedge fund managers' former colleagues will be found in this directory.
- *Polk's.* Polk's provides a list of banks according to region, usually with officers listed. However, many of the older books are significantly outdated and the banks represented have been bought out by other banks, making it difficult to find interview sources still at these institutions.
- *Standard Directory of Advertisers.* This is a geographical list of companies with officer listings. For hedge fund managers, finding a source here will be quite a stretch but at times, this just might work.
- *Directory of Corporate Affiliations/International Affiliations.* This alphabetical index of companies gives a relatively comprehensive list of officers with titles. It also provides locations and satellite office numbers, regional numbers, and so forth.
- *Standard & Poor's Register.* This registry furnishes an alphabetical index of companies, directors, and officers, typically high echelon executives.
- *Encyclopedia of Associations.* Here you'll find a list of associations that are typically hard to verify. Subjects may reference on a biography that they're members of some organization, like the Ukranian Fraternal Organization or the International Christian Esperanto Association. While

the members of these organizations will not have business-related experience with the subject, typically, at times they may be able to comment on how the subject has handled himself on a committee or a project, say.

- *Martindale Hubbell.* A geographic and alphabetical lawyer directory that is irreplaceable if your manager ever practiced law.
- *Burwell Directory of Information Trackers.* This is a directory of technology companies and their officers.
- *Who's Who in Finance and Industry.* This source has excellent biographical information, but subjects aren't always listed (though many of the more established ones are).

GOOGLE

As a means of augmenting the pay databases, Google has its place. Given the nature of the Web, information tends not to date back as far, and the searches are clunkier and less likely to be as precise in their results. Still, Google will help, at times, discover the name of a person who may have attended a conference with the subject, or cowrote an article, or, for a smaller former employer, provide a name of a former, possible coworker. Feel free to play around with Google, so long as you recognize it is no panacea.

OTHER

When you have exhausted leads provided by public records research, and have called sources provided by other sources, but still feel that you need to do more interviews, you may have to consider cold calling. I don't mean picking up the phone and asking people to buy some stock you are selling, though one aspect of this is the same. Given that hedge fund managers have typically spent their careers in the financial services industry, often at very large organizations, it is possible, although not extremely time efficient, to smile and dial in hopes of reaching people who once worked with the subject manager. To increase your odds of success in this often dreary venture, be sure to research departments in which the subject has worked; reviewing business terms and informative articles regarding what may be esoteric subject matter will help you appear knowledgeable of an interviewee or prospective interviewee's specific area of expertise, and thus convince a person in an organization to forward you to the appropriate interviewee.

Once you have a company number and get through to someone, look for the pertinent department head. Although some might suggest going to human resources to get the name, a receptionist in the particular department is more likely to look in their directory if it's a large company. Ask if the receptionist knows of anyone that was around during your subject's tenure by giving approximate dates. If no former colleagues remain, just get the names and then look for their phone numbers via methods described in the next section.

In a specific example of productive cold calling, consider the time when you might have to call broker/dealer firms, where some hedge fund managers have labored previously, and you don't have a name for a prospective interview subject. *Step one:* ask for the Compliance Officer. Compliance Officers are usually aware of any violations committed by employees because they may reflect, indirectly, on them. Additionally, Compliance Officers, experience has shown, typically will at least provide you with the name of the subject's superior, your primary goal.

HOW DO YOU FIND SOURCES' CURRENT CONTACT INFORMATION?

Chapter 5 described at length how to go about ascertaining where a subject has lived, who his spouse is, when he was born, and so forth. In much the same way, the sources and methods outlined in that chapter are now used to locate a potential interview source's current contact information. Naturally, this takes no effort when the source remains at a company that the subject manager has left. But when a source has left the fund in which you might invest, or has since gone on, like the manager, to leave the company for which they both had worked at one time, finding the source can be no easy feat.

As mentioned above, the best possible source of information about the fund in which you are considering investing, the proverbial canary-in-the-mine, is an individual who has left the fund recently. Though a receptionist's departure might not create any interest, even a marketer could have valuable insight into what is happening at a fund right now, something that a background search is not designed to detect. More critically, a recently-departed portfolio manager or an analyst is a potential gold mine of otherwise hard to get real-time insight.

To find people who have left the fund in question, start with the obvious places: the news, corporate records, and regulatory records, any or all of which might tell you where the person is working now. If that fails, you'll need to proceed with searches designed to reveal the person's home phone number. Although this is more awkward than calling the source at work, you can mollify the source by explaining what has occurred and offering to call during work hours, once the source has furnished a daytime number. Meanwhile, here are some tips at getting that home phone number:

1. Try to find out everything you can about the person's full name and states/cities where you know he has worked. You can then cross-reference this information with any of the Internet phone books (good ones include Searchbug, superpages, and anywho.com). Also keep in mind that occasionally, the good oldfashioned 411 method may yield results different from those on Internet phone books.
2. Search Nexis news files, or a file named Finder, located in a Lexis library. If this fails to reveal useful information and the person has a common last name, google or dogpile (a search engine combiner, of sorts) their last name and a key word, like the name of the company where they worked or "arbitrage," say, something related to what they do. Sometimes this will bring up a wedding announcement that provides another family member's name, who might have a listed number.
3. Search identification sources using the person's name and last known work address in an effort to develop a home address and possibly a phone number. If no number is found, consider sending an overnight letter.
4. Ask other sources who *also* worked with the subject and the interviewee. People have each other's numbers.

HOW TO GET A SOURCE TO RETURN A MESSAGE

You've identified some good people to call about your subject manager. You've figured out where these people work now. You've prepared yourself, both with specific questions and with a general outlook on how to proceed with the interview. Now the only thing that remains is how to get the source to actually pick up the phone.

Two schools of thought exist here; I'll discuss both, but know going in that once you go with Option 2, you won't be able to return to Option 1 (sort of like the inexplicable metal spikes at auto rental return garages—you just can't back up).

Option 1. Leave a message that is deliberately vague, in the hope that this will pique the interviewee's curiosity. I'm not at all suggesting that you lie, and in fact, am dead set against that. But leaving people wanting more can be an effective strategy, and may earn you a return call simply because the source wants to know what is happening. Once you are on the phone, the techniques described below will allow you to sink the hook in for good.

All well and good, but how do you do this? Say something like, "This is Joe Smith, and I am calling you about a person you worked with at

Prudential. Please give me a ring at (516) 555-1212 when you have a second. Thanks." What you haven't said here, as you can plainly see, is the name of the subject; while it may seem counter-intuitive, you'll find that people's natural curiosity will at times trump their inclination to remain anonymous and on the sidelines.

Option 2. Be specific. This method, which entails saying, quickly, who you are, why are you calling, *and* about whom, also has the ancillary but critical benefit of demonstrating that you are not going to waste the busy source's valuable time. If you know by their title alone, or by their role in an organization, that a source is likely to be pressed for time, Option 1's vagueness will be ineffective and may even backfire. Calling a portfolio manager at a hedge fund about a former colleague, for instance, lends itself to Option 2 right out of the gate; this person is not likely to allow his curiosity to overcome his desire to focus his day on what he does every day: making money. A better approach to this source would thus be, "This is Joe Smith, and a client has asked us to research Sam Jones, who news stories indicate was your partner for a few years. Please give me a ring at (516) 555-1212 when you have a second. Thanks." If message one does not result in a return call, you might then try to step up the pressure by appealing to the person's sense of ethics, desire to help other people, or simply their wish to be polite. "This is Joe Smith. I recognize that you are busy but anything you can share about Mr. Jones will certainly help him. . . ." This statement ties the subject's interests to the interview source's and is obviously best used when you are certain or nearly certain the two had an amicable relationship. A slight tweak in the language plays to a different theme, that of the need to be polite and helpful. Here, replacing "him" with "me" can result in a return call from a person who feels that information they have to share is important and should be known to someone seeking to do business with their former colleague, and might even feel guilty for not sharing it. Naturally, to the degree that you can show that you have things in common with the source, business-wise, the greater chance of success this has. Still another slight alteration here, like saying, "This is Joe Smith. I recognize that you are busy but my investment committee is holding up a decision pending talking to you about Mr. Jones, so a few minutes would be most appreciated," plays to a source's feelings of self-importance, and can be unusually effective. Here again, the message should be accurate; I used an example that should not be taken verbatim if the statement is blatantly false.

As mentioned above, the one thing you can't do is go out of order; once you have been specific, you give up the opportunity to be vague. Having said this, I'd argue that in most circumstances being specific does offer a better chance of success, and would therefore advocate this approach for the typical message you leave.

Though the use of an assistant has become increasingly rare as voice mail systems entrench themselves into the business world, if a manager's firm does have a person answering the phones, you have options not afforded to you when a machine is standing in your way. Assistants not only know the subjects in many instances, they usually also know the way the interviewee feels about the subject, and are certainly aware of their boss's schedule and preferences.

When you contact a source, and reach an assistant who asks if you'd like voice mail, I'd recommend using this method first (with the techniques outlined above). However, your next move should be redialing and speaking to the assistant directly. Your goal initially will be to determine whether the manager prefers to use e-mail or voice mail. (I am a serial e-mailer but many people, of course, reply much sooner to a verbal message.) If e-mail is the answer, get the source's e-mail address, then send a brief message explaining what is happening (similar to Option 2). Also mention that you were advised by Mary, the assistant, that the source favors e-mails over voice messages. Acknowledge the weaknesses in your position; that is, express in your e-mails (or your voice mails, for that matter) that you realize they won't call you while the market is running, and that they are busy running a business. Then indicate that you'll only need a minute or so, and have only a few specific questions. These demonstrations of concern for the source and knowledge of the source's industry makes you appear less like a market researcher stumbling around and may just be the secret password you need to get the source to open up.

Lastly, what about those times that the source actually picks up? Below are details of how to generate useful information from the source. But first, a quick pointer on one possible introduction you can use. (I stress that this is only one way of handling the opening moments of a call). "Hello my name is —, I'm calling from —. . . . Stop me if this gets a little confusing [this makes the interviewee concentrate harder—no one likes to be the kind of person that is easily confused] our client is considering doing business with Mr. Smith and wanted us to speak with you about your time with him at —."

HOW TO ENCOURAGE A SOURCE TO SPEAK CANDIDLY

I think what this book has lacked, among other things, is a catchy, hopefully soon to be overused acronym that sums up everything you need to know in a purportedly easy-to-remember fashion. So here goes: the key to interview success is PEC, or *Preparation, Emotional Connection and Conversation.* Cute, huh?

PREPARATION

The most fundamental element of interviewing success is preparation, which in turn, leads to the development of rapport. Prepare yourself by reviewing, again, the public records that first turned you onto this source. Mention that you saw a news story reporting that the source and the subject traded bonds together at Lehman's London office. Note that a corporate record listed the interviewee alongside the subject as an officer of an entity. Explain that you saw an SEC file in which the interviewee and the subject were listed as directors of a public company. Remind the interviewee about the lawsuit citing the source and the subject as codefendants. All of these statements, ideally made at the onset of the interview, will help you move past the "tell me all you know about Randy" type question that inevitably produces a stilted answer, if you receive one at all.

Preparation also will help you anticipate when an interviewee might be hostile to a subject, thus guiding your query. Here preparation is akin to reconnaissance. Your early efforts are critical to understand the likely reaction of the interviewee to being called, out of the blue, by someone he doesn't know. This knowledge in turn is critical to your success in keeping the source talking. Clear examples of those almost certain to have an adverse opinion of the subject include someone who has sued the subject manager; someone who fired or had some other work dispute with the subject, according to news accounts; or even an ex-spouse. While each of these interview sources would be handled slightly differently, the central theme still applies: the more you know before you call, the better you'll be able to engage the source in a fruitful discussion.

EMOTIONAL CONNECTION

A lot of interviewing ultimately comes down to reading the personality and motivation of the people with whom you are speaking, and establishing an emotional connection with them. Now some of this can be anticipated if your preparation (there's that word again) was productive; when you read a news story, for example, you will be looking for any hints of discord that might affect the way a source perceives a subject, and thus may influence the way that source reacts to your questions. The U.S.-based business press, regrettably, is often not very explicit when it comes to conflicts. More often than not, you'll have to learn how to interpret what is not being said, rather than what is. A story remarking that a subject has been replaced at a particular fund by another person (your potential source) and offering absolutely no reason for this departure may be (I stress, may be) indicating that the departure was not entirely voluntary. Taking this into account prior to getting on the phone will help you be more nimble in your interviewing effort.

Anticipating a source's likely reaction to your questions can only get you so far. During the call, you'll have no choice but to think on your feet. Here is where preparation takes a different turn; rather than preparing for the call by trying to determine how best to establish rapport, here you'll prepare to overcome standard interview roadblocks (as will be explicated by specific examples in the sidebar below) by being able to understand and categorize them immediately as they are occurring on the call. Most importantly, this is the time when you'll be forced to "read" a source and react accordingly; this is not easy to do, by the way, on the phone, when non-verbal cues are by definition unavailable to you.

The read and react theory is turned into practice by understanding how a source feels about the subject specifically, and how the source feels about the interview process itself. Let's assume that you have sensed, based on the replies to your first few questions, that the source has a negative opinion to share, but is reluctant to do so. The game now hinges on your being able to tap into whatever emotion might motivate the source to open up. For some sources, anger might work. For others, it might be empathy, a way of sharing the experience with the source. For still others it might be getting them to empathize with the client, who they may want to "save." There is no one right answer here, and often you'll need to trot out multiple approaches. At the end of the day, recognize that paying close attention to the cues the source gives you, combined with the ability to adjust, while being honest and, dare I say it, caring, will yield the best results, even in the stickiest situations.

For some specifics, proceed to the box entitled "Overcoming Interviewing Objections."

OVERCOMING INTERVIEWING OBJECTIONS

Your goal in interviewing is to get the source speaking about his knowledge of and experience with the subject. Sources will have questions and fears that, if handled incorrectly, may end up preventing you from reaching this goal. Sources may want to know who you are, whether it's okay to speak with you, whether their names are going to be used in a written report and, if so, in what manner. The following will help you reach your goal of getting the source to discuss the subject, rather than dwelling on these concerns.

Be Prepared—Yes, I am saying it again. Know before you begin an interview what you hope to gain, what the most important questions are, and how the source is likely to react (this is especially important if the source may try to avoid answering). Preparation begins with identifying particular concerns. Important questions should be written down, so they are not overlooked. And by having facts at the ready, such as what deals the subject and source have done together, you will develop rapport.

First Name—Address a source by his first name. You otherwise will come off sounding like a supplicant and possibly will command less respect.

"Yes" or "No" Questions—Don't ask yes or no questions, unless you want a yes or no response. Such questions give your source an easy out, should the question be specific enough for the source to evade addressing what it is you want to know, or mentioning something new. General questions are ideal, for they neither presume knowledge nor betray ignorance unnecessarily. Recall, too, that even phrasing is important: ask "Who was his boss?" rather than "Do you remember his boss's name?"

Much of the success you'll have in overcoming the Yes/No question dilemma will come from remembering one thing: your goal is to let the source do the talking, not you. This is obvious but invaluable and is sometimes counterintuitive to an inexperienced interviewer. People hate silence. The interviewer must command the silence. It's as simple as that; the interviewer must reign in a natural desire to fill silences. Even an awkward feeling question such as "what was your experience working with Ms. Jones" is superior to "was your experience favorable," etc. Everyone knows that. What people forget is that it is uncomfortable for the interviewer to ask an awkward question, and thus the interviewer often will retreat to comfort by talking more than is necessary and optimal (and in many cases providing suggestions as to how to answer, like was is favorable? Was it good?). Remember, the uncomfortable silence is your, the interviewer's, friend.

Be Persistent—The trick to getting a successful interview is often nothing more than really wanting to get it. Of course this isn't enough, but when someone tells you "no" or "I don't know," especially when you're trying to locate someone, make them tell you why or where else you can look. Often times you'll find that if you persist you'll get

(continued)

OVERCOMING INTERVIEWING OBJECTIONS
(*Continued*)

more information than you did initially. Don't be afraid to call people back several times. Ask secretaries when they expect your source to return so you can call back then.

Say What?—Act surprised when a source doesn't want to comment. This works better when the source sounds like he wants to say something, but is unsure if he should, or is afraid he may get sued. Ask why the source doesn't want to comment; for example, if the source says, "I don't think I should say anything," respond with, "Hmmm... O.K.... I just thought since you two were partners (or worked together) you would have a lot to say about him. Why don't you want to comment?" Give the impression that you are genuinely surprised by the source's reticence. Also, a good thing to keep in mind is that sometimes people don't want to speak because they fear being sued or have been contacted by a lawyer. Flat out ask this. Usually they will either say "yes" or "no, but..."

Wear My Moccasins—If a source repeats that they feel uncomfortable talking about the subject, ask them to imagine themselves in your position. "Wouldn't you want to know a little about who you are dealing with?" "I need your help. I'm not sure if this person is a risk." Remember, you are looking for an emotional trigger, and for some people the emotion you can count on to work is empathy.

Start Slow; Say What You Know—Often times it is best to ask the source those questions that you are confident the source will be willing to answer, like when the source met the subject, how long they worked together, etc. Provide encouragement by mentioning specific, unimportant facts about the subject that you do know. This may put the source at ease, and give him the feeling that you're not on a fishing expedition. When the source is talking, and you have developed a rapport, come back to the tough questions.

Note that this must be balanced against the fact that many of the people you call are very busy and don't have a lot of time to spare. When this is the case, start off by saying, "I know you're busy so I'll be brief..." This is where knowing exactly what you want to ask comes in handy. It is essential to prioritize your questions and be sure that you come away knowing the basics: the source's relationship to the subject, as well as the source's view of the subject's overall performance, reason for departure, and how the source would compare the subject to this peers. Many times your honesty and respect for their time will be appreciated and rewarded with direct answers.

I Just Need a Minute or Two—When you first get interview subjects on the phone, state that you just need a minute or two. It eases their concern that they are going to have to spend a lot of time on the phone with you. Ask your most important questions right off the bat; get into the fuzzier stuff later. (This can seem contradictory to advice given above; you'll need to analyze the source's mood quickly and determine whether to get right to it or slow play.) If the interview subject holds you to your "minute or two" comment then your most important questions will be answered. More likely, once disarmed by how little time you plan to keep the interview subject on the phone, the interview subject will spend as much time as you need talking to you about the relevant subject matter; often a one or two minute conversation will become 20 minutes.

A corollary to this is what I call "pulling a Columbo." As the interview nears a close, say, "Oh, and one last thing…" At this point people are relieved to hear that the interview is over and are generally either caught off guard or will answer your question just to get off the phone.

Teach Me—Give the impression that you are eager to learn and, if necessary, more ignorant than you are. Ask sources to explain deals or situations to you. Ask for examples and anecdotes. People like to be teachers. Cultivate this with expressions of interest and wonder ("Really?," "Wow," "I did not know that," "Oh, that makes sense"), and then raise and re-raise questions, even those the source previously had declined to address. If you're enthralled, and hang on the source's words, the source may not want to be so stiff and lose the audience. Also, don't be afraid to ask what something means. If your source likes to hear himself speak, there's a chance he'll start to explain and then remember things about the subject you wouldn't have known to ask.

In conjunction with the "teach me" style, you might consider also blowing a little smoke your source's way. Say things like: "I need your help," or "in doing my research I've found that you'd likely be the best person to speak with regarding Mr. Smith." Still another way of phrasing this is to state, "Although you're not listed on Mr. Smith's

(continued)

OVERCOMING INTERVIEWING OBJECTIONS (*Continued*)

reference list, given that you were his boss, it seems that you'd be the best person to speak with to get an accurate depiction of his tenure at —."

No Comment, But . . .—If a source says no comment to more than one of your questions, but doesn't hang up, keep asking questions. Ask the "Big Question." Ask questions where a no-comment might be helpful, such as, "would you do a deal with him again?" and, "As his former partner, would you say he's competent, trustworthy?" etc. No comment here, of course, is not a very good sign for the subject.

Next, suggest possible interpretations of a 'no comment,' especially ones you do not think the source will affirm, to compel the source to elaborate. Offer suggestions: "Are you saying no comment because you're afraid (of litigation, for example), because of a personal difference, or because of something he did?" Also, here is the time to ask whether the source's reserve is attributable to the subject specifically, or whether the source does not comment on anyone. Even this answer can be hugely valuable.

If you keep getting no comments you can try putting the source in your shoes. "If you were me, and got no comment, where would you look next?" Finally, you can let the source stew for a couple of days and call him again. If by then you've got some information tell him about it and ask him if he can fill in some gaps. (What you should not do is introduce negative information or editorialize.) The source will by now see how serious you are and may want to help.

Commiserate—If a source was harmed by the subject and doesn't want to talk, commiserate: "Yeah, I can understand that. He seems to have really screwed you. You must be really pissed off." Then relay something you already know about how the source got "screwed." Make the source go back to the time of the unpleasant event; make him relive it. Once the source is riled up, he probably won't want to hang up.

Challenge the Source—To be used rarely and when nothing else seems to be working, or when a source makes a sweeping statement but then will not back it up with any specific detail. Challenge question: "Well is this some kind of personal dispute, or is there something here that I need to know about?" If the source says, "I think there's something you should definitely know about." Then you can say, "Great. Please tell me so that my client can have all the information it needs to make a decision." The point here would be to have your source distinguish himself as credible, and not merely griping, if the comments are negative. Be persistent with your follow-up questions so your source cannot make wide, baseless statements or accusations. Ask the source for someone else who can substantiate his comments, and as always, ask for specific examples and wherever possible, corroborating documents.

SPECIFIC STRATEGIES FOR GETTING TO THE "TRUTH"

First, know that there is simply no real way to ever "prove" that a source is telling the "truth" absent strapping them to a lie detector machine (which itself can be fooled, as George Costanza proved). Neither you nor an investigator you hire is the CIA, the police or a prosecutor; moreover, even with prosecutorial or police powers, there is nothing to stop people from being misleading or untruthful (as Congressional inquiries into steroids and possible presidential misconduct have certainly demonstrated). The best you can do is demonstrate that what you report you were told is indeed what you were told.

This notwithstanding, there are ways, albeit imperfect ones, to help substantiate the likely veracity of a source's claims. It is important to reiterate that these methods revolve around the idea that corroboration can be found, plausibly, in the form of specific examples, documents, and other sources able to comment on the same issue.

The first way of getting to the accuracy of a source's statements is demanding details. The trick here is the interviewer's play between sympathy and skepticism. The interviewer initially gets the source to speak freely by over-sympathizing with anything the source has to say. If the source is sharing a decidedly negative opinion of the subject, the interviewer already has broken through with sympathy. Once done, though, at some point the interviewer must seek to vet the source's

(continued)

SPECIFIC STRATEGIES FOR GETTING
TO THE "TRUTH" (*Continued*)

claims, doing so by literally switching gears to the position of the skeptic:

1. Ask for details, including specific examples. One ploy to get interviewees to be descriptive is by purposely making some small mistakes with regard to facts; this can prompt a source to correct you, and in the process lead to the conversation flowing more freely.
2. If the source resists, explain that while what he has told you is crucial, it is more credible if he can explain in greater detail what he means. For example, "Our clients (we) are poised to listen seriously to what you have to say and your information is very valuable, but (A) I don't understand what you are saying or (B) We'll need to hear in greater detail what you mean in order to explain the risk here."
3. When that works, return to sympathy. Expressions of surprise and sympathetic disbelief can be surprisingly effective. "He did that?!" "Wait!? "Excuse me. Can you please explain that further?"

Once the conversation has resumed on this track, it will often be harder for you to get the source to stop talking rather than the reverse. Now is when you move to stage two: documents. A source who provides documents authenticates his declarations. If the source blathers on about the subject manager being litigiousness, ask him to direct you to the court where those suits have been filed. If the source talks about the manager lying about his returns, have him show you the audited figures. And so on. Documentation equals proof.

Finally, never let the source (really, any source) off the phone without asking for other people you can speak with who can substantiate that source's impressions. As an aside, in many instances the people Source One provides end up presenting an entirely different story, so long as you do not tell Source Two what Source One said, and proving that people's perceptions of a situation vary wildly. This furthers the notion, also, that the "truth" is only what people think happened. Regardless, the more people you speak with, the more comfortable you can feel with the tableau of impressions you receive, and the more likely you are to uncover kernels of the manager's behavioral patterns that seem to fit with your own view of that manager. And it is ultimately these patterns that matter the most, for they dictate how the manager is likely to react going forward, giving you a huge head start in how you can efficiently handle difficult scenarios that may arise in your investment relationship.

Wait the Source Out—Remember from our Yes/No discussion above that most humans are off-put by silence in a conversation, and therefore will seek to fill it. Don't be like most people. When you ask a hugely important, and perhaps difficult question, if the subject pauses, simply shut up. And wait. Not that this is a game of chicken, but chances are that if you remain steadfast in your quiet, eventually the source will break and respond. Moreover, you have nothing to lose with this method, except possibly some sweat.

WHAT TO DO WHEN THE SOURCE STARTS ASKING THE QUESTIONS

Despite all your preparation, desire, and skills, many sources will not be opening up like the Red Sea for Moses just because you ask them to. They may turn the tables and first pepper you with questions; your job now is to assuage their trepidations and make them feel comfortable that this process is normal and natural, and not a police inquiry. Consider, too, that a source may feel antsy if he has either very negative information, in which case the over-riding fear is often of being sued, or if he has totally positive information, when the source is actually seeking to protect the subject, not help you. In the former situation, you should assure the source that his comments will remain for your internal use only (of course you need to back up this statement by actually acting on it). It is true that unlike a newspaper, you would, in practice, have to reveal a source's name in the event a hedge fund manager became angry enough at your refusal to invest, sued you, and knew that the reason for your decision was based on the source's comments. Of course, this is a fantastic series of events that is controllable almost entirely by you. First, it is seldom in your best interests to be this specific in your rejections. Moreover, even if you do say that your decision was based on your due diligence efforts, you are under no obligation, ethically or legally, to be more forthcoming, and in fact, the less said, the better. Even in a situation where you'd like to discuss what the source said, to gauge the subject's response, saying exactly who the source is will not add much to the discussion.

If you do not wish to take this tack, go the route of having the source provide you with the names of people less likely to feel consternation about being interviewed. Meanwhile, explain your position to the source, and sometimes, to your surprise, they may just speak freely anyway, having appreciated your candor.

In the latter case, you'll want to explain to the source that his positive feedback will undoubtedly help the subject, not hurt him, as the client seeking to do business with the subject manager will be heartened by these type of independent compliments. By framing the situation this way, you should be able to abate the source's worries and proceed with the interview.

Specific questions you may encounter, and ways to deal with these, follow:

a. I want to speak first with the subject, before speaking with you: Tell the source that this is fine. While you would not want to promote this, it is worse to give the impression that you are hoping to conceal your actions from the subject, or anyone. *Demystify*. Again, feel free after saying you think this is fine to ask another question, though don't anger the person so much that a second interview will no longer be possible.

b. The Source says they can't talk, period: Find out one thing at least: is this a general policy the source or the company they work for have, or is this specific to the subject?

CONVERSATION

This I cannot stress strongly enough: being conversational is vital to your ability to garner the most possible information from people you are interviewing. Everyone can tell when a person calling them is reading questions from a list; almost no one will respond positively to this. So how do you talk in a conversational way? If you have been paying attention at all (and I understand why at this point you might not be), you'll know that Step One is, yes, preparation. Prepare yourself, as stated above, for how the source might perceive your questions. Prepare your list of questions (see below) but only to have them as a handy guide, something to help you remember what to ask if the conversation hits a lull. In states allowing you to tape an interview (see Chapter 14 for a discussion of how this works) you might consider doing so; alternatively, it might be wiser to. And mostly, prepare yourself mentally for the call prior to getting on the phone by going over exactly what you are seeking to learn via this interview.

Solid preparation will lead to productive conversation. Conversational interviewing, in turn, allows you to take the interview in whatever direction it may head. This is why I stress that you should have your basic questions written down (below); doing so will make you comfortable in the tangents that a true conversation inevitably takes, for you know that you can always get back to your elemental queries later.

Conversational interviewing is, at it might sound, something of an oxymoron. The net effect you are seeking is to come across as being the source's colleague, rather than as an interrogator. Speak to the source with this in mind. Laugh at their jokes, and tell some of your own. Be empathetic. Really listen. Pretend this is a friend talking to you about last night's game, or shoes she just bought (if that's your bag). Have a conversation.

STANDARD INTERVIEW QUESTIONS

Familiarize yourself with the following questions, or ones like them, so that you can say them naturally. There is little reason that these basic questions should be unanswered at the conclusion of an interview. Also, by having a list, you can easily add to it as the interview progresses and still keep focused on the discussion.

Whatever you do, however, don't sound like you are reading these questions from a piece of paper. Remember, be conversational—put these questions into your own words (watching out for, of course, the yes/no trap).

1. How did you meet the subject? What do you think of him?

Remember, should you know the answers to these questions already, which I'd strongly encourage you to discover as part of the preparation discussion above, these questions would be framed more as a way of having the source confirm the information you have rather than as a question designed to elicit an actual response.

2. What are the subject's strong points? What could he do better? (Remember, always ask the source to cite specific instances in which the subject has demonstrated whatever quality the source has attributed to them. One way of doing this is to ask, "What event or business dealing, do you think, best exemplified Mr. Smith?")

Crucial here is your timing and phraseology. Asking these questions simultaneously will make you sound like you are reading, something you'll remember from the conversational portion of the above discussion is a death knell to an interview. Instead, ask about strengths first. Later, you can ask, gently but persistently, about "weaknesses," but emphasizing in your choice of language phrases that will likely bring out a reply. Rather than asking for a laundry list of the subject's weaknesses, ask how the subject might improve his performance. Commiserate here too by tossing in that of course, everyone has something they could do better (as this is true, it is not as if you are "fooling" the source). These little steps will go a long way to making the source feel comfortable that indeed, you are not out to "get" the subject but are only interested in getting information that a client might consider pertinent. Another critical phrasing item is something you likely have heard before: never ask a Yes/No type question unless this is the format in which you want to receive an answer. Saying "are there any areas in which Mr. Shain can improve?" will almost always yield a one-word "No"; asking "in what areas can Mr. Shain improve?" does not provide the interview source with a convenient excuse to not reply.

3. How would you rate the subject compared to others with whom you have worked in the same capacity on a scale of one to ten. Why?

A comparison forces the source to get past platitudes, and often will allow you to measure how the source really feels about the subject, even when they say strictly positive things. A source who goes on and on about how great a subject is, then ranks the subject as a 6.5 out of 10, is probably telling you something. And when asked why they are providing a ranking that is inconsistent with their other responses, they may go on to tell you something they had hoped to avoid saying, and that is more critical than anything else they have said to that point.

4. In what position would the subject not excel? What environment do you think their skills are best suited to?
5. Why did the subject leave the company? By the way, never ask, "Do you know why the subject left?" This will generate a simple response: "No."
6. What is the manager's relationship to junior employees? Colleagues? Bosses? How does he handle working on a team? How does he deal with

second guessing? Do others he worked with agree with your assessment? If not, what would they say?

7. What is the subject's management style? How does/did that contribute to low or high turnover among analysts who work(ed) with the manager?

8. How does the subject handle down times?/Stress? When times are tough, how has the subject reacted?

The idea here is that all hedge funds will encounter troubling periods. How a manager handles losses, for example, might say more about them than almost anything else you develop. Do they go into a shell, and become unable to trade? Do they go to the opposite extreme, becoming a riverboat gambler worthy of the affections of Doyle Brunson? Ultimately, the real question is whether they will tell you the truth in these situations, or whether you'll need to be a better interrogator than the late Johnnie Cochran to get a straight answer.

9. How does the subject's prior work experience prepare him for what he is doing now?

You are trying to determine, for example, whether the subject has traded before, or been an analyst but not a trader. This question should help you focus on the idea that it is not enough to know the companies that employed the subject, or the divisions in those companies, or the subject's title. No, what you need to know is how in reality they spent their day.

10. What should a client know prior to doing a deal with the subject?

This is an excellent, open-ended question that can take you in a lot of different directions. You might learn about flaws the source had not formerly discussed. You might hear that the subject is honest, a great trader but incredibly abrasive and someone who has difficulty holding onto staff. Or you might be advised that there is simply nothing else of importance, and that a client should rest easy when dealing with this manager.

11. Would you work with the subject again?/Would you invest with the subject? Do you?

These are examples of Yes/No questions that are actually effective, for here you actually want a Yes/No answer, not a wishy-washy speech.

12. Who else worked closely with the subject? Who else is familiar with the subject's work history? What is their contact information? (Again, do not ask, "Are there others who are familiar..." as you will give a source a chance to say no.)

This type of question can also help you deal with a source who is completely unwilling to speak about the subject. Ask the source who you should talk to. If the source replies, "Well no one that is still here would remember the subject," tell the source that you understand, and that all you need are the names of people who were there, as you will then find those people on your own. Sound confident, and keep at it.

Also, when a reference is given by an interviewee, it can help to wait a few hours before calling the second source. Often, Source One will brief Source Two that you will be calling; Source Two often will speak more candidly knowing someone else has already commented on the subject manager.

Be sure to ask any specific manager-related questions, such as relevant news items, litigation, etc. Also, many situations will raise questions that are unique to that person—knowing what you need to find out in advance is essential, and goes back to the P in PEC.

Finally, always ask questions about claims made by the subject manager on a biography. A previous employer is the person best suited to tell you whether the manager in question really headed a fund, say, versus having played a minor role in the decision making process. Simply put: are the biography's cited accomplishments the manager's, or someone else's?

OTHER TIPS

Tip 1: Log creation. Were you to conduct interviews yourself, I'd recommend that you document your efforts. Here, you can keep track of your sources' names, phone numbers, how they know the subject, how you found their name initially (news, corporate record, SEC, another source, etc.) and any other relevant information used in your interview research, including sources' assistants' names, difficulty level of the interview, etc. I strongly encourage you to also record how you found the person, including both the dead ends as well as the information that ultimately proved fruitful. If you ever need to reach this source again, knowing where not to start can be a bigger time saver than knowing where to start.

The document should also trace the arc of your full efforts; by noting not only the people you reached, but also the people you tried to call and couldn't find, as well as people who never called back, you'll be able to go back later, if necessary, and continue in your efforts to contact people familiar with the subject (while possibly saving yourself time by not repeating previously fruitless efforts).

An example of an interview log is found below.

Subject's Name:
Firm Name:

Contacts:

Name:
Company:
Affiliation to Subject:
Phone:
Email:
Details (that is, left voice-mail, e-mail, interview transcription, etc.):

Name:
Company:
Affiliation to Subject:
Phone:
E-mail:
Details (that is, left voice-mail, e-mail, interview transcription, etc.):

Tip 2: Always compare the list of sources you develop with the references furnished to you by the subject manager. At times, the subject's omission of a boss or longtime co-worker can be equally as telling as what that person eventually says to you in an interview.

Tip 3: Look for indications of conflict, including lawsuits, terminations, resignations and/or rivalries described in news and other sources, when seeking interview sources. This should be thought of in terms of balance; because most of the business press takes a rather complimentary approach to its subjects, antithetical opinions should be sought.

Tip 4: If the interviewee seems to have a certain animus for your subject, press for information regarding the subject's education, previous work experience, etc. The interviewee may have knowledge about discrepancies in your subject's past and has demonstrated a motivation to speak. Note, here you'll always want to then go on and verify, independently, anything the source asserts.

Tip 5: In those instances where you have specific, verified information at your disposal, and you think a source is being untruthful about the situation in question, repeat what they have said several times but in subtly different ways, angling towards what you think the truth might actually be (this of course presumes, again, that you have facts to support your position). A source eventually may get fed up and re-state their view, which may yield new, more accurate information.

Tip 6: Becoming a decent interviewer is not hard. But being a great interviewer is rarely learned, it is just there. A lesson we have learned after watching scores of people try to do interviews is that the interviewers who are successful really want to get sources on the phone. This attitude, unfortunately, is not something that can be easily transmitted externally; either you feel this way, or you don't. Given this, if you decide to do a lot of interviews on your own, I'd recommend that you measure the results your staff is achieving and then have interviewers who are thriving become your interview "specialists." For while the rest of this chapter can make a poor interviewer adequate, even above average, no book can provide the ultimate key to a consistently excellent interviewer: innate desire.

Tip 7: Develop your own short-hand, and stick with it. This will help you record discussions, while keeping the tone conversational. As soon as the interview ends, fill in your notes with specifics, as this moment of clarity will recede as time and interruptions take their inevitable toll on your memory.

Tip 8: Be available. There is nothing worse than struggling mightily to get a source to return a call, then being on the phone with someone else. Alert your staff that they should interrupt you, find you, page you or whatever, when you are awaiting an important return call.

WHAT NOT TO DO

Learning from your own experience can be painful, which is why it is almost always profitable to learn from someone else's, instead. Below are some tips on things you shouldn't do when interviewing sources about a hedge fund manager.

1. Do not introduce negative information about the subject to people who have no reason to know it. Remember, conversations can and do get back to the subject, so be ultra-professional. (Saying something like "I heard the manager visits prostitutes" for example, is probably not a good idea. Now if the source happens to be someone who sued the subject, alleging that the subject fired him for not visiting a prostitute with the source, then feel free to discuss this. The operative word here, in other words, is "introduce.")

Along these lines, don't jump to conclusions and pester your interview sources with inappropriate questions, like, "Mr. Smith has had a couple of restraining orders—do you think he is a violent person? Have you ever witnessed him acting out violently?" Instead, be subtle: "What do you think of Mr. Smith's management style? Are there any issues or patterns we should be aware of?"

Another situation that develops here is what information, provided by one source, can share with a second source. If Mr. Johnson has been interviewed, and you are now speaking with Mr. Kelly, do not tell Mr. Kelly that Mr. Johnson said the subject was "difficult" to work with, and could he corroborate that. One, you should not generally be disclosing the names of other sources unless you were given clearance to do so by that source. Beyond this, you do not want to color the second source's opinion by sharing with him information from the first. This does have its limits, however; if source two, Mr. Kelly in our example, is not opening up at all, you might consider phrasing a question this way, "I have heard that the subject manager can be a difficult co-worker. Other people disagreed with this assessment. How would you describe him?"

2. Don't lie. Subterfuge and pretexting may very well have a place somewhere, but not when it comes to checking out hedge fund managers. Play things straight, using the techniques described above, and you'll get what you need while being able to sleep at night.

3. Don't interrupt, or talk over the source. Let people speak. If someone is rambling, let them; do not interject until you're sure that the interviewee has stopped talking.

4. Don't tear through your questions. Most answers will lead to another question. Take time to formulate good follow up questions and feed off of the source's answers. Again, don't worry about uncomfortable silences; if anything the source will want to fill the void with more commentary.

5. Don't say you are looking for a "reference." If the source feels positively about the subject, you are at best setting yourself up for an unfettered endorsement. Worse than this, though, is that you are setting the tenor of the interview, as opposed to letting it evolve naturally. And worse still, if the source is even mildly ambivalent about the subject, he may just refuse to talk at all, hearing the word reference and believing that this is not a position he is comfortable taking.

6. Finally, do not hang up the phone when the questions you think you want answered have been answered. Allow for more information to develop in the course of your interview. This harkens back to the conversation angle discussed at length above.

RECAP

1. Identify sources via public records and subsequently, via other sources.
2. Find sources' current contact information by using same techniques used to find subjects. Persistence is crucial.
3. Before doing an interview, be prepared. Preparation= rapport=success.
4. Be conversational.
5. Try to tap into the interview source's emotional connection to the subject.
6. Watch your phrasing. Do not ask a Yes/No question unless you want a Yes/No answer.
7. Wait out silences. Silence is your friend.
8. Always ask for specifics and examples.
9. Ask for corroboration, both in the form of other interview sources and documentation, as well as via additional interview sources.

CHAPTER 13

What You Think Is Helpful, But Isn't

So far, this book has focused on teaching you how to investigate hedge fund managers, learn their backgrounds, tendencies, reputations and even their warts—all with an eye toward predicting their future behavior and ultimately how much risk you'll be taking on by adding them to an alternative investment portfolio. This chapter, however, will embark on a different mission: here, I'll talk about, and hopefully debunk, some of the myths about investigations and what makes them successful.

SUPER SECRET SOURCES

How many times has an investigative firm called you, or told you in a meeting, that their firm is staffed by ex-FBI, CIA, DEA, KGB, or PTA members? A quick glance at the websites of many, if not most, firms in the PI world reveals a cornucopia of cool-sounding spy acronyms, all designed to get an institution to say one thing: "We don't have anyone who's worked at the CIA, so we better hire those guys, because they do." But before you pick up the phone, consider asking yourself a different question, "What is the PI selling here?"

What the PI in question is selling, in effect, is access. Access to information currently maintained by the government. Information that is otherwise inaccessible to the average person, or institution.

This yields a problem. If the PI is selling access to information that others can't access, either one of two things must be true:

1. The government's most classified data, that which is held by some of its most secretive agencies, is being sold to the highest bidder, provided that person happened to have worked at a secret agency before. And

somehow this is going on all the time, with no one in the government being discovered or penalized for these actions.
2. The PI is full of it.

Okay, Monty, I'll take door number 2. It's not as if, after all, the CIA has a hedge fund division, teaching the latest and greatest investigative techniques to a squad of operatives who'll subsequently be able to parlay this into private practice (at least I sure hope it doesn't, what with a bearded Islamist, initials OBL, still on the loose). In reality, it is incredible to believe the notion that somehow our nation's investigative agencies, tasked with protecting us from terrorists, stopping bank robbers, spying on other nations, and combating the drug scourge (full disclosure: as a libertarian, I think the drug "war" is complete folly, but that, too, is for another book, one already done well by Jacob Sullum of *Reason*), have the time, inclination, and skill to compile dossiers on hedge fund managers, too. And if I am right, and I am as confident of this as I am that the sun is coming up at some point tomorrow, then what PIs are doing is no more than clever marketing, itself certainly not illegal, but ultimately not useful to you, the institutional investor, either.

What I'd suggest is that when you are told of the qualifications of the PI's staff, ask simply how this affects the work produced. This is the easiest, most direct way of ferreting out the above, though it is unlikely that most PIs will be forthright about what they hope remains an alluring mystery.

OFAC

According to Lexis, this is how to access OFAC files,[1]

> *The Office of Foreign Assets Control ("OFAC") file is designed as a reference tool providing actual notice of actions by Office of Foreign Assets Control with respect to Specially Designated Nationals and other entities whose property is blocked, to assist the public in complying with the various sanctions programs administered by OFAC. In addition to the OFAC content the enhanced file contains FBI Fugitives including 10 Most Wanted, Most Wanted Terrorist, United Nations Sanction list, World Bank of Debarred Firms list, Politically Exposed Persons (list of Chiefs of State and Cabinet Members of Foreign Governments), Commodity Futures Trading Commission (list of Regulatory and Self-Regulatory Authorities that have received exemptions under CFTC Rule 30.10), Office of Comptroller of Currency list of Unauthorized Banks, and*

Interpol European Union Most Wanted (Recent Event Red Alerts), Bank of England (Consolidated list) and a one-time Special Alert list issued from FinCEN.

The latest changes may appear here prior to their publication in the Federal Register, and it is intended that users rely on changes indicated in this document that post-date the most recent Federal Register publication with respect to a particular sanctions program in the appendices to chapter V of Title 31, Code of Federal Regulations. Such changes reflect official actions of OFAC, and will be reflected as soon as practicable in the Federal Register under the index heading "Foreign Assets Control." New Federal Register notices with regard to Specially Designated Nationals or blocked entities may be published at any time. Entities and individuals identified are occasionally licensed by OFAC to transact business with U.S. persons in anticipation of removal from the list or because of foreign policy considerations in unique circumstances. Licensing in anticipation of official Federal Register publication of a notice of removal based on the unblocking of an entity's or individual's property is reflected in this publication by removal from the list.

Wow. Sounds ominous, almost as scary as when the Delta House was put on Double Secret Probation. And, ultimately, just as nonsensical, and worse, very distracting. What I wondered is how many people are actually on this "list." More specifically, how many of those on the list are hedge fund managers? My guess is extraordinarily few, in fact, zero; anecdotal evidence certainly supports the zero hypothesis, as in reviewing thousands of hedge fund managers, I can't remember finding a single item from this source. Reviewing the OFAC list (http://www.ustreas.gov/offices/enforcement/ofac/sdn/sdnlist.txt), I confirmed my theory (and made some money for my optometrist) by not finding a single recognizable hedge fund manager on this list.

As this search is part of Lexis, and is simple to do, it certainly can't be harmful to look. Just remember not to feel any huge sense of security if your hedge fund manager is not here.

SOCIAL SECURITY NUMBERS

The investigative industry's dirty little secret is that with a person's home address, one can obtain that person's social security number. But why bother? The only, and I repeat the only, reasons any investigator needs a social security number, as elucidated in Chapter 5, is to help determine where a subject has lived, and thus what courts need to be searched, and to distinguish information that relates to the subject from that which merely involves another person with the same name. The importance of this latter point cannot be overstated. It is no one's fault that many people share the same name; I'd argue that more damage is done by inadvertently confusing two people with the same name than by simply deducing someone's social security number. That said, consumers' concerns regarding identity theft are real and valid. Below is what I believe to be a simple solution, so simple that obviously somewhere I am missing the motivation of the powers that be (banks, insurance companies, and everyone else who routinely ask for our social security numbers) in failing to seize an opportunity to easily address a growing problem.

ELECTRONIC EYES: WHAT THE COMPUTER KNOWS—A SPECIAL REPORT; ON LINE, HIGH-TECH SLEUTHS FIND PRIVATE FACTS

An article entitled, "Electronic Eyes: What the Computer Knows—A special report; On Line, High-Tech Sleuths Find Private Facts," was typical of many recent stories relating to this topic: the article's premise is that "the world of computer technology and information marketing ... has turned private detectives into a vanguard of privacy invasion."[2] In other words, private citizens better be alarmed that their personal lives are no longer personal, because of the power of the computer. The article is misleading; more importantly, the solution to privacy invasion lies not in eliminating computer-based information (unfeasible) or in denying access to this information ("information brokers" now routinely access information that they're denied to). Rather, the defense against this "privacy invasion" is simple, and two-fold: eliminate the use of social security numbers as passwords, instead using a PIN, like those used for bank debit cards, and secondly, actively pursue and prosecute information brokers and investigators who obtain information illegally.

The use of a PIN rather than a social security number as a password would dramatically increase consumer's privacy protection. The telephone and other scams mentioned in the article would no longer be effective, as an information broker would have no access to this PIN.

Information brokers who do manage to circumvent these procedures should be prosecuted and jailed. The article lumps together legal and illegal information gathering, then infers that this information retrieval is immoral. Of course, obtaining information on medical histories, phone records, credit cards, stock accounts, bank accounts, and tax records is already illegal, and, ergo, immoral. To properly analyze the morality of computer data retrieval, one must focus on whatever information is accepted by law. Combining the illegal and legal merely obfuscates the issue and potential solutions, while inflaming public fervor.

Society needs no new laws, but rather must start enforcing the ones that exist. My firm routinely receives literature from information brokers advertising their ability to retrieve information that is not legally available. Why do these companies broadcast their illegal behavior, seemingly without fear of the law? Because news stories like this one refer to them as "data moles." (Interesting that bank robbers with high-tech body armor aren't called "money moles.") It's time that these information brokers be called what they are, crooks. And it's also time for banks, credit card companies, insurers, doctors, and other businesses to cease asking for a social security number as a password, and instead have us all use a PIN.

CREDIT REPORTS

Credit reports, discussed further in Chapter 15, are available with, among other things, a signed release from the hedge fund manager. In the old days (you know, when we old-timers walked five miles to school, uphill, each way), credit reports had more value because they imparted more otherwise unavailable data than just whether someone has paid a Sears card on time. Nowadays, most of the "negative" items that a credit report mentions, including bankruptcies, tax liens, court cases, and other similar matters, are recorded elsewhere, as well. What's more, these records are stored in publicly searchable arenas, not requiring a release from the subject. So what's left of the valuable portion of credit reports is solely the hedge fund manager's actual credit history. And although on occasion this can prove useful, given the rare case in which a hedge fund manager is not paying his credit cards, mortgage, auto loans, or student loans on time, or in the situation where the manager is extremely young (and thus has not left much of a trail to follow via other sources), far more often than not this usefulness will be outweighed by the negative reaction many hedge fund managers will have to institutions seeking to review their credit.

RECAP

1. A lot of what you might think is helpful is really marketing-influence nonsense.
2. Comprehensively reviewing and analyzing public records, combined with interviews of independently developed sources, is what makes due diligence effective.

CHAPTER 14

The Law

A fair number of laws affecting background reviews relate primarily to outside vendors, rather than to an institution that is doing its own research. Still, it is always useful to understand the law, not only for the situations in which you use an outside firm for background reviews, but also for your own edification. On occasion your internal staff may question you or, more likely, present a misleading case based on something they have overheard and misinterpreted.

FAIR CREDIT REPORTING ACT (FCRA)

The FCRA applies to two discrete events in the investigative universe. The first relates to potential employment matters, while the other has to do with credit reports.

A. Employment Investigations

An investigative agency conducting research that might affect the employment status of an individual has in almost all instances several obligations per the FCRA (these are trumped, by the way, by an ongoing fraud review). Foremost among these is that the subject of the review must be advised of the report and sign a release authorizing its preparation prior to the report (see Addendum 14.1 for a copy of an FCRA employment release). Other conditions include:

- Before an adverse decision is made (meaning: the subject does not get hired, or is fired), the subject must have an opportunity to review the report. This legislation stemmed from the belief that consumers were being effectively blackballed by information that may not have even pertained to them, with no ability to correct said data.

- Subjects currently residing in California, Minnesota, or Oklahoma have a right, based on their respective state laws, to view a report regardless of whether an adverse action was taken or not.
- If interviews are conducted, the interviewees must be alerted, in advance, that their comments may be viewed by the subject, in light of condition number one, outlined above.
- None of the data from an employment matter can be reused.
- Criminal and civil matters that antedate the report by more than seven years cannot be disclosed; it is crucial to understand, however, that this does not apply to employees who earn $75,000 or more.
- Aside from the release, the potential employers must sign an end user certification, attesting to the fact that they understand and are abiding by the relevant FCRA provisions. See Addendum 14.2 for a copy of a sample document.
- A buyout situation can also be an employment scenario if the individual in question is not an owner (an owner of a firm, by definition, cannot be fired, and thus cannot have his employment affected) and if the buyout shop would seek to have a person fired rather than merely walking away from a transaction if something significantly negative were found about the employee in question.

   None of these factors means anything to an institution seeking to invest in a hedge fund. Don't be swayed by anyone who tells you otherwise. Except in the instances in which an institution is looking to hire staff for its firm, investment situations do not fall under FCRA (these situations are not considered consumer reports and are more akin to Dun & Bradstreet commercial products and the like, as evidenced in the attached FTC opinion letter (Addendum 14.3)). Even in those situations where are you looking to bring on internal staff, you are allowed to conduct, on your own, any research on a candidate you wish except for a credit report (see below) without asking for permission; remember that FCRA (Addendum 14.4), as it relates to reports, applies to third-party, consumer reporting agencies, not you.

B. Credit Reports

   Under no circumstances can you run a credit report without a release from the subject authorizing this (again, ongoing fraud investigations are an exception, but this does not apply to this conversation). Moreover, a release is not fluid; each time a credit report is procured a new release is necessary.

   As will be explained in Chapter 15, some credit agencies require other items as proof of location. Essentially, the credit agencies need to ensure that the end user of the credit report (you) is a real entity, located at the address you claim to occupy.

NCIC

As alluded to in the previous chapter, it is not uncommon for investigative agencies to claim, explicitly or implicitly, that they have access to information that you as a private citizen don't. Aside from the gargantuan leap in logic it takes to believe that not only do secretive governmental agencies possess information about hedge fund managers, but they are also willing to sell such information to those who wish to buy it (provided the buyers used to work at the governmental agency in question), it must be pointed out that laws exist to prevent this very thing from occurring. One of these relates to the National Crime Information Center, better known as the NCIC. Its website makes it eminently clear that the information collected here is not available to the public: "NCIC is a computerized index of criminal justice information (i.e.—criminal record history information, fugitives, stolen properties, missing persons). It is available to Federal, state, and local law enforcement and other criminal justice agencies...."[1]

Misuse of this data, I can say from first-hand observation, was rampant at one time. Rules have been tightened over the years, however; one of the newer requirements forces the law enforcement official using the system to log in, and presumably captures the search. This means that it is no longer possible for a source to sell access to this system to a former colleague seeking to learn whether a person is in the system. The website states, "All records in NCIC are protected from unauthorized access through appropriate administrative, physical, and technical safeguards. These safeguards include restricting access to those with a need to know to perform their official duties, and using locks, alarm devices, passwords, and/or encrypting data communications."

In addition to the fact that the NCIC's information is not public, it should be understood that the data itself is not infallible. According to the website, "data contained in NCIC is provided by the FBI, federal, state, local and foreign criminal justice agencies, and authorized courts." A figure that has been tossed around is that 20 percent of the information the NCIC would like to capture is actually entered in the system. One hypothesis that might explain this has to do with incentives; what incentives do state and local entities have to be 100 percent vigilant in their reporting of data? It can certainly be argued that doing so helps everyone, but when it comes at a personal cost (that is, more work for the already overworked public law enforcement person) it is not hard to imagine why compliance is not routine.

The long and the short of it is simple. Criminal records need to be searched area by area, based on an examination of where a manager has lived and worked. There are no legal shortcuts to this.

GOVERNMENT MONEYMAKING IDEA

Like many people I sometimes fall into the easy trap of criticizing the government without offering any solutions. Today, I am breaking free of my self-induced bonds and offering free advice. As illuminated above, the government does not sell NCIC data; it merely collects, then makes available this data to other governmental, judicial agencies. Part of the reason for this, I suspect, is the "innocent until proven guilty" theory that is a bedrock of our society. It would be hard to counter the notion that a person who finds himself in the NCIC database after an arrest but who later turns out to be proven innocent should have a further stigma attached to his record by having this record even more widely disseminated. That said, what if the NCIC information were to be segmented in two categories: arrest records, and convictions. The convictions portion of the database could then be bundled and sold to say, Lexis, at a huge price, for the perceived value of this information would be quite high (although the average hedge fund manager has not been convicted of a crime, you can see that searches done for other reasons, including preemployment for numerous, low-level employees might yield different results based on the nature of the people involved). If the NCIC were to pay some of the money it received to the local and state agencies reporting in, the data would be that much more robust (as techies love to say and as I have desperately waited 200+ pages to say once) and thus, even more valuable.

TAPING INTERVIEWS

When conducting interviews with references (almost but not quite a complete waste of time) and independently developed sources (refer back to Chapter 12), one school of thought suggests that taping the calls can be extremely useful in that it frees up the interviewer to be entirely conversational, rather than being concerned with frantic note-taking efforts. The hurdle here, however, is that although many states permit this taping, with no advance notification to the other party (this is termed "one-party consent," with you, the interviewer, being the one party consenting), others don't. The following 12 states, in fact, require "all party" consent when recording conversations[2]:

California	Massachusetts
Connecticut	Michigan
Delaware	Montana
Florida	New Hampshire
Illinois	Pennsylvania
Maryland	Washington

The courts have not yet totally sorted out which law will prevail when a person calls from a one-party state like New York to a person in a two-party state court like California, although rulings tend to indicate that the two-party consent standard will be upheld. To be safe, and until national standards are firmly established, it is certainly best to err on the side of caution by not taping any calls to individuals located in two party states.

PRETEXTING

The recent Hewlett-Packard scandal has caused a minor uproar over the use of an investigative technique known as pretexting. A similar scenario involving a hedge fund, albeit a matter that has received far less attention, is David Einhorn's accusation that an Allied Capital "agent" illegally obtained his phone records. Here's some background:

Pretexting means different things to different people. What the HP investigators were purportedly doing—posing as a John Smith to get that John Smith's phone records—is not kosher. In fact, it is also not permissible to pose as any real person to get records of another person; pretending to be John Stossel doing an investigative piece on a John Smith, for example, also does not fly. Pretending to be a fictional person and seeking information about a John Smith can, however, be legal in certain instances.

The above, however, are classic examples of distinctions without a difference. I say this because pretexting simply has no place in hedge fund investigations, so whatever fine-tuned legalities of the situation might exist are irrelevant. For your purposes, simply keep this in mind: be wary of boasts of access to super-secret sources, or connections to current or former federal agents. Hedge fund background reports do not involve espionage. Instead, the task is to master the art of assimilating all legal methods and sources to provide business intelligence in a relevant manner. This approach will yield more business-relevant information than any other, while keeping the risk of negative attention at its lowest possible point.

RECAP

1. Most laws involving private investigations have little bearing on hedge fund research.
2. Some investigative firms flout the law to gather data.
3. Using an investigator that does so can and will cause you heartache, eventually.

CHAPTER 15

Credit Reports

WHO CAN ORDER THEM?

Credit reports are available from three major credit agencies: Trans Union (http://www.transunion.com/), Experian (http://www.experian.com/), and Equifax (http://equifax.com/). Though each has its own way of doing things, at least one agency requires three of the following from the end user (in this instance, you, the institutional investor) prior to reviewing a person's credit:

1. A copy of three (3) recent end user's employment applications.
2. A copy of the end user's filed Articles of Incorporation, sales tax records, or state/federal tax records.
3. Copies of two end user utility bills (one bill from 2 different utilities).
4. A copy of end user's business license.
5. A copy of end user's business credit report.

Any firm that reviews credit for you should be able to procure, rather easily, numbers 2 (from online Secretary of State records) and 5 (a Dun and Bradstreet profile). Item number 3 is typically the simplest to provide the vendor, then; phone records, heat bills, electric bills, gas bills and other similar invoices all serve the purpose.

In addition to the above, Fair Credit Reporting Act (FCRA) regulations make it clear that prior to reviewing someone's credit in anticipation of a business transaction, the subject must sign a release authorizing the review of that credit. See Addendum 15.1 for such a release.

As for whether you, the institution, can access credit reports directly, that is a question to pose to the credit agencies directly, for their rather Byzantine regulations are both complicated and ever-changing. Note, meanwhile, that credit reports are inexpensive and easy to retrieve; their value, as discussed below, is dubious, however, so don't get sucked into spending a lot of money on these reports.

THE VALUE OF A CREDIT REPORT

Since you have by now read Chapter 13, "What You Think Is Helpful, But Isn't," you already have a hint about my opinion of the relative worth of credit reports. As a reminder, credit reports were at one time quite valuable because they had information that other sources didn't. As things like tax liens, judgments, court cases, and bankruptcies became ubiquitous via searches of other online records, all without the rigmarole of a release from the subject, utility bills, and so forth, the value of a credit report has plummeted.

Still, credit reports do have one thing no one else has: payment history on car loans, vehicle loans, student loans, and credit cards. And like the theory of tax liens (if a hedge fund manager cannot manage his own financial affairs, why let him manage a piece of yours?), the credit report can play a role in your due diligence efforts. Just remember that unlike other sources, this one comes with a price tag, the hedge fund manager's scorn.

As an aside, one other advantage of credit reports, albeit a minor one, is that they do provide some employment data: a credit report often has a reliable record of one or more companies for which the subject has worked and the date the information was reported. This can be helpful in placing a manager at a particular place at a certain time, especially when the company will not verify employment and no news or corporate information places the subject there. This said, credit reports will not provide start and end dates, and will in no way replace the process of establishing, then verifying, a subject's full employment history.

DO CLIENTS TYPICALLY WANT THEM?

Very rarely are institutions, in our experience, reviewing credit reports on hedge fund managers. The problem with credit reports is the upside/downside ratio is just too low. Hedge fund managers are notoriously secretive. Asking them to fill out a lengthy release, replete with a ton of legal mumbo jumbo, is like trying to get Imelda Marcos out of a shoe store. It just isn't going to happen. Moreover, they may react aggressively, and given that you want to have a long-term relationship with them, starting off on this type of footing is, for many institutions, just not worth it.

HOW TO READ A CREDIT REPORT AND WHAT TO LOOK FOR

As an investor, your attention should be paid to those items that indicate any type of financial issue, whether these are termed "current negative" accounts, "previous negative" accounts, collections (as you can surmise, these are initiated when the credit grantor has exhausted other means of having the creditor pay an outstanding bill), charge-offs (this is the final, worst stage and indicates that the credit grantor believes the account will never be paid, and is thus "writing it off"), judgments, liens, or bankruptcies. A summary of this information is typically located near the top of the credit report, after the person's name, address history and other identifiers are shown; the following is an example.

THE FOLLOWING CREDIT SUMMARY REPRESENTS THE SUBJECT'S TOTAL FILE HISTORY

PUBLIC RECORDS: 0   CURRENT NEGATIVE ACCTS: 0   REVOLVING ACCTS: 7
COLLECTIONS: 0   PREVIOUS NEGATIVE ACCTS: 0   INSTALLMENT ACCTS: 0
TRADE ACCTS: 7   PREVIOUS TIMES NEGATIVE: 0   MORTGAGE ACCTS: 0
CREDIT INQUIRIES: 2   EMPLOYMENT INQUIRIES: 3   OPEN ACCTS: 0

In this example, the person had flawless credit, with all "negative" accounts marked with a zero reflecting the fact that at no time did the person have any delayed payments, liens, collections, or judgments. This won't always be the case, as some reports are littered with accounts that are or were past due.

Not all "negatives," of course, carry the same weight. The manager may have been 30 days late once on a VISA card; this clearly is not a concern when compared to, say, another credit card in which the manager was 90 days+ late, on many occasions, and ultimately resulting in a collection taking place. As has been reiterated in chapter after chapter, what you are looking for is a pattern of behavior, with the following being the factors that should be stirred into the credit stew:

1. The number of accounts that have been or are now termed "negative."
2. The frequency these accounts have been negative.
3. The dollar amounts in question.
4. The current standing of these accounts.

Using the Trans Union credit key, attached at Addendum 15.2, you will be able to deduce the answers to the above. First, some definitions are in order. Current negative accounts are those accounts where the creditor (the subject) is now behind on payments. Previous negative accounts, then, you can see are those where the creditor made late payments at some point in the past but is currently paying on time. Previous times negative totals are the number of payments that were made past the allotted time period; one previously negative account might itself have been paid delinquently 10 times over a three year period, while another might have been paid late only twice (in that instance, the previous times negative number would be 12).

The source of "negative" accounts can be obvious, such as those characterized as a collection, charge-off or "settled for less than full balance," which is an account that was, well, settled for less than the full balance owed. Other times, however, which account that is or was negative may not be as apparent, as per the following example.

```
***EMPIRICA 95 SCORE +710 : 001,010,002,013 ***
**TRANS-ALERT**HAWK-ALERT**SEE END RPT
TRD=19 NEG=1 PUB=0 COL=0 INQS=5 BAL=$221K HC-CL=$889K-71.9K
TRADES
SUB.NAME/ACCT# SUB#/TERM OPND HICR DVER/CLS BAL/MAX.DEL
PAY.PAT/HIST MOP


GUARANTY MTG F 6379003   1/87 $57.5K 4/98A   $0   $0   211111111111 M02
        4/98C           11X11X11111
C               *TRANSFER /VAREALESTATEMORTGA   23   1   0   0

SEARS    B 6256458   5/85  $8499 2/03A  $7385 $0   111111111111 R01
    $8400           111111111111
I               /CREDIT CARD 48   0   0   0

DILLARD    D 4456015 1/86  $5127 2/03A  $0   $0   XXXXXXXXXXX1 R01
    $7500   12/01P           111111111111
A               *CREDIT CARD LOST/STOLEN/CREDIT   46   0   0   0

EXNMBLE/MBGA  O   10/85  $1205 2/03A  $457 $0   111111111111 R01
    MIN46 $2000           111111111111
I               /CHARGE ACCOUNT 48   0   0   0
```

Reading this gobbledygook almost makes me yearn for a 50-page complaint in a multicount lawsuit (almost). While I put in some eye drops, check out a credit tool aimed at consumers seeking to decipher their credit reports, provided by BCS Alliance (http://www.bcsalliance.com/ z_howtoreadreport.html). Though you are not the end user the company had in mind, the site is still quite instructive, and should be combined with the aforementioned credit key to answer any questions you may have.

Per the BCS Alliance site, accounts are rated as follows:

0 = Approved, but account is too new to rate or not yet used

1 = Paid as agreed

2 = 30 or more days past due

3 = 60 or more days past due

4 = 90 or more days past due

5 = 120 or more days past due or is a collection account

7 = Making regular payments under a wage earner plan or other arrangement

8 = Repossession

9 = Charged off account

Given this, you will look for accounts that are rated with a two or higher, as reflected both by the series of a dozen or so digits, in most accounts these being all ones, under the category "Payment Pattern," as well as by the current rating, noted typically on the far right of the second line of each account. In the accounts above, three accounts are rated "R01;" the R indicates the account is a revolving credit account (an unimportant distinction for your analysis) while the 01 denotes that the account is being handled perfectly. The Guaranty Mortgage account, on the other hand, is shown as "M02," showing that it was once 30 days late. Be aware, too, that exceptions and explanations for late payments do exist. Here, a transfer of the mortgage account occurred. In these instances it is not uncommon for an account to be listed as late even if the creditor is not at fault, and this information should be viewed with this in mind.

Similarly, small hospital or other medical accounts often represent legitimate disputes or matters awaiting insurance resolution.

The third item on our list, you'll recall, is the dollar amounts in question. Two numbers to look for here are the past due amount (numbers 21 and 39 on Addendum 15.1, Trans Union's credit key) and the maximum delinquent amount (number 42). The former is the amount the account is past due at that moment or at the last time it was past due; the maximum amount is what you think. Do not look for numbers in the millions here; remember the accounts being measured are monthly payments for credit cards, mortgage loans, and the like, and thus a few thousand dollars is more typical.

Lastly, below are real-world definitions for further credit report terminology, some of which may sound threatening, while you may have heard of other items but misunderstood them.

Trans-alert. Despite its worrying sound, the word "Trans-alert" in a credit report carries little to no meaning for the investor. An alert might be raised when the entity pulling the credit report uses an address that might not be the manager's current address. The report then sounds the alarm, averring, "current input address does not match file address(es)," adding that this "requires further investigation." Actually, no it doesn't.

Another, equally irrelevant reason (to an institutional hedge fund investor) for a Trans-alert occurs when the consumer has had his credit reviewed four times or more in the last 60 days. While this may very well indicate that creditors are troubled by payment problems, causing them to relook at the person's credit, this itself would typically occur only when payments are late, something that you will already see on the report.

Hawk-Alert. These alerts are normally sounded when there is some reason to believe that the consumer's social security number has been used fraudulently. While this is indeed something the consumer himself should be acutely aware of, it has little to no bearing on the investor. (The exception here would be if it is clear the person really has used two social security numbers. The problem is that proving this is almost impossible without going to the Social Security Administration or some similar agency directly; doing so, unfortunately, will lead to an investigation and if it turns out a simple conflation-type error was made, as is typically the case, the subject will not likely be very happy with you.)

Empirica "Score." A person's credit score, in essence, reflects the likelihood the person will default on an account, based on a series of factors known only to G-d and the credit agencies. (Actually you can obtain more information about this by reviewing a factor sheet provided by the credit agency, but don't bother.) The reason I'm not keen on this score is that it takes straightforward details that should concern you and mixes them with things that won't, creating a number that seems simple enough but which is actually convoluted. For example, a creditor who cancels old, unused credit cards (as people are often instructed to do) may find his score adversely affected because the average amount he now owes on his remaining cards has increased. Stick to reviewing the total number of accounts that were or are negative, and whether any collections or charge-offs occurred, and you'll get the information you need.

Public Records: Ranging from bankruptcies to judgments and liens, along with notations that the latter groups have been satisfied (paid), these are covered elsewhere, and better, as discussed earlier.

RECAP

1. To pull credit, you need a release and proof of identity.
2. Credit reports may not be available directly.
3. Reports do show lax payment history.
4. Delinquencies can be a yellow flag.
5. Asking for a credit release may rankle a manager.

CHAPTER 16

Warning Signs:
Red and Yellow Flags

My review of thousands of hedge fund managers for more than a decade has led to a few observations about what information concerns institutions, along with what should concern them (this book is attempting, among other things, to marry these two). The following highlights indicators that can alert you to individuals who may be less than forthright in their assertions and in turn their business dealings, and/or who present an outsized risk when compared to others with whom they compete. All in all, the key to making this information work for you, as noted over and over in this book, is developing a full picture of the manager's patterns of behavior, adding this insight to your operational due diligence results, then comparing that to the reward side of the ratio as well as to your own internal tolerance of risk.

RED FLAGS

1. Bankruptcy

Of the thousands of hedge fund managers our firm has reviewed, only a handful has filed for personal bankruptcy. This is an opportune moment, by the way, to point out that the circumstances of a business transaction greatly influence the perception of the information being reviewed. A venture capitalist seeking to finance an entrepreneur not only will not likely be off-put by the entrepreneur having once declared bankruptcy, he may actually be secretly pleased, considering this something of a sign of an enterprising spirit. In this world, spectacular failures can be worth far more than a string of small successes. Compare this to a hedge fund manager, whose sole aim is to manage someone else's money. An institution looking at a manager who has declared bankruptcy at some point is going to find it hard to think anything other than that this person is a riskier bet than other places the institution can put its money. Moreover, if the manager's fund was to collapse, and somehow the press learns of the bankruptcy, the resultant adverse publicity could be nightmarish.

2. Fraud

The one thing that more than anything keeps investors up at night would be the concern that one of their managers might commit fraud. Although this book has stressed repeatedly that a background report, by definition, is not designed to reveal current fraud, proper, comprehensive, analytic background due diligence can and will reveal behaviors and history that, taken together, might show a higher than average risk of a future blow-up. One of these pieces of history, naturally, is a previous situation in which the manager was accused of fraud. Critical to ascertaining the relevance of this will be both viewing the outcome of the matter, as well as reading actual documents in which the charges are detailed. The reality of the situation is that the outcome is not nearly as important as the specificity of the charges, as well as whether the incident was isolated or part of a pattern of similar allegations. Recall from Chapter 6 that most lawsuits ultimately are dismissed, though more important to remember is that this has absolutely nothing to do with the merits of the suits and almost everything to do with the idea that courts encourage settlements and discourage trials to unclog the legal system. So don't get hung up on the idea that fraud was never "proven." Instead, view the documents, compare them to the rest of the material you have seen, conduct interviews, and then decide.

3. Criminal Actions

Criminal actions, both felonies and misdemeanors, obviously call for serious attention. Here again, you'll want to look at whether the action was a one-time incident, or part of a series of criminal suits. Another critical factor is the timing of a suit: a DUI filed when the manager was 21, while not excusable, is not going to bother you as much as one filed when the manager was 40. Similarly, a recent DUI filed against a manager can indicate that the fund being managed is having trouble, causing, or at least contributing, to the manager's drinking problem.

Finally, do not assume that if a criminal suit does not involve a "business" issue, it is unimportant. While it is certainly accurate to portray a suit alleging business crimes as more problematic than one relating to more personal matters, the latter can still be pertinent. A manager accused of hitting someone in a parking lot, or of soliciting a prostitute, could generate just the type of press an institution doesn't need. Although this behavior may not have anything to do with how smart the manager is, how good a trader the manager is, or what the manager's staff thinks of him, it still exhibits a disturbing lack of judgment, especially if the incident occurred within the last few years.

4. Two Social Security Numbers

This is a very tricky area that I hesitate to even discuss. The difficulty with this area is the lack of certifiable evidence that a subject definitively used two social security numbers. The reason for this dilemma is that in most instances, the presence of a second social security number associated with a subject manager is either easily explained, as in the situations where a spouse's number gets confused with the manager's after they seek a joint auto loan, say, or is the result of a mistake made by one of the credit agencies or other identification sources who tabulate this data. Although most of the instances where a second number appears can be explained away by either of the two scenarios, a third, disreputable explanation exists: the manager is or has actively used two numbers. At this point you may be asking yourself how you'd even ascertain whether this has occurred or not. The main method of doing so is seeing different numbers used in different records, as opposed to just via an identification source (which, as noted earlier, can be prone to error). Popular examples include finding one number on a biographical release and another on a bankruptcy or a tax lien, which segues into the reason why most people who use two numbers do so, that is, to hide a piece of their past they don't want an investor knowing about. Unfortunately for them, and fortunately for you, not only doesn't this method work (since a skilled search of records will reveal that these bankruptcies and liens do relate to the subject), but it also tells you something else about the subject's character, or more aptly, lack thereof.

As an aside, I have spoken with a representative from the Social Security Administration about this topic. This official indicated that using two social security numbers is at best improper and possibly illegal. A person can be issued more than one social security number only by mistake or miscommunication (for example, if a person had been issued a number but was not aware of it, and the person then applies for a number, and the Social Security Administration does not notice that a number had already been issued for the same person, then the use of two numbers is merely improper—the result of an error). If, however, the person has *knowingly* employed more than one social security number—regardless of whether he had been mistakenly issued two—this misuse is illegal.

YELLOW FLAGS

1. Biographical Misdeeds

Errors of omission or commission are amongst the most common items we run across in hedge fund manager reviews

An error of omission refers to a manager's leaving off a portion of his employment background, typically, from a biography presented to the institution. Recall from the chapter on verifying credentials that early biographical history is often simply not specified, and is not nearly as much of a concern, if it is one at all. Some institutions, truth be told, ask for only the past 10 years of history; a manager in his mid-30's or older necessarily will be omitting items from his background using this yardstick.

These types of errors become more troublesome when a manager fails to mention an entity where he worked between two other reported tenures. First, bear in mind that a reason for such an omission always exists, as my former partner was fond of reminding clients. This reason may not be nefarious, but it is there, and it is up to you to determine what it is. It could be as simple as the manager took a job he regretted almost immediately, and left so soon that he decided to simply not discuss this further. Or it could mean that the subject had problems, such as lawsuits, poor performance, or other matters, at the unmentioned firm. Still a third option is that firm itself failed; here your task will be to ascertain whether the subject contributed to this demise, or was prescient in jumping ship, or both.

Errors of commission usually involve titles or dates not agreeing with what was found via the independent verification of the person's biography. A few months here or there, pshaw, you might be tempted to say. But as with many temptations, this one is not healthy. Fudging dates often occurs because the subject manager did not leave the previous job voluntarily; fudging titles is invariably a way of making the manager's credentials seem to be more than they really are. The former is certainly not a lock to be true but nonetheless requires further review to uncover the facts behind the misstatement. The latter, conversely, is doubly worrisome, as you are now dealing with an inexperienced manager prone to lying (read: Sam Israel).

Another error of commission, albeit one that is rare, is a manager embellishing personal credentials. From purported Olympic gold medals to awards bestowed by government officials, some people observe no bounds in their embellishments.

One final note here. When reviewing hedge fund blow-ups, post mortem, over the past several years, a hallmark is a fund run by a manager whose career accomplishments or college education fell short of what he claimed. Scott Sacane of Durus, recently sentenced to a prison term for securities fraud, is a good example. A biography of Mr. Sacane cited in a newspaper wedding announcement indicated that Mr. Sacane was a graduate of the University of Colorado.[1] The University of Colorado, however, indicated that Mr. Sacane attended the University from September 1984 to December 1990, and again from January to May 1993, but did not receive a degree. Whoops.

Another recent example is Angelo Haligiannis of Sterling Waters (at the time of this writing, still on the lam). Mr. Haligiannis reportedly left NYU in his junior year, telling people that he had graduated early.[2]

One hypothesis for why this matters: if a person is willing to be untruthful about something seemingly so minor, what will he do when a real problem, such as declining performance, occurs?

Overly Vague Statements   If a manager has worked for Goldman Sachs, he won't describe it as a New York–based financial company. He might, however, describe a stint at Rooney Pace that way (see p. 266). Another example from the back files: a subject's biography stated that he had advised various individuals and institutions, with a concentration in "developing financial systems and incubating hedge funds . . . ." If I knew what this meant, I am sure it would sound great. Meanwhile, how about citing an actual employer?

Sometimes what is missing can be more telling than what has been included. Biographies lacking the normal details like the name of an employer, the company's location or the dates employed are all worrisome indicators of future vagueness at a time when an institution will need specifics.

Unverifiable Credentials   As mentioned in Chapter 9 on verifying credentials, financial people who describe their military service often use terms like "top secret clearance," or Special Forces. A plausible explanation is that people's biographies cite only those accomplishments that make them look good, and so we are seeing a skewed result here because those who have ably served in the military but received no particular honors simply don't mention their service. It is also possible that truly good con men know that military credentials are extremely difficult and time-consuming to confirm.

I Was the Youngest Ever. . .   I was the youngest managing director in so and so investment bank's history. I was the youngest person to be made vice president in my division, ever. I was the youngest person to have a meeting with my boss on a Tuesday in September. While only two of three of these claims are like those that people sometimes make, they all have about as much value. Certainly there are situations where someone legitimately was the youngest [fill in the title here] at [fill in the company here]. However, more often than not this boast cannot be substantiated. What's more, this is a static claim made in a world that obviously changes by the moment. One day you were the youngest ever, another, well, you weren't. Finally, from what I have seen, a certain type of person feels the need to label himself this way; this person is often not the secure, qualified financial wizard with whom you are seeking to invest.

Grandiose Self-Descriptions Let the following excerpt from an actual subject resume submitted to our firm stand as an example of those who truly over-sell and frequently underdeliver. *"I have achieved success through a seemingly limitless reservoir of energy, stamina and a rigid devotion to the work ethic. My pedagogical skills are unsurpassed and I am a 'Mover and a Shaker' while remaining loyal to the company goals. I have superb oratorical skills and my motto is, 'THE IMPOSSIBLE JUST TAKES A LITTLE LONGER.'"* [All capitals courtesy of the subject.]

2. Now I'm a Hedge Fund Manager

In the early days of hedge funds, and pretty much continuing until circa 2000, hedge fund managers had pretty much the same pedigree. A typical manager attended Harvard, received an MBA from Wharton, worked at Goldman, then for Tiger Management, before striking out on his own. When in early 2000 the initial public offering (IPO) market dried up, almost overnight, a bit of a chain reaction occurred. Venture capitalists and private equity shops suddenly had no clear exit strategy for their investments. High yield debt lenders can't lend if deal flow is nonexistent. And investment banks and underwriters started laying people off. Around the same time, hedge funds became increasingly popular, as institutional investors sitting on gobs of cash needed somewhere to put it. Although the causality and the linear description above may be simplistic and debatable, the result was not: more and more frequently, people began reinventing themselves as hedge fund managers.

A common trend was the investment banker who became a hedge fund manager. Although on the surface this is not as far a reach as, say, the amusement park owner (below) leaping into the hedge fund pool, many individuals are in the hedge fund space for one primary reason: lack of alternatives. And though you might be tempted to applaud their resourcefulness in turning a lay-off in their field into an opportunity to join another, it may be better to clap for them on the sidelines. For the difference between people who have been investment bankers and those who have actually traded is gigantic.

Aside from the classic influx of investment bankers to the hedge fund world, we have seen pharmacists, entertainment industry folks, engineers, even amusement park operators redefining themselves as "hedge fund" managers (though they might be better thought of as heat seekers, people whose skills include identifying a hot industry, then getting in it). As the popularity of the hedge fund industry exploded, the reinvention of an individual as a hedge fund manager became a common trend. Though this reinvention is not, by definition, immoral and certainly not dishonest, the risk of failure here can be higher than with someone who has gone through the hedge fund apprenticeship process, actually trading, failing, and, most of all, learning.

Two Tales from the Crypt

1. A former engineer and academic became a systems person at an investment bank, then ran research for a fund before starting his own fund. A former partner indicated that the manager had almost been fired from a previous trading job after his superiors concluded from his presentations that he had nothing behind what he saying and was in essence trading blind.[3]
2. A mergers and acquisitions professional moved to money management, then to a dot.com, then back to money management. This kind of shifting from one hot industry to the next, or in the world of super heroes, a shape shifter, doesn't always portend disaster, but it clearly warrants a second and third look.[4]

3. Litigation

As discussed at length in Chapter 6, if you are like most institutions your greatest fear is investing money with someone who turns out to have a criminal history. Although this is a legitimate concern, the number of hedge fund managers who have this type of blot is incredibly small. Far more common, and of perhaps even more significance, are civil lawsuits, both those filed by the manager as well as those against him. These civil lawsuits tell various cautionary tales, as categorized below.

Distractions   A manager currently embroiled in a divorce, especially an acrimonious one, may be a great trader, honest, and a fabulous businessman, under normal conditions. But few would argue that a divorce is not, at least, somewhat distracting, and at worst, almost all-consuming.

Personality Issues   A hedge fund manager who sues the landscaper is someone who fights for his rights. A manager who sues the landscaper, the electrician, the pool man, and the fence guy, conversely, is someone who is unafraid of the legal system, and may be just a bully or a crank. Once again, we return to the pattern of behavior theory, which holds that people's previous behavior is an accurate predictor of how he will act in the future. If you don't mind dealing with someone who sues every time something doesn't go his way, that can still work out fine. Just don't be shocked to find yourself staring at a sheaf of legal documents if something goes awry in your relationship with the manager.

A similarly significant threat is if the prospective manager is the defendant in lawsuits filed by the four people contracted to do work for him. A series of $2,000 judgments naming the manager as debtor may seem trivial given the dollar amounts. Consider, however, why a successful, presumably wealthy businessperson is not paying the person who cuts his grass. Whether it is simply a case of being disorganized, or a more significant personality trait issue, you are relying on the judgment of this person, something these suits may call into question.

Ethics   In a litigious society, it is no surprise that employers sometimes sue their former employees, and vice versa. Where this rises to yellow flag level is when, you guessed it, the manager has sued or been sued by more than one previous employer. Even one such suit, however, can demonstrate troubling ethics, and thus requires that the suit's complaint be studied, as opposed to relying on an index saying merely that a breach of contract allegedly has occurred. Most of these suits will charge that the ex-employee breached a noncompete or a nonsolicitation agreement. This can be a serious issue, but it really is more of a problem if the former employee is told by the courts that the new business is not to begin until the noncompete period has expired. Even so, a monetary fix (that is, paying the former employer to ignore this provision) will frequently be enough to deal with this. Similarly, an employee suing over severance pay or an unpaid bonus should sound few alarms, unless this has happened several times (in which case, though the manager might have been correct, you still might worry about the matter of good judgment in selecting firms with which to work and in pursuing lawsuits at the expense of pursuing a career).

Some suits between managers and their former employers, however, can be harbingers of problems, shining a light on a manager's ethics and revealing behavior that looked better in the dark. One example here is an action alleging that the manager stole computer programs and used these to start a competing business. The details matter here; trade secrets cases, as with most suits, can go either way, so you need to review documents and conduct interviews to get a better feel for what really happened. Focus on the specifics and on whether the story makes sense. Did the manager really need these programs to start the business? Was the manager at all entitled to this material? What did the manager take? Does the manager admit to taking anything?

4. Multiple Job Switches

Although few people would call for a return of the days when people worked for one company until they got the gold watch on retirement day, holding a series of posts for less than 18 months is not the type of biography that inspires a lot of confidence. Terms like "industry veteran" and "decades of experience" sound impressive but when dissected, even with a dull scalpel, it is difficult to get past the fact that someone who has held 7 jobs in 10 years, even within the financial industry, is at best someone who won't stick around at the fund in which you are investing and at worst a person you wouldn't want to stick around at the fund in which you are investing.

One manager we reviewed worked for nine firms in eight years before striking out on his own. Although this is not as much of an issue for commodities traders, who do tend to bounce around more than other hedge fund managers, it still reflects quite a bit of movement. And when examined a little more closely, a disturbing picture emerged.

Company 1. Not shown on the subject's biography; expelled from NFA membership several years after the subject left.

Company 2. Company president advised that the subject put in a trade, tried to stop it, but did so errantly, effectively putting in the losing trade twice. The subject purportedly didn't notice until the next day. The broker for which the subject worked had to pay out; the subject promised to reimburse his firm but never did, according to the president.

Company 3. Defunct.

Company 4. Defunct.

Company 5. Defunct.

Company 6. Defunct.

Company 7. Several NFA and CFTC arbitrations filed against the firm but none citing the subject.

The subject's time at these seven entities occurred in an eight-year time span. Although he certainly can't be blamed for the demise of the middle four entities, his reverse Midas Touch is nothing to boast about. As mentioned previously, if you discuss a specific incident with a manager, almost all of them will have a reassuring, reasonable-sounding story about that event. However, nothing can really explain away the totality of a career. A person who has not demonstrated that he is helping to make his employers successful is either not very good or has terrible judgment in selecting employers, something that can be overlooked if it happens once or twice, but is harder to forgive when it happens this often.

5. Square Peg/Round Hole

Determining the level of risk a hedge fund manager poses is not, unfortunately, as simple as codifying whether the person is a good trader and is honest. Of course those two qualities are absolutely necessary, but they are not exclusive. A relatively recent phenomenon in the hedge fund industry is the increased membership to the billionaire boys club. The thing about a billion dollar fund is that it requires the hedge fund manager to manage not just money, but people too. A billion dollar fund is no longer the type of entity that can get by with the trader, an analyst or two, and a secretary; no, now the fund needs a staff. With staff inevitably comes staffing problems, whether they be people upset at their compensation, personality battles between employees, or boss/employee style issues. A good manager has to figure out how to handle all of these matters, in an ever-changing landscape, and may not have the necessary experience to do so, even if he is well intentioned. Pay problems are a factor in almost every business, but are probably more intense the more money is at stake. Analysts and researchers are not stupid by nature; with the plethora of hedge funds that exist today, they see little reason to hang around a fund that is either not doing well (thus costing them a bonus) or that is but is not paying them what they perceive to be a fair wage (remember, a hedge fund's returns are very public, so analysts know what their bosses are making). This latter issue is obviously within the management team's control, to a large degree, but it can be difficult to navigate this when one has no roadmap of experience to turn to.

Another somewhat common scenario is the trader who is superb at making money, but a disaster at making friends. I am not referring here to a socially inept manager, one who prefers a computer screen to a cocktail party (I think most institutions would actually find this encouraging). No, here I am referring to the person who is so abrasive, even for hedge fund industry standards, that staff defections are routine, and the ability to build a team just is not there. Returning to the idea that a large fund requires a larger team, it necessarily follows that the person or people at the top need to be able to manage that team in order to have the fund succeed. Be on the lookout for high turnover, even if it initially starts with seemingly low-end folks, for this can portend disaster.

Another thing that occurs is a different portrait emerges of a subject from interviews with former colleagues from the one painted by a relatively staid business press. This demonstrates, too, the point that interviews will almost always be valuable, even in situations where the person looks "clean," because interviewees speak to information that records simply don't have.

One example is the person who was described as brilliant but arrogant, condescending, and ultimately very isolating. This latter quality led to many bridges being burned, and to a dysfunctional, and ultimately underperforming, firm.

In a separate case, interview sources professed great confidence in one partner, but not the other, who was described as an extremely intelligent person but one who lies about anything, even small things, in order to get what he wants. Unfortunately for partner number one, this is not a good sales feature.

Finally, you have the person who is successful at one thing, but who describes himself as another. A good marketer can be immensely helpful to a hedge fund. A good marketer who puts himself out as being a trader, by contrast, would not bode as well for that fund's chances of success.

6. Olio

Well-Publicized, Ostentatious Charitable Giving   When people hear this, they sometimes recoil, readying themselves to pounce on me with a statement like this: "What's wrong with giving to charity (expletive deleted)?" The point here is not, of course, the charitable giving itself. Many hedge fund managers undoubtedly are major contributors to various charities; the problem arises when this giving is done to confer legitimacy on a person who does not deserve it. The most famous example is Robert Brennan, not a hedge fund manager but someone who demonstrates this idea to a tee.[5] Mr. Brennan was for years a significant donor to Seton Hall University, a Catholic school based in South Orange, New Jersey. This paid off in spades for Mr. Brennan, who had a recreation center at the school named for him and who was routinely lauded in the press by some of Seton Hall's priests, despite the fact that fairly early on it was clear from the charges levied by regulators that the money he was giving to the school, in ever more public fashion, was stolen, in effect, from people who trusted him because of the veneer of respect his public giving gave him. Pretty twisted, and cynical, but I think quite accurate.

The lesson here is that people who are real givers often want no part of the acclaim that the recipients want to bestow upon them. People who are giving in order to manipulate the views of others, effectively turning themselves from discarded crust to upper crust, are the ones to watch out for. If you see pairings of appearances at incredibly public functions with contributions to hospitals, the ballet and other prominent arts, or, as above, schools, look out. And if you see a guy boarding a helicopter, shouting "Come fly away with us!" (the infamous slogan of First Jersey Securities, uttered un-ironically by Mr. Brennan just before customers' money flew away), run.

Reverse Midas Touch: Entities That Fail After a Subject's Departure

Some people have a knack for making every employer, or at least every unit in every employer, better. Others have a knack for just being in the right place at the right time, joining companies or industries just as those companies or industries take off. Then there are the people who signal the end of an era, mostly without even knowing it. When cab drivers are becoming day traders, and bragging about their sudden financial wherewithal, you know the decimation of that field cannot be far behind. (Note: naturally none of this applies to real hedge funds that trade this way and have proven themselves to be successful. I am referring specifically to people jumping into this career simply because some guy in pressed khakis on late night television told them how easy it was.)

With hedge fund managers, an expanded news search, something that should be part of every due diligence review and is directly the opposite of the so-called negative news search (as you'll recall from Chapter 7), which misses this information and in fact often even misses the very negative news it purports to be designed to find. (Okay, I have taken a breath and am back.) The expanded news search is designed to tell you what happened to a company before, during, and after a subject's arrival. To accomplish this, the search has to be conducted for articles, well, before and after a subject left a firm; this is done not only by expanding the years of the search, but also, critically, by searching for articles citing the entity but not the individual manager. This is how you'll find stories that refer to a company doing poorly, say, after a subject left, but not discussing why that had occurred. Admittedly, it will be hard to discern if legal actions, significant financial losses, or mass employee exoduses were at all a consequence of the subject's actions, but clearly this requires an answer. Since news stories will not generally be enough, here you'll need to start interviewing former coworkers. I have seen this play out both ways, note. On some occasions, you approach interviews thinking, based on all the news you have read, that the subject almost had to have been the reason, or a reason, why his former employer fared so badly, only to be surprised to find that the subject was the only good thing going for the entity and just did not have enough support to save it. Here, you might approve of, even compliment, the subject's far-sightedness in leaving an entity that was clearly troubled beyond his abilities to save. Other times, the manager was a catalyst to the problems, and sought to depart before this became obvious. Either way, the combination of the expanded news search and conducting independent interviews will help you uncover times when a subject has been at a failed firm, and what he did to help or hinder the decline. Following a path of failure is central to avoiding one of your own.

One more note here. The Midas Touch refers, you may recall from your Greek mythology, to the legendary King Midas, who was able to turn everything he touched into gold. People with the Reverse Midas Touch touch things and watch them turn into garbage. Sometimes the question to ask yourself is not whether the person's explanations for the various failures and problems make sense, but whether you care. For if Branch Rickey is to be believed, that is, that luck is the residue of design, then the corollary probably stands up: continuous bad "luck" may not be luck at all, but may simply relate to something that person does, and you may not want to pay to find out what that something is.

Timely Shifts Between Industries   This is somewhat similar to the afore-mentioned multiple job switch flag. However, here the person is not just job hopping, but is also moving from one industry to another, usually mirroring changes in the economy. An S&L lender cum dot-com entrepreneur cum hedge fund manager is probably not what you are looking for when you think of a seasoned hedge fund.

Oops: There Goes That Regulatory Rug   One yellow flag that has little to do with the manager's actions, per se, but that might prove to be debilitating is when the manager makes money via a new and potentially controversial investment tactic like market timing, or some tactic that is not yet illegal but frequently the subject of debate and possibly, regulatory probes. An entity that professes to make money in only one way, especially one that is coming to the attention of regulators, may not be able to switch gears, even if they tell you otherwise.

Below is a handy guide to distinguishing between events that probably won't and shouldn't cause you any alarm (marked by number ones) and those that should cause you to examine things more closely (marked by twos and threes). As with everything else, use this information as a guide, compare it to what you know, both from an operations standpoint, your site visits and other intelligence you have gathered, then weigh the positives on the numbers side, stir in your overall risk tolerance level, add ice, and blend.

CREDENTIALS

Education—Accuracy

1. Everything on biography, including dates and major, is true per schools in question.
2. Minor differences found in year of graduation, major, or degree type.
3. Subject did not graduate when biography or other records indicate he did.

Education—Pedigree

1. Received undergraduate and graduate degrees from Ivy League or similar-level schools.
2. Received undergraduate and possibly graduate degrees from lesser-regarded schools.
3. Received no degree.

Employment History—Accuracy

1. Everything on biography, including dates and titles, is accurate according to employers in question.
2. Minor differences found in titles, dates of employment, or omissions of employers from biography.
3. Significant differences found in titles (for example, analyst versus vice president), dates of employment (more than three months off, but only when served for less time than claimed, not more, which is usually an unimportant severance-related issue) or omissions of several employers from biography.

Employment History—Pedigree

1. Worked for large investment house or well-known hedge fund, as a trader, for three to five years plus prior to striking out on own. Must be combined with a total of seven to ten years total work experience, and no more than three positions per decade.
2. Worked for above but not as a trader. Less than seven to ten years actual work experience.
3. Little to no actual trading experience. Moved from industry to industry, as well as from job to job, five times or more in a decade. Worked for known boiler-room firms (see sidebar, below).

LITIGATION

Bankruptcy

1. Business subject worked for petitions for bankruptcy but subject exercised no control over said business.
2. Business subject controlled or in which subject was high-level officer petitions for bankruptcy.
3. Subject petitions for personal bankruptcy.

Fraud

1. See the above bankruptcy criteria for directions here.

Criminal Matters

1. Subject accused of misdemeanor but found not guilty.
2. Subject convicted of misdemeanor, like DUI, but at age 25 or less *and* occurring more than 10 years prior to the present time *and* no other similar issues found.
3. Subject convicted of felony, or multiple misdemeanors, or single, recent misdemeanor with aggravated circumstances.

Civil suits—Defendant (individual)

1. No suits found. One personal injury or divorce from more than 5 years prior to the present and making no claims of physical abuse, alcohol problems, or other similar matters.
2. Multiple suits found, but none focusing on business-related issues. One suit by previous employer or involving another significant business issue: allegation of fraud, failure to pay for business services, and so forth. Ongoing divorce (distraction) or previous divorce alleging alcohol problems or physical abuse. Multiple divorces (two to three).
3. Multiple suits found, all focusing on business-related issues, with the exception of specific to investment-type cases (e.g. short seller sued for allegedly trying to influence share price). Multiple suits involving significant business issue. Multiple divorces (four or more).

Civil suits—Defendant (Corporation)

1. No suits found. One personal injury, trademark, or minor failure to pay for professional services (under $5,000, more than five years old) suit.
2. Multiple suits found, but none within the last three to five years, none naming individual subjects also, none resulting in judgment of greater than $50,000. One suit involving rare, nontraditional claim—including, for example, failure to pay rent, failure to pay for prime brokerage services, or other similar matters. One suit resulting in judgment of less than $200,000.
3. Multiple suits involving significant business issues. Multiple suits also naming individual subjects and involving business issues not specific to investment-type matters. One suit resulting in judgment of over $200,000.

Civil suits—Plaintiff (individual)

1. No suits. Multiple suits (two to three) in an extremely broad time frame (ten years plus).

2. Multiple suits against prior employers. Multiple suits (three or less) in a broad time period (more than five years) excluding divorce. Multiple divorces (two to three) or one ongoing divorce.

3. Multiple suits (four or more), excluding divorces, in a narrow time period (less than five years). Multiple divorces (four or more).

Civil Suits–Plaintiff (Corporation)

1. No suits. Multiple suits (two to three) in an extremely broad time frame (ten years plus).

2. Multiple suits against prior employees. Multiple suits (five or less) in a broad time period (five years plus), excluding suits filed by activists or similar investors.

3. Multiple suits (more than six) in a narrow time period (less than five years), excluding suits filed by activists or similar investors.

Tax liens (individual or corporation)

1. One tax lien for less than $1,000 *and* satisfied (paid) *and* more than 10 years from present time.

2. Multiple tax liens or one recent unpaid lien for more than $1,000 or any lien for more than $25,000.

3. Multiple unpaid liens for more than $25,000.

NEWS COVERAGE

Level/Amount

1. Number of stories found consistent with type of investing (distressed, activist, short sellers or similar styles expected to generate more press than classic long only), role in organization (higher title = more press) and length of career (the longer in business the more stories one would expect).

2. Fewer stories than one would expect per above. Typically one would expect at least one business-related article per year of service in investment field.

3. No press found, or only personal citations (wedding announcements, charitable donations, and so forth).

Tenor (Positive/Negative)

1. All articles either benign or positive.
2. Multiple articles negative but all focusing on one particular topic.
3. Multiple articles negative involving multiple topics.

REGULATORY

Registered

1. Company registered as an investment advisor with the SEC or similar designation with other regulatory body.
2. Neither company nor individual registered with SEC, NFA, NASD, or state regulatory body.
3. Subject claims registration that is inaccurate.

Infractions

1. No infractions.
2. One infraction in which procedural problem occurred. Multiple infractions found (two to three).
3. Multiple (more than four) infractions or one infraction in which fine resulted from trading violations. Subject claims no infractions but infractions do in fact exist.

Licenses—Accuracy

1. All licenses claimed proven to be held and current.
2. License proven to have been formerly held but no longer current, though biography implies it is.
3. License never held, or Series exams not passed when claims made to contrary.

IF YOU SEE THESE ON A BIOGRAPHY, BEWARE

As with almost all background information, a manager who has worked for one of the firms below merits closer inspection, though perhaps not immediate "run for the hills" status. Managers who worked for one of these entities, among others (because firms that have been termed "boiler rooms" or "bucket shops" change names so frequently, no list can be exhaustive) shortly after leaving college, and for only a short time, can probably be given a pass. But anyone who worked for one of these firms for longer than six months (a period of time long enough to know what kind of outfit was being run), or started at one of these entities long after already beginning a financial career (again, at a time when they probably should have known better) or

(continued)

IF YOU SEE THESE ON A BIOGRAPHY, BEWARE (*Continued*)

worked for more than one such entity, definitely has something of a black mark.

- Rooney Pace
  This firm was expelled from the securities industry in 1988.
- D.H. Blair
  According to news stories, this firm was investigated by the NASD and the SEC for allegedly practicing the pump and dump scam. This illegal practice occurs after a perpetrator buys low-priced, typically thinly-traded stock shares, then pumps up the purported value of these shares, inducing investors to buy in. Subsequently, the "scammer" sells out, making a profit, while the stock price craters, taking the investors' money with it.[6]

  On August 13, 1997, NASD Regulation, Inc. announced that D.H. Blair & Co. Inc., had been fined $2 million, and was to repay approximately $2.4 million "to investors who were over-charged as a result of excessive mark-ups in 16 securities, and of other fraudulent conduct." "NASD Regulation also found that D.H. Blair... created an artificial 'profit' in [two of] the securities that allowed the preferred customers of one of the firm's senior managers to benefit by selling their stock back to the firm. Thereafter, D.H. Blair's brokers used the artificial increase to solicit new investors to purchase these securities, without disclosing the circumstances of the price increase."[7]
- HJ Meyers & Co., Inc.
  H.J. Meyers & Co., formerly known as Thomas James Associates Inc., was a Rochester, N.Y.-based brokerage firm that closed in September 1998 and subsequently was forced into Chapter 7 Bankruptcy in April 1999. H.J. Meyers had at its peak 500 employees in 15 offices and was renowned for selling "high-risk investments in penny stocks." One co-founder, Brian Thomas, was barred for life from the securities industry in 1990. The other, James Villa, filed for Chapter 11 bankruptcy in June 1999.[8]

  To those that followed the firm, its demise was about as shocking as learning that eating two Big Macs every day isn't so healthy. Consider that in July 1996, H.J. Meyers was handed "one of the biggest payouts in the history of National Association of Securities

Dealers regulation—more than $1 million in customer paybacks and fines."

Also coming as no surprise was H.J. Meyers "neither admit[ing] nor den[ying] wrongdoing."[9]

On June 16, 1997, *Forbes* Magazine wrote a piece provocatively titled, "Wall Street's Hall of Shame"; "Here are the worst brokerages in America, singled out by state securities regulators in their recent enforcement actions."[10]

- Investors Associates (Hackensack, New Jersey, and 16 branches)
- Meyers Pollock Robbins, Inc. (New York City, 30 branches)
- Duke & Company, Inc. (New York City)

Separately, per *The Boston Globe*, January 21, 1988, Massachusetts securities regulators sought to shut down five penny-stock dealers, Duke among them, for "defrauding Massachusetts consumers by employing aggressive sales tactics from out-of-state 'boiler rooms.'"[11]

- Biltmore Securities, Inc. (Ft. Lauderdale, Florida, three branches)
- First United Equities Corp. (Garden City, New York)
- LT Lawrence & Co./Lawrence & Co. (New York City)
- Toluca Lake Securities Corp. (Toluca Lake, California, 11 branches)
- Josephthal & Co.
  Securities Week reported on January 31, 2000, that Josephthal and three high-level executives, CEO Dan Purjes, Paul Fitzgerald, and Matthew Balk, "face NASDR charges of fraud and unfair business practices with investors." According to the article, "Over the last ten years or so, Josephthal & Co. has been the target of 105 arbitration claims, not including two pending cases filed recently on behalf of customers who claim that Josephthal brokers pushed unsuitable investments on them, failed to disclose the investments' inherent risks and, in one case, made trades while under NASD suspension."[12] Since 1992, "five states have taken actions against the firm and/or certain Josephthal brokers for . . . illegal offering of penny stocks, employing unlicensed brokers, failure to reasonably supervise sales practices, unauthorized

(continued)

IF YOU SEE THESE ON A BIOGRAPHY, BEWARE
(*Continued*)

trading, failure to disclose material facts in connection with the offering and sale of securities and selling unsuitable securities."

The recent charges occurred immediately following a similar incident that Josephthal settled with the NASDR (that one to the tune of more than $500,000).

■ First Jersey Securities (run by the aforementioned Robert Brennan, now serving a federal prison sentence) and Stratton Oakmont.

According to a January 31, 2000 *Securities Week* article, Josephthal was not the worst, for what that's worth. "Josephthal's spotty record does not place it in the category of a Stratton Oakmont or First Jersey Securities, two notorious bucket shops, according to one state securities regulator...."[13]

Regarding Stratton Oakmont, the NASD permanently expelled the firm in late 1996.

On December 5, 1996, NASD Regulation, Inc. announced the permanent expulsion from the securities industry of Stratton Oakmont, as well as Oakmont president Daniel M. Porush and head trader Steven P. Sanders.

"With this expulsion, NASD Regulation has rid the securities industry of one of its worst actors," said NASD Regulation President Mary L. Schapiro....

Barry R. Goldsmith, NASD Regulation's Executive Vice President of Enforcement added, "In less than a decade, Stratton Oakmont amassed one of the worst regulatory records of any broker/dealer firm. The firm has been the subject of numerous disciplinary actions brought by the NASD, the Securities and Exchange Commission (SEC), and state regulators involving fraud, market manipulation, sales practice abuses, and failures to adequately supervise its employees."

Need more? Well, the NASD piece has it, for those with a strong stomach.

Stratton Oakmont joined the NASD in April 1987. Since June 1989, the firm managed to accumulate 12 NASD and NASD Regulation disciplinary actions, with charges ranging from "securities fraud" to "inducing customers not to cooperate in Association investigations."

One of the lowlights included an SEC action (settled by Stratton in early 1994) in which Stratton was accused of committing securities fraud through its "boiler room" sales operation.

Stratton subsequently and unsurprisingly failed to obey the terms of this settlement. This led to real trouble: in February 1995, the SEC obtained a permanent injunction against Stratton, "enjoining it from violating the terms of the March 1994 administrative order." Yep. Pretty tough, that SEC. Now don't do that again, Stratton, you naughty company, or we'll tell you not to do it again, again.[14]

- Brauer & Associates; Adler Coleman; Hanover Sterling

A December 15, 1997, *Business Week* story discussed mafia influence in the brokerage field. "Business Week's chop-stocks investigation shows that the Mob is far more active on Wall Street than might appear from the public pronouncements of regulators and law enforcement officials. Among the firms that have allegedly been subject to Mob influence or ownership are the New York office of Brauer & Associates Inc., a Florida-based brokerage where stock promoter James P. Minsky was briefly employed, and Adler Coleman Clearing Corp., a former clearing firm. Adler went out of business in 1995, after the demise of Hanover Sterling & Co., a noted chop house."[15]

- Stuart James

Per the New York Times, in mid 1990 Stuart James was fined by the NASD. more than $2 million for overcharging, in "one of the largest fines ever levied against a brokerage firm by the NASD."[16]

According to several news sources, the Securities and Exchange Commission ultimately revoked the firm's registration for various violations regarding the sale of small stocks in 1993. SEC records show that the brokerage had "engaged in a ... cynical and horrendous fraud of literally monumental proportions."

Check out http://www.sec.gov/litigation/opinions/34-38815 .txt if you are still curious.

CHAPTER 17

Conclusion

"**S**ince 2002, we have filed more than 50 cases against commodity pool operators and hedge funds that have committed violations under the Commodity Exchange Act. This is one more example of our aggressive enforcement against those who use deceptive techniques and claim to manage hedge fund money," said Gregory Mocek, Director of Enforcement at the CFTC.[1]

Commodities expert Jim Rogers is the latest prophet of doom ... for both the private equity and hedge fund industries. "Right now we have 25,000 to 30,000 hedge funds around the world.... We don't have that many smart 29-year-olds in the world." He added, "I assure you, we're going to see a lot more blow-ups."[2]

And, because hedge funds functioned until recently with almost no oversight by the Securities and Exchange Commission, the industry has been more susceptible than regulated investment vehicles to attracting the less principled or trained managers.[3]

Flying in the face of these Cassandras, and despite the supposed risks and the near-certain expectation of second-guessing, or worse, for institutions choosing hedge funds that end up blowing up, those in the know understand that when compared to other combinations of debt and equity investments, hedge funds are a must for their portfolios. Hedge funds provide outsized returns, with low correlation to equity markets. As SMU's Ed Easterling put it so well, a hedge fund does not have to beat the market all the time to win; if it flags the market during up times, yet preserves capital in market downturns, it will come out far ahead at the end.[4]

Supporting this was a recent set of statistics compiled by Credit Suisse Index Co., Inc., entitled "The Hedge Fund Industry Rocks Both Bear and Bull Markets," and demonstrating that "the long and short term outlook for hedge funds makes them a favorable investment vehicle in both bull and bear markets...."[5]

Oliver Schupp, president of Credit Suisse Index Co., Inc. averred that hedge funds are accurately characterized as "a diverse portfolio of asset classes," and thus comparing them to traditional single-asset class market indexes is "misleading and inaccurate."

Other findings included these:

- In 2006, 9 of the 10 Credit Suisse/Tremont Hedge Fund Index sectors produced positive results.
- The Credit Suisse/Tremont Hedge Fund Index suffered almost zero drawdown in the past ten years, ending December 2006. This is critical when compared to results of most major equity markets indices, which according to the study lost an average of more than 40 percent during the bear market years that spanned from 2001 through 2003.
- During 2002, HEDG gained 4.4 percent. In contrast, according to the study, MSCI World, S&P 500 and DJ EuroStoxx all lost approximately 20 percent.

But speak to any institution nowadays and you'll inevitably hear this refrain: Over the past decade, the talent pool of hedge fund management has been and continues to be diluted as finance professionals and others from all walks of life (many with little or no trading history), lured by potential payouts and autonomy, flood into the alternative investment marketplace, where they compete with seasoned money managers for institutional dollars.

As this book has demonstrated, this dilution has been a significant factor in the number of hedge funds that falter for any reason except for simple failure to raise enough capital. The flight of Michael Berger in March 2000 after squandering approximately $400 million from his fraudulent Manhattan Investment Fund heralded the potential for disaster in a marketplace that is purportedly unchecked by the constraints regulating traditional securities. And although it can be argued that Mr. Berger's Ponzi resembled a hedge fund in name only, the lasting perception of many, fueled rightly or wrongly by the press, is certainly that this was a hedge fund disaster of then-epic proportions.

Perhaps presciently, Paul Roye, director of the investment management division of the Securities and Exchange Commission, issued this warning in the April 30, 2002, *Financial Times*: "As hedge fund assets have grown, we have also seen an unfortunate growth in hedge fund related fraud. . . . Many hedge fund managers are inexperienced and the industry's opacity creates the potential for fraud."[6] As is well known, the SEC apparently heeded its own alarm, subsequently and temporarily, by mandating tighter controls on hedge funds.

These concerns were heightened by surveys revealing an alarming number of alternative investors that were not practicing adequate due diligence. According to *Reuters*, May 20, 2002, recruitment firm TMP Worldwide released a survey warning that investors are piling into a market where few firms employ due diligence staff. "We were surprised somewhat that only seven of the 18 (firms) polled provided data for a head of due diligence. This suggests that the idea of assigning a senior-level executive with exclusive responsibility for looking into the accounting and legal paperwork of hedge funds in which a fund of funds is considering investing does not have widespread acceptance in the industry."[7]

Is this just ancient history? Are institutions' due diligence practices now so sophisticated, so refined, that the Michael Bergers of the world would have no shot at accumulating, much less losing, hundreds of millions of dollars? The responsibility of appraising the risk associated with a fund and its management ultimately falls on the institution. And bemoaning the fact that the hedge fund world is no longer small enough to be called a club is as useful as fretting about kids needing too many compliments today versus two decades ago, when not getting yelled at was enough. The reality is that the market for alternative investment vehicles has become too saturated for institutions to count on reaching out to their industry contacts to keep away speculators looking to harvest a ripe market. For an institution, knowing what you are getting yourself into has become far more difficult. New investment opportunities are often presented with innovative strategies but are operated by fledgling managers with scant or even obscure track records. In 1997, fewer than 1,000 hedge funds existed; ten years later this figure has been placed as more than 9,000 worldwide. This explosion in the number of hedge funds has made the people due diligence component of risk analysis a much more difficult process than in years past, while at the same time contributing to a corresponding decline in the quality of the backgrounds of the managers who are running these hedge funds. Relying on a network of contacts to identify the reputation of a prospective manager is now a decidedly insufficient gauge.

Luckily you don't have to. You may still know a lot of people in the industry, and they may know still other people, but this Game of Telephone approach is now not only ineffective, but unnecessary. Although the past decade has wrought tremendous upheaval in the hedge fund world, increasing the number of funds nine- or tenfold and drawing managers from practically every conceivable profession, this same period has seen the dramatic, continued advancement of computer-based data sources whose information, when gathered, collated, analyzed, and combined with that developed from manual sources, allows for insight that was heretofore impossible to garner.

Background due diligence that systematically gathers and analyzes public records and information from independent interviews allows investors to qualify fund managers and weed out those that represent undue risk. Fund managers that display questionable judgment, or worse, leave evidence of this that even contacts in the elite hedge fund community can no longer accurately identify.

The above-referenced Michael Berger lied about his age, experience, and credentials in order to depict himself as more qualified than his true credentials and actual performance warranted. John Whittier of Wood River had a four-pack of mid five-figure tax liens, his business failed to pay its rent, and he was sued for more than a million dollars for allegedly not paying a broker for a stock. In biographies, the now-jailed Scott Sacane claimed a college degree he did not actually have. And on and on. None of these items, however, would come to light by "asking around," for all of these individuals were renowned for their charm, or their oratory skills, or some combination of personal appeal and intellect.

The frequency with which discrepancies between what managers present about themselves and what is really accurate about their past is, based on our reviews, significantly higher over the last few years than it had been 10 years ago. Then, it was rare to find an issue worthy of concern in a manager's past. Most managers were easily identifiable in the industry. They attended Ivy League schools, began their careers at top Wall Street firms and gained industry experience at the few esteemed hedge funds before striking out on their own. This is no longer true.

No investor can afford to enter the burgeoning hedge fund market unaware of the risks involved. With the asset class (or more accurately, classes) attracting talent as well as trouble, understanding the qualitative backgrounds of fund managers is more important than ever. Thankfully, this isn't the movie *Castaway*, and you aren't Tom Hanks, forced to go it alone with few resources and fewer chances of success.

A few years ago, the term "transparency" was all the rage in the hedge fund community. At any conference, you could be sure to hear at least half a dozen speeches on transparency issues. I like to think of background due diligence as transparency of the people, an aspect of transparency that can be very instructive when choosing a hedge fund manager. It is certainly understandable that hedge fund managers are more transparent about their techniques *after* you have invested; after all, you wouldn't expect or even want them to disclose their competitive secrets to you or anyone else prior to an investment, since before long their secrets wouldn't be, well, secret. But being okay with not knowing exactly how they are trading is not the same as being okay with not knowing exactly who they are, and what they have done before, and whether they have been sued, and what their former colleagues think about their chances of success at trading on their own and running a business. You must know these things before investing.

By making manager due diligence a standard part of your overall due diligence process, and by looking for patterns of behavior that typically indicate future problems are looming, you can have your cake (invest in hedge funds) and eat it too (not worry that they're frauds). And by doing due diligence correctly, whether internally or externally, or some combination of the two, you can ensure that your institution makes money, not headlines.

Throughout this book chapters have been summarized in an effort to highlight significant points. Towards that end, here is a recap of the recaps, a summary of the most important features.

RECAP OF THE RECAPS

The Whys of Background Due Diligence

1. Hedge funds are not a passing fad.
2. There are more than 9,000 hedge funds: more choices but also far greater chance of picking a lemon.
3. The press feasts on blow-ups.
4. Most hedge fund frauds and blow-ups receiving press are not hedge funds at all, but this doesn't change the results of the negative attention.
5. Warning signs before the blow-up almost always appear.
6. A manager does not have to be a criminal to blow up; even distractions can do it.
7. As funds get huge, managers need to manage people, not just money. Can they?
8. Ad hoc methods like calling on industry contacts are no longer an efficient or effective means of conducting due diligence on people.
9. The U.S. regulatory apparatus is not designed to prevent blow-ups from occurring.
10. Systematic due diligence on management combined with operational due diligence allows for a definitive reduction in blow-up risk.
11. Reviewing managers is not only wise, but also may be considered a fiduciary duty.
12. A manager's past is an excellent predictor of his future actions; a person's behavioral tendencies tend to get repeated, especially in times of stress.
13. Discovering past behavioral patterns greatly enhances present decision making by predicting and dealing with future problems, before they happen.

14. Due diligence is the way to discover these patterns.
15. Learning how to recognize these patterns is critical.

The Hows of Background Due Diligence

1. No identification information, no due diligence.
2. Home address=social=past address history.
3. The more identifiers you find, the more relevant your other results will prove.
4. Always ask how your researchers how they determined information related to the subject.
5. Identification takes time, but no time you spend will be better spent.
6. Broad-based court searches are best.
7. Still, broad searches must be supplemented with targeted searches of the regions where the subject manager has lived and worked.
8. Search state and federal courts, as far back as economically feasible.
9. Search courts either online, or manually, for those courts not covered online.
10. There is no online source, or even combination of online sources, that completely covers every state or federal court in the country (not even close, frankly). *You must conduct manual searches to fill in gaps left by online resources.*
11. *You must obtain actual documents.* This is to determine the import of a suit (and often, even what it was about, with the Paul Westervelt Bayou whistleblower action being a recent, fabulous example of this), to learn the outcome of the suit, as well as to learn whether it relates to your subject manager or simply someone else with the same name. Not doing this is the single biggest failing of most people's due diligence efforts and can be deadly to your reputation and bottom line.
12. Any description of a suit should describe how the suit involves the subject, indicate the amount in question, describe what happened, and explain the status of the suit (open, closed, judgment, settled, etc.).
13. To determine whether a suit names your subject, compare identifiers, such as middle name/initial, spouse, age (meaning a suit was filed when your subject would have been a minor), addresses, employers, signatures, and sometimes, social security numbers (though civil cases will not have this magic pill).
14. Because a suit is dismissed does not mean it had no merit. Most suits are settled out of court, and do not result in judgments; *this does not mean the defense did nothing wrong.* (Of course, the argument can be made that people settle nuisance suits. This always has to be taken into account and measured against the next point, that is, the Pattern.)

15. Always, always, look for a pattern of behavior. Was a single suit filed? Or numerous actions? Was a subject repeatedly accused of the same type of behavior, over a significant amount of time? Does the manager invest using strategies that naturally lend themselves to suits, like distressed deals or activist investments, or is he a straight long/short or other type of investor? Are the suits that are filed unusual for a hedge fund manager?

16. Know what it is that you are looking to accomplish. Do you care mostly about making returns or avoiding bad press? Are you concerned with a manager's personality? Are you a public institution, beholden to rules not affecting private institutions?

17. Ask for help. A good investigator will be answer the above questions, and place the subject manager on a continuum for you. Investigators won't be able to tell you what to do, nor should they, but you'll be armed with information to add to your other analyses, information that is critical but often not presented.

18. Use multiple news databases.

19. Read everything you can, not just those things you think will reveal prior or continued wrongdoing.

20. Cross-check, compare, and contextualize news data.

21. Look for inconsistencies in biographical assertions versus what the news is reporting.

22. Seek sources for independent interviews.

23. Search the NFA, NASD, SEC/IARD, and SSA.

24. Most regulatory searches can be done online.

25. Many hedge funds are registered as investment advisers, through the SEC, although currently they do not have to do so.

26. Disciplinary actions, or disclosure events, are available on most websites.

27. Biographical errors of omission or commission can be a powerful indicator of future problems.

28. Obtain at least a biography and a release from every manager; a questionnaire can also be useful.

29. Most schools and large firms now require a release to verify data.

30. Verify precise dates to reveal gaps.

31. Ask the subject to explain any discrepancies or gaps. Verify additional information you are given.

32. Look for a pattern of mistruths, half-truths, or untruths.

33. With corporate records searches, do not assume you know what you are looking for; do not search merely for data on corporate entities about which you already know.

34. Be nimble: amend your search strings as new information arises in your searches.

35. Record the names of individuals listed alongside your subject in corporate records; consider interviewing them.
36. The Internet has a specific niche in hedge fund research, but can't and shouldn't replace news searches, court retrievals, and the like.
37. Blogs are rife with current industry knowledge and occasionally clue you in, before anyone, to a key person departing a fund (the canary in the mine).
38. Identify possible interview sources via public records searches and subsequently via other interview sources.
39. Find sources' current contact information by using same techniques used to find subjects.
40. Before doing an interview, be prepared. Preparation = rapport = success.
41. Be conversational.
42. Watch your phrasing. Do not ask a Yes/No question unless you want a Yes/No answer.
43. Wait out silences.
44. Always ask for specifics and examples.
45. Ask for corroboration, both in the form of other interview sources and documentation, as well as via additional interview sources.
46. Look for patterns. Look for patterns. Look for patterns.

The Whens and Whos of Background Due Diligence

1. Background due diligence needs to be done on every manager; cherry picking leads to bad apples. If a deal is worth doing due diligence on at all, it is worth doing it correctly.
2. Due diligence knows no shortcuts.
3. Due diligence takes time. Start early to avoid panic.
4. Comprehensive due diligence means attending to details, not avoiding searches to save money and time.
5. Databases are tools, not commodities. Vastly different results may be achieved depending on who does the research. Don't think of databases as key-punch, data entry.
6. A lot of what investigators portray as helpful is really marketing nonsense.
7. Do not accept a menu of research choices; all news sources, and all court records, should be reviewed in every case.
8. Some investigative firms flout the law to gather data.
9. Using an investigator that does this will cause you heartache, eventually.

What to Remember If You Choose to Outsource

The problem for most institutions lies not in the desire to conduct effective background research, but in the ability to know it when you see it. A wide disparity exists between the skills hedge fund investors typically have and the skills needed to know whether the information being presented is all that there is, whether it is important, and most critically, whether it even relates to the subject manager or another person with that same name.

Presentation is not superfluous. Most of what passes for due diligence comes in the same form, a check list of some kind focusing heavily on the sources reviewed rather than the information found. Unfortunately, by organizing the data this way, much of its meaning is stripped away. Even when crucial facts are right there, they are not seen by a person who is either concentrating solely on plopping data into a prefabricated format, or who is not even reading what has been found, or worse, both.

Is this a harsh assessment? Maybe, but there is no question it is also accurate. The problem facing an institution is the lack of experience that is needed to see through what is essentially a charade, something designed to look like due diligence when in reality it is often little more than an elaborately designed series of plugged-in online data. A written narrative of a manager's history, while more time-consuming to write and to read, nonetheless does what due diligence is supposed to do; that is, it presents the facts about what a manager has done before, what issues the manager has faced along the way, how that manager might fare compared to others in his field, and ultimately, what risks an institution will face in investing with that manager. Although it is more difficult to prepare, the reason the written narrative succeeds in this effort is that it forces the researcher/writer to make connections between disparate pieces of information, connections that form the very essence of due diligence.

Here's an example. Firm A reports all news information it gathers in a section entitled "media." It goes a step beyond many other firms by at least searching the news (though it only searches Nexis) not just for "negative" information (recall the pitfalls of doing so as outlined in Chapter 7) and it even prepares a short summary of several of the articles. One of these was a newswire announcing that the subject manager had been hired in 1999 as a portfolio manager for a Morgan Stanley fund. In the section devoted to the subject's employment history, meanwhile, the firm has gone ahead and actually sought to verify, independently, the dates and titles given on the subject's biography, again giving it a leg up on the all-too-many firms that rely instead on whatever they might find in news and other sources regarding someone's career. The verification efforts are plugged in to the report, but clearly no effort is made to actually read the data, as a two-year gap, from

1999 through 2000, is present in the manager's work history, based on the verification information discovered, *but is not mentioned in the "report."* What's more, the research revealed enough information to fill in this gap, or at least to start to do so, based on the newswire piece mentioned above. An institution quickly scanning this "report" would almost certainly, like the so-called expert, not pick up on this discrepancy. More importantly, the institution would then be missing what is plausibly the most troublesome aspect of the subject's history, as in most instances people do not omit jobs they have held unless they had a reason for doing so.

Here is another scenario: you have a retrospective article written in 1998 about the subject's activities at a former employer back in 1986. This information belongs in a discussion of the subject's 1986 work history, not in a chronological arrangement of news stories from oldest to most recent. Putting business history into context matters; it is the story that counts, not the source.

The converse of this, the written narrative approach produced by Firm B, would not only reveal and discuss the gap in the employment history based on the initial verification results, but would then actively seek to determine what the subject manager might have been doing during this time frame. Following this, interviews would be pursued to ascertain why the omission occurred. Finally, the institution itself would be prodded to speak with the manager directly, asking general questions about the person's work history first, in a further effort to gauge the manager's forthrightness. All of these techniques may seem obvious, but this makes the fact that so few people take the time to do them even more startling.

The second leg of the making connections tripod has to do with the sources reviewed. To make connections, one needs, you guessed it, the connectors. Eliminating vital research steps like obtaining actual court documents or searching multiple news sources for all stories naming the manager, not just those that mention the word "crook," is without question more difficult, more expensive, and more protracted. But until there is another way of searching and retrieving these and other things discussed throughout this book, the difficult, expensive, and protracted way will have to suffice. For the alternative really isn't an alternative at all. Not if minimizing risk is your goal.

Lastly, we come to expertise. With experience and specialization comes expertise. Some people see an Impressionist painting and see a mess, whereas others find the meaning and the beauty amidst the jumble of colors and forms. Background research, too, produces something of a mess. Many hedge fund managers have been mentioned or featured in hundreds of news articles, have invested in scores of companies, sat on numerous boards, held many jobs in various cities across the country, and have been no stranger to the legal system. Piecing together the career of such a manager is not necessarily a straightforward enterprise and is by no means available at the mere push of a button. But the due diligence expert knows how to sift through the mountain of words and create something cogent, something that speaks to the manager's history in a way that puts the institution in a position to understand its risks in investing with the manager, the signs it should heed going forward as well as the mechanisms for dealing with those issues, in advance.

Summing it up with a list, here are things to keep in mind when outsourcing.

1. A good investigative firm will not tell you when to invest or not invest.

    Aside from the liability issues associated with this type of pronouncement, the investigator only knows the risk side of the risk/reward ratio, and in fact, only knows one (albeit an important one) part of the risks inherent in the deal. While an investigator should be able to point out possible problems, certainly, and even place the subject manager on a continuum compared to other managers previously reviewed, telling you when to invest is presumptuous and not in your best interests. A high-quality report points out inconsistencies, discrepancies, and gaps but ultimately lets these items speak for themselves.

    Some methods for determining the importance of the information with which you are being presented include these:

    a. Ask the investigative firm what other institutions do when viewing said data.

    b. Ask how common an occurrence the event in question is, and how many managers the investigative firm has reviewed (so you can tell the size and thus relevance of the survey pool). Recall that two alarming items in the Wood River blow up were the suit for failure to pay the landlord and the suit for failure to pay the broker on a failed trade; the reason both of these were so alarming is not only that they indicated a history of lawsuits, and not only because they reflected poor judgment and/or business practices, but also primarily because they are such rare suits to find regarding a hedge fund.

    c. Always think about, determine and remember what is critical to your investment, decision-making process. Do you care solely about a return on investment (there is nothing necessarily wrong with this approach)? Are you concerned about your image if the subject fails, and investors, in turn, question their decision to place money with you? Are you nervous about fallout from negative press coverage of the manager, and possibly you, in the case of a blow-up or other problem?

A fund of funds whose primary desire is to net a certain amount for its clients might be tempted, therefore, to invest with a manager who has demonstrated the ability to make money but who has, say, a minor criminal conviction in his history. Conversely, an endowment, particularly a public one like, say the University of Maryland or some other similar state school, might think this piece of history is too fraught with danger given how the endowment is set up and perceived.

2. Reports should not include mountains of data that are unrelated to the subject. This cannot be emphasized strongly enough. An investigator handing you 500 pages of news stories and a shrug when asked whether these articles regard the subject, or someone else similarly named, has only handed you a stack of problems and increased your liability in the process. Similarly, the investigator needs to be able to sort out information you have already seen, and deemed relevant and even scary. If your research, for instance, turns up sanctions against what appears to be the subject, the investigator needs to be able to ascertain whether these sanctions actually do involve your manager, and thus are cause for concern, or don't, allowing you to breathe easier.

3. A report should be written clearly. No fancy legal jargon, no cop-talk, no discussions of who reached out to whom. Just plain English, telling you where the subject has worked, what happened at those posts, and what issues or problems present themselves with this manager.

4. A report should explain the import, or lack thereof, of the items it discusses. Facts shouldn't just be listed, they should be explained. A lawsuit being dismissed, for example, is not an indicator that the suit had no merit; if the report doesn't tell you this, you might make an assumption that could adversely color your decision.

5. A report should always integrate data into sections relating to the subject's career, as opposed to organizing sections depending totally and solely on where the information was found. Reading a section discussing three different news stories mentioning three different subjects won't be of much use to you; reading a news story, then a lawsuit, then an interview, all about the same topic, will.

6. Similarly, a report should not make you, the institution, do extra work. This means that information from various biographies, for instance, should be placed in chronological order, so that you can see, contextually, the outline of the subject's career, rather than grouped together by source of the biography, which is irrelevant. This also means that the report should not ask you whether you want to obtain court documents, or search a certain news file; if you had the knowledge and time necessary to make such a determination, chances are you would not need to outsource in the first place.

7. Where information was not available in public records, a report should suggest steps, such as interviews, to fill in the holes left by the earlier research.

8. A report should always include court searches of each and every city, state, and country where the manager has lived and worked. Now more than ever, people move around, and it is the researcher's job to track them.

9. Litigation should be described in terms of who did what to whom (allegedly), when, how much money was being sought, and what the outcome of the action was. Back-up documentation should be included as well.

10. A report should always point out biographical discrepancies and gaps. This information should compare what has been reported on different biographies, to information given directly by the employers, stated in SEC or other corporate/regulatory records, and reported on in the news. Remember, gaps can indicate that a manager left a previous position involuntarily. Discrepancies speak to a subject's character. Also along these lines, information about other posts held, whether found in Secretary of State records, SEC-type files, identification sources, credit reports, or news stories, should be mentioned, particularly if the subject's biography omitted these stints.

11. A report should always attribute the sources of the information it presents. Not doing so or fuzzying up the descriptions is usually a method designed to make the report appear sexier and more valuable than it is (I have seen reports wholesale copy a seven-page credit report or a five-page Dun & Bradstreet profile, clearly in the interest of increasing page count). On this point, look for the use of quotes when negative information is being reported; without this it will be unclear whether the information is the researcher's opinion (which is not what you are looking for, necessarily) rather than what has been stated or charged by someone else.

12. You should not end up with more questions than when you started. Plenty of situations will be unresolved based on a public records review. Suggestions for methods to resolve these, though, should always be present. (*Hint:* a typical suggestion is to conduct interviews with individuals deemed to be familiar with the incident in question.)

13. Interviews are almost always useful but do come at the cost of absolute discretion. Still, in situations where the subject is very young, and thus public records information is scant; where an issue has arisen and public records point to a possible problem but interviews would help flesh it out; where litigation—regulatory or another problem—has occurred in an entity where the subject worked, but where there is no clear idea

how or if the subject was personally involved; or where research has uncovered an entity omitted from a manager's biography, interviews are strongly suggested and should be pursued.

As alluded to above, and as described in our very first chapter, the increased concern of fraud in hedge funds stems from the flood of money that has come into the industry over the past few years. With the money has come a huge increase in the number of managers. Many have come and continue to arrive from large hedge funds, where they held junior positions. But many others are coming from less traditional backgrounds, simply following what might seem to be easy money. Dual concerns emerge: the ideal of hedge fund managers who are experienced specialists is no longer omnipresent, and perhaps more alarming, fraud perpetrators who follow the hot industry du jour are creeping into the field. And as they blend into the much more populated and less known crowd of today's hedge fund managers, it is increasingly more difficult to ferret them out.

The very nature of the hedge fund industry, with its purported lack of transparency and lack of regulation, does not help the fight against fraud. Neither does the capacity issue that hedge fund investors face. Because investors may get shut out of certain established and successful funds, they can find themselves going to newer managers who come with the risk of more unknowns. The *Wall Street Journal* recently reported that the 100-largest hedge funds now control approximately 67 percent of the money in the hedge-fund universe, a 20 percent rise from 2003, according to Morgan Stanley's prime-brokerage unit. What's more, the 300 hedge funds with $1 billion or more control almost 85 percent. This said, according to *Hedge Fund Daily*, the article added that "because there are so many investors interested in hedge funds—and the largest ones are often closed to them because of their size limits—smaller firms would be more than happy to roll out the welcome mat for them."[8]

Not only that, but investors sometimes feel compelled to go after new managers because the best returns are often found in a fund's first few years. Although there are many ways in which fraud may have an easier time harvesting in hedge funds, the reality is that fraud creeps into any hot sector: from telecommunications to real estate, from the Internet to hedge funds.

Fraud is a worst-case fear of hedge fund investors. Several recent blow-ups within the industry have focused attention on this very real threat. But investing in a subpar manager, and not realizing the envisioned returns, is another, more prevalent risk investors must minimize. Comprehensive background investigations can play an important role in weeding out managers who pose a strong fraud risk. At the same time, effective due diligence can also be an important tool used to identify those managers whose backgrounds more generally suggest that the possible reward of investment is not worth the evident risk.

In the end, there may be no sure-fire way to prevent fraud. No matter how diligent a fund of funds or an individual investor is, if people want to steal, they will find a way. That notwithstanding, bringing together thoughtful and layered due diligence to hedge fund investing is the best way to minimize the risks of the fraud threat as well as subpar manager selection. Institutions have to lie in their own bed, but if you do not succeed in this regard, you will be held liable by your ultimate authority, your clients, who will not hesitate in moving their money elsewhere.

So get to it.

Notes

CHAPTER 1

1. PerTrac. February 26, 2007 (http://pertrac.pertracnet.com/per0020/web/ me.get?web.websections.show&PER0020_1220).
2. Gregory Zuckerman, "Despite Bumps, Hedge Funds Push On," *Wall Street Journal*, January 3, 2007 (http://users2.wsj.com/lmda/do/check Login?mg=wsj-users2&url=http%3A%2F%2Fonline.wsj.com%2Farti cle%2FSB116768640652364139-search.html%3FKEYWORDS%3 Dhedge%2Band%2Bfund%26COLLECTION%3Dwsjie%2F6month).
3. "JPMorgan Tops U.S. HF Manager List, Up," Institutional Investor .com. March 2007 (http://www.dailyii.com/article.asp?ArticleID= 1243355&LS=EMS121645).
4. "Big Hedge Funds Are Still Control Freaks," *Hedge Fund Daily*. Institutional Investor.com, February 2007 (http://www.dailyii.com/ article.asp?ArticleID=1241982).
5. Stacy-Marie Ishmael, "The Hedge Fund Life-Cycle: A Theory," *Hedge-World* (http://ftalphaville.ft.com/blog/2007/02/08/2395/the-hedge-fund-life-cycle-a-theory).
6. "Institutions Put More Assets into Hedge Funds—Survey," *Reuters.com*. March 2007 (http://www.reuters.com/article/mergers News/idUSN2038472420070320).
7. Lisa Haines, "Schwarzenegger targets California's pension deficits," *Financialnews-US.com*, January 3, 2007 (http://www.financialnews-us.com/?page=ushome&contentid=1046868989).
8. "Russell Pension Report 2007 Forecasts a Significant 'Breaking Up of the Herd,'" February 12, 2007 (http://www.russell.com/News/ Press_Releases/PR20070212_US_p.asp).
9. Eurakehedge (http://www.eurekahedge.com/news/07_feb_BNY_HF_ survey.asp).
10. Riva Froymovich, "Hedge fund assets reach $1.89 trillion," *Investment News*, March 19, 2007 (http://www.investmentnews.com/apps/ pbcs.dll/article?AID=/20070319/REG/70319044/-1/BreakingNews04).

CHAPTER 3

1. Paul Adams, "Dadante Admits Stock Fraud," *baltimoresun.com,* August 17, 2007 (http://www.baltimoresun.com/business/investing/bal-bz.ferris17aug17,0,6635566.story?track=rss).
2. Paul S. Atkins, "Speech by SEC Commissioner: Remarks Before the 9th Annual Alternative Investment Roundup," January 29, 2007, U.S. Securities and Exchange Commission (http://www.sec.gov/news/speech/2007/spch012907psa.htm).
3. Jenny Anderson, "Winners Amid Doom and Gloom," *New York Times,* March 9, 2007 (http://www.nytimes.com/2007/03/09/business/09insider.html?ex=1331096400&en=7db67ab8dbfe982b&ei=5090&partner=rssuserland&emc=rss).
4. "Impatience No Virtue For This Hedge Fund," Institutional Investor.com, February 27, 2007 (http://www.dailyii.com/article.asp?ArticleID=1242028&LS=EMS120997).
5. Alistair Barr, "Keel Capital Hedge Fund to Shut Down: Firm Cites Lack of Short-Selling Opportunities, Restrictive Strategy," Marketwatch.com. February 26, 2007 (http://www.marketwatch.com/news/story/keel-capital-shuts-down-citing/story.aspx?guid=%7BBBDB6214-7D08-45D7-9BB7-31D4C05DB7C4%7D).
6. "U.S. Hedge Funds With $35B Call It Quits In '06," Institutional Investor.com, March 2007 (http://www.dailyii.com/article.asp?ArticleID=1259468&LS=EMS123036).
7. "Special report: Managed accounts and operational risk," Terrapin.com (http://terrapinnmedia.com/go.asp?/bTER001/mQ34J83/u0GT84/xEW7N6).
8. "More from Managed Accounts USA in New York," All About Alpha.com, March 15, 2007 (http://www.allaboutalpha.com/blog/2007/03/15/more-from-managed-accounts-usa-in-new-york/).
9. "Unlocking Keys To Hedge Fund Failures," Institutional Investor.com, January 2007 (http://www.dailyii.com/article.asp?ArticleID=1118163&LS=EMS116953).

CHAPTER 4

1. Jenny Strasburg and David Scheer, "Fund Manager with NFL Clients Fined $20 Million," February 12, 2007, Bloomberg.com: Worldwide (http://www.bloomberg.com/apps/news?pid=20601087&sid=a.2AWe540D9I&refer=home).
2. "U.S. Securities Exchange Commission, Litigation Release No. 19999," February 12, 2007 (http://www.sec.gov/litigation/litreleases/2007/lr19999.htm).

3. Monee Fields-White, "Kirk Wright's Razzle-Dazzle Play," Bloomberg Markets, October 2006, (http://www.bloomberg.com/news/market smag/wright.pdf#search=%22%22kirk%20).

CHAPTER 6

1. "USGS Frequently Asked Questions," USGS.com (http://interactive2 .usgs.gov/faq/list_faq_by_category/get_answer.asp?id=785).
2. "Public Access to Court Electronic Records Login Form" (https://pacer .login.uscourts.gov/cgi-bin/login.pl).
3. Nolo.com (http://www.nolo.com/definition.cfm/Term/79C0EE18- 349B-4FC1-8F73F7860BAF2528/alpha/N/).
4. See Addendum 6.7.
5. Addendum 6.8 on the web site (http://www.wiley.com/WileyCDA/ WileyTitle/productCd-0470139773.descCd-DOWNLOAD.html).
6. Christopher C. Faille, "From the Bayou of Connecticut to a New Home at Northeast Securities," *HedgeWorld Daily News*, May 16, 2002.
7. Neil Behrmann, "Background of Samuel Israel III and Commodity Traders,' View on How Bayou's Funds Disappeared," *Infovest21 News,* September 6, 2005.
8. Ibid.
9. "Third Broker Pleads Guilty in Bayou Hedge Fund Scam," AP, December 15, 2006 (http://www.northcountrygazette.org/articles/ 121906HedgeFund.html).
10. Roddy Boyd, "Burning Hedges: Onetime Whiz Kid Knew How to Cover Tracks," *New York Post*, December 17, 2006.
11. "Institutional Investors Lining Up to Recoup $200 Million Losses—Attention Turns to Wood River Auditors, Counsel & Financial Professionals as Circle of Responsibility for Hedge Fund Fraud Widens." *PR Newswire*. March 2, 2006.
12. "Wood River Hedge Manager Charged with Fraud," (http://consumer-fraud.legalview.com/news-articles/302926/).
13. LawFuel.com. November 08, 2006 (http://lawfuel.com/show-release .asp?ID=9475).
14. "Conversion," 'Lectric Law Library (http://www.lectlaw.com/def/c309 .htm).
15. "Implied Covenant of Good Faith and Fair Dealing," The Free Dictionary.com (http://legal-dictionary.thefreedictionary.com/implied+ covenant+of+good+faith+and+fair+dealing).
16. "Breach of Fiduciary Duty," Legal View (http://fiduciary.legalview .com/).

CHAPTER 8

1. "Fraud, Market Conduct Among Regulators' Hedge-Fund Concerns," Stock Investment, Fraud, March 8, 2007 (http://www.stockinvest mentfraud.com/pdf/detail.cfm?id=208619&article=TRU).
2. "Regulators mull new hedge fund rules," Investment News. June 5, 2007 (http://www.investmentnews.com/apps/pbcs.dll/article? AID=/20070605/FREE/70601045/-1/INRegulatoryAlert03).
3. U.S. Securities and Exchange Commission, Litigation Release No. 19999, February 26, 2007 (http://www.sec.gov/litigation/ litreleases/2007/lr19999.htm).
4. Letting Hedge Funds Conscience Be Their Guide," Institutional Investor.com, February 2007 (http://www.dailyii.com/article.asp? ArticleID=1241986&LS=EMS120251).
5. "Agreement Among PWG and U.S. Agency Principals on Principles and Guidelines Regarding Private Pools of Capital," U.S. Treasury Press Release (http://www.treasury.gov/press/releases/reports/ hp272_principles.pdf).
6. "Donaldson: New Hedge Fund Limits May Not Be Enough," Insitutional Investor.com, January 2007 (http://www.dailyii.com/article.asp? ArticleID=1126684&LS=EMS117593).
7. Alistair Barr, "Altering Regulations for Hedge Funds Not the Answer: Steel," MarketWatch, February 27, 2007 (http://www.marketwatch. com/news/story/altering-regulations-hedge-funds-not/story.aspx?guid= %7B543975CB-05BE-4BFC-A2A0-19124512EFFB%7D).
8. Ed Easterling, "Hedge Funds: Myths and Facts," April 10, 2007 (http://www.crestmontresearch.com/pdfs/HF%20Myths%20Facts.pdf).
9. "Why So Few Securities Fraud Cases Are Criminally Prosecuted," August 30, 2000, Knowledge@Wharton (http://72.14.209.104/search?q= cache:JAkc2pZr4R8J:knowledge.wharton.upenn.edu/createpdf.cfm%3 Farticleid%3D230+robert+brennan+prison+sentence&hl=en&ct=clnk &cd=10&gl=us).
10. "New York State Attorney General Report on Micro-Cap Stock Fraud," December 1997 (http://www.oag.state.ny.us/investors/ microcap97/report97a.html).
11. "What is IARD?" IARD.com (http://www.iard.com/WhatIsIARD.asp).
12. "About NASD," NASD.com, May 2, 2007 (http://pdpi.nasdr.com/pdpi/ disclaimer_frame.htm).
13. "NASAA History," NASAA.com (http://www.nasaa.org/About_ NASAA/NASAA_History/).
14. http://www.nfa.futures.org/BASICNET/FAQ.aspx frequently asked questions.

CHAPTER 9

1. Matthew Goldstein, "Bitter Medicine for Whiz Kid Sacane," TheStreet.com, July 30, 2003 (http://www.thestreet.com/pf/markets/matthewgoldstein/10104871.html).
2. "Smith & Wesson Big A Stickup Man," CBS News.com, February 27, 2004 (http://www.cbsnews.com/stories/2004/02/27/national/main602686.shtml).
3. Infoplease.com (http://www.infoplease.com/askeds/state-most-colleges-universities.html).
4. After entering the site, first click on "Overview" to begin the process.
5. Corporate Affiliations.com (http://www.corporateaffiliations.com/content/cn_home.asp).
6. "Military Personnel Records,"Archives.gov, (http://www.archives.gov/st-louis/military-personnel/).

CHAPTER 13

1. In Lexis search on lexis library docket;ofac. Two other sources provide the same information: (http://www.instantofac.com/ and http://www.treas.gov/offices/enforcement/ofac/).
2. Nina Bernstein, "Electronic Eyes: What the Computer Knows—A Special Report: On Line, High-Tech Sleuths Find Private Facts," *New York Times*, September 15, 1997 (http://query.nytimes.com/gst/fullpage.html?res=940CE4D61638F936A2575AC0A961958260&sec=technology&spon=&pagewanted=2).

CHAPTER 14

1. National Crime Information Center, January 18, 2006, (http://www.fas.org/irp/agency/doj/fbi/is/ncic.htm).
2. Thomas, Ralph, "Covertly Recording Telephone Conversations," 2006 (http://www.pimall.com/nais/n.recordlaw.html).

CHAPTER 16

1. "Moran/Sacane," *Worcester Telegram & Gazette* (Massachusetts), May 10, 1992.
2. Robert Kolker, "Take the Hedge-Fund Money and Run," *New York Magazine*, October 30, 2006 (http://www.rgm.com/articles/nymag.html).
3. First Advantage Investigative Services, LLC, Proprietary report.
4. Ibid.

5. For earlier background, see "Seton Hall University Presents Governor Keating with Honorary Degree, Check for Victim and Family Relief Fund," (http://www.state.ok.us/osfdocs/nr5-22.html). For later developments, see "Professors at Seton Hall Want Convicted Trustee to Resign," *The Chronicle of Higher Education* (http://chronicle.com/che-data/articles.dir/art-42.dir/issue-09.dir/09a03502.htm); "Setback in Stone," *legal affairs* (http://www.legalaffairs.org/printerfriendly.msp?id=954); "1983: Penny Stock Swindler-Celeb," *Philadelphia Business Journal* (http://www.bizjournals.com/philadelphia/stories/2002/08/05/focus2.html).

6. TheStreet.com, glossary (http://www.thestreet.com/financial-dictionary/pump-and-dump.html).

7. "D.H. Blair and Top Officials to Pay $4.9 Million in Fines and Restitution," NASD Regulation, Inc. August 13, 1997, (http://www.nasd.com/PressRoom/NewsReleases/1997NewsReleases/NASDW_010511).

8. "Troubled Company Reporter," bankrupt.com, September 3, 1999: Vol. 3, No. 171 (http://bankrupt.com/TCR_Public/990903.MBX).

9. Will Astor, "NASD Case Misleading, H.J. Meyers Chief Says," *Rochester Business Journal,* Vol. 12, No. 16, August 2, 1996, 4.

10. Gretchen Morgenson, "On Sleazy Street," *Forbes Magazine,* June 16, 1997, 262.

11. Richard Kindleberger, "Mass. Regulators Accuse 5 Penny-Stock Dealers of Fraud," *Boston Globe,* January 28, 1998, C5.

12. RJ, "Josephthal Has a Long Record of Run-Ins with Regulators and Customers," *Securities Week,* January 31, 2000, Vol. 27, No. 5, 1.

13. Ibid.

14. December 5, 1996 press release (http://www.finra.org/PressRoom/NewsReleases/1996NewsReleases/P010592).

15. Gary Weiss, "The Mob is Busier than the Feds Think," *Business Week,* December 15, 1997 (http://www.businessweek.com/1997/50/b3557008.htm).

16. "N.A.S.D. Fines Stuart-James," *New York Times,* May 14, 1990, Late Edition, 6 (http://select.nytimes.com/gst/abstract.html?res=F3061FF63C5E0C778DDDAC0894D8494D81&n=Top%2fReference%2fTimes%20Topics%2fOrganizations%2fN%2fN%2eA%2eS%2eD%2e).

CHAPTER 17

1. "U.S. Commodity Futures Trading Commission Files Anti-Fraud Action Against New York Hedge Fund Cornerstone Capital Management, LLC and its Operator, Atlanta Resident Joseph T. Profit II,"

(Release: 5288-07). Commodity Futures Trading Commission, February 6, 2007 (http://www.cftc.gov/opa/enf07/opa5288-07.htm).

2. "Not-So-Jolly Predictions from Rogers," Institutional Investor.com, February 2007 (http://www.dailyii.com/article.asp?Article ID=1234181&LS=EMS118893).

3. Mike Tierney, "Risky Dealings Smash Nest Egg," *Atlanta Journal-Constitution*, March 19, 2006.

4. Ed Easterling, "Hedge Funds: Myths and Facts," *Crestmont* Research, April 10, 2007 (http://www.crestmontresearch.com/pdfs/ HF%20Myths%20Facts.pdf).

5. "New Credit Suisse/Tremont Hedge Fund Index Research Reveals That Hedge Funds Indices Are Not Directly Comparable To Their Traditional Counterpart," February 14, 2007, *Hedge Index* (http:// www.hedgeindex.com/hedgeindex/en/PressRelease.aspx?cy=USD&Doc ID=476).

6. Paul Taylor, "US Maintains the Status Quo: REGULATION," *Financial Times*, April 30, 2002, HED1.

7. Elif Kaban, "Fund of Hedge Fund Executive Pay Tops $4 Million," *Reuters News*, May 20, 2002.

8. "Slimmer Pickins For Smaller Hedge Funds," Institutional Investor.com, April 2007 (http://www.dailyii.com/article.asp?ArticleID= 1328416&LS=EMS125460).

Index